Transforming Teacher Education

Reflections from the Field

Transforming Teacher Education

Reflections from the Field

Edited by
DAVID CARROLL
HELEN FEATHERSTONE
JOSEPH FEATHERSTONE
SHARON FEIMAN-NEMSER
DIRCK ROOSEVELT

HARVARD EDUCATION PRESS
CAMBRIDGE, MASSACHUSETTS

Library of Congress Control Number 2006939811
Paperback ISBN 978-1-891792-33-5
Library Edition ISBN 978-1-891792-34-2

Published by Harvard Education Press,
an imprint of the Harvard Education Publishing Group

Harvard Education Press
8 Story Street
Cambridge, MA 02138

Cover Design: Anne Carter

The typeface used in this book is Adobe Jenson Pro.

For Vito Perrone and Judith Lanier,
two organizers for democracy

Contents

Acknowledgments

Our dedication tells something of Team One's debt to Judy Lanier, the visionary dean who made all our work at Michigan State University possible, and hails Vito Perrone, of the North Dakota Study Group, who has taught us so much about teaching, learning, and schools. We also want to acknowledge the encouragement of our many other friends and colleagues in the Study Group, this generation's representatives of the long tradition of democratic, progressive education from which we draw ideas and inspiration. And had we not been privileged to know Deborah Meier, Patricia Carini, and Theodore Sizer, three extraordinary practitioners and organizers, we might have imagined the work at MSU very differently.

On the MSU campus, we salute Henrietta Barnes, the farsighted and yet intensely practical chair of the department in the first years of the new five-year program. Henrietta showed by example how the chair of a large department can support a cluster of dedicated though troublesome practitioners. We also want to thank the outstanding group of teacher educators who led the other teams in the new MSU teacher certification program during the difficult yet heady first decade: Andy Anderson, Tom Bird, Laura Roehler, Cheryl Rosaen, Sandra Wilcox, and Lauren Young. We borrowed ideas and practices from these colleagues and huddled with them about troubles. We occasionally quarreled with them, but now we insist that, whatever our disagreements, these colleagues contributed to an astonishing culture at MSU, one in which teacher education was the decisive priority, and nothing in the world seemed more important.

A special thanks to Randi Stanulis, coleader and, in the end, the last faculty leader of Team One. Also thanks to the last team coordinator, Judy O'Brien; to the wonderful team secretaries, Judy Redding and Tena Harrington; to Sharon Schwille and Trudy Sykes, who always saw what we were aiming for and helped us to get there; and to Bruce Rochowiak, principal of Averill Elementary School, who supported the work of the Team in a hundred ways. Of all the MSU faculty members past and present who contributed to our enterprise, we are especially indebted to Laura Apol, Sandra Crespo, Brian Delany, Jenny Denyer, Nell Duke, Patricia Edwards, Susan Florio-Ruane, Joyce Grant, Arden Moon, Lynn Paine, Deb Smith, Gary Sykes, Charles Thompson, Chris Wheeler, and Suzanne Wilson. We appreciate, too, the colleagueship of all of the amazing doctoral students who helped to shape the culture and curriculum of Team One and are now reshaping teacher preparation at universities across the United States and beyond: Paul Conway, Mark Enfield, Paula Lane, Cathy Reischl, Shari Levine Rose, Kara Suzuka, and Steve Swidler.

We are unendingly grateful to all the teachers and principals—too many to list—who supported the work of Team One over the years and to our students past and present, who have so often shown us the way.

Introduction

This is a book about our efforts as passionate, committed practitioners to develop a high-quality teacher education program in a large and bureaucratic public university over the span of a decade. Some would wonder whether the goal is worthwhile, let alone possible. In his first annual report on teaching quality, then Secretary of Education Rod Paige (2002) called for the abolition of professional education as it currently exists and recommended replacing it with streamlined certification requirements that emphasize what is really important: verbal ability and content knowledge. Although subsequent reports took less extreme positions, they still expressed considerable skepticism about the role of teacher education in improving the quality of teaching and learning in our public schools.

As insiders to teacher education, we, too, are critical of much that goes on in our field. We lament the disregard for serious content knowledge, the preoccupation with techniques, the reliance on unexamined practice. We agree that teacher education too frequently promotes unrealistic goals, offers scant intellectual fare, and fails to provide prospective teachers with the tools to realize their aspirations and society's expectations (Dewey, 1904/1964; Lortie, 1975).

We understand why this is so. Immersed for many decades in the difficult work of teacher preparation, we have learned that helping prospective teachers develop sophisticated understandings of subject matter, students' thinking, and the creation and management of classroom learning communities—the whole, complex package—is hard, intellectually demanding work. We have seen that nourishing curiosity about children's ideas; mathematics, science, literature, and art; and the workings of the wider world as the cornerstone of professional development is relatively uncharted territory. We know that all too often we fail to accomplish all of our goals for our students.

Given what we know about the complexities of teaching and the great difficulties that beginning teachers experience, however, dismantling university-based teacher education rather than investing in its improvement seems shortsighted. It also ignores compelling empirical evidence that quality teacher education makes a demonstrable difference in teachers' practice, in their satisfaction with teaching, and in their willingness to stay in the profession (Cochran-Smith, 2004; Darling-Hammond, 2000; Grossman, 1990).

This book tells the story of a small group of colleagues at Michigan State University, locally known as "Team One," who enacted a high quality, culturally ambitious version of teacher education in a big, public university. It addresses current challenges in teacher education by describing and investigating some of the complexities all teacher educators face in their efforts to create and sustain passionate teaching in standards-based, field-centered programs. We offer a rare portrait of what it takes to do quality teacher education for the elementary grades on a large scale in the kind of institution that prepares the majority of our nation's teachers, but we are also talking to all teacher educators in institutions large and small, public and private. What we have to say can also be useful to those designing alternative routes to teaching. And finally, we are appealing to a larger public willing to concern itself with a vital and often buried issue in American education: how will we staff our children's schools with competent, caring, and thoughtful teachers?

Here we explore the challenges encountered as we have tried to prepare prospective teachers, most of whom are middle-class, white women who attended suburban and rural schools, to teach children different from themselves—poor, African American, and urban—using pedagogies that differ sharply from those they knew as students in public and parochial schools. Even though many teacher education programs are smaller than ours and structured in different ways, decades of conversations with colleagues at other institutions convince us that teacher educators at other colleges and universities struggle with the same dilemmas and seek solutions to related problems. There are, we are sure, many ways to do good teacher education; yet it may be that the most effective programs have certain themes and practices in common. This book is a case study that aims to advance our conversation about what quality teacher education looks like and why it is hard to create.

We develop five broad themes across ten chapters.

First, a serious teacher education program must address the central tasks of learning to teach (Feiman-Nemser, 2001), ensuring that teacher candidates have subject-matter and foundational knowledge and skills as well as the commitments and tools to continue developing their practice. Left to their own devices, new teachers are unlikely to embrace intellectually ambitious approaches to teaching subject matter for the long haul, overcome prejudices about what children from backgrounds different from their own are capable of learning, or be disposed to base instructional decisions on evidence about their students' thinking. While teaching must eventually be learned in the doing, the knowledge, skills, and dispositions that teachers bring to their work influence not only how they teach but what they can learn from their teaching. Examples of central tasks in learning to teach include learning to be at home in subject matter; learning to see and hear children, especially those whose backgrounds differ from the teacher's; earning intellectual and moral authority; and constructing a teacher identity.

Second, a good teacher education program must continually work to develop in each student a new adult and professional identity as a teacher committed to the growth of children and to knowing and teaching subject matter in intellectually engaging ways. This involves supporting teacher candidates as they undertake the difficult transition from student to teacher, while at the same time stretching their ambitions for children's growth and for teaching for understanding. Some students make this move fairly readily, while others have considerable difficulties. A teacher education program has to find effective ways to help those who struggle with this transition while exercising professional judgment about those who may not be ready to teach.

Third, given the contradictory mandates and the divided mind of the American public about reform in education, teacher educators must help prospective teachers develop intellectual habits and a capacity for judgment that will allow them to embrace and negotiate the tensions and dilemmas in their work. This means, for example, holding students to common standards while helping them grow individually and meet their own standards. It also means introducing teacher candidates to new images of good teaching while supporting them in achieving their own pedagogical goals. It involves working daily in problematic practice sites torn by bureaucratic demands and by contrary visions of students, subject matter, and teaching.

Fourth, teacher educators need to create structures and a culture that support the ongoing learning of all who work with prospective teachers: mentor teachers, graduate students, and faculty teaching in the program. For example, most programs have trouble finding enough collaborating teachers who practice the kind of ambitious teaching they are trying to promote. If teacher educators do not work intensively with collaborating teachers, prospective teachers' time in the field will only reinforce the traditional images they bring from their own apprenticeship of observation. Similarly, neither university professors nor graduate students teaching in a program are likely to know all they need to. Without the structures and culture to support experimentation and collective inquiry on the part of all those involved, teacher education will remain a low-impact enterprise.

Fifth, experiences in schools are at the core of the prospective teacher's learning of teacher education, a stark fact that teacher educators ignore at their peril. A big challenge for Team One and for any field-based program is developing enough placement sites and mentor teachers to support a year-long internship. We deliberately use the word "develop" since we could not count on large numbers of classroom teachers who both modeled the kind of teaching we advocated and knew how to use their teaching and classrooms as sites for novice-teacher learning. Continuous field development has to be a key priority for a good teacher education program. This challenge confronts all brands of teacher education, including condensed programs that rely on new teachers to learn to teach on the job.

No summary list can do justice to the complexities of a good teacher education program. The five themes above represent our effort to map the complex terrain of Team One. Their deeper meaning derives from the vision of teaching and schooling that brought us to teacher education in the first place. All of us had shaped and been shaped by the educational opportunities and upheavals of the 1960s and '70s. In one way or another, we were products of open education and the civil rights movement. In one way or another, we all came to share a vision of teachers as activists, artists, and intellectuals. A former teacher at the University of Chicago Laboratory Schools, Sharon Feiman-Nemser came out of the teacher center movement. Dirck Roosevelt, David Carroll, and Susan Donnelly had all taught at the Prospect School in Bennington, Vermont, where they were steeped in child-study approaches that were the trademark of that fascinating and influential progressive experiment. Helen Featherstone taught in an alternative school in Roxbury, Massachusetts, and edited the reformist *Harvard Education Letter*. A former editor of the *New Republic*, Jay Featherstone wrote about British primary schools in the 1960s and later served as the principal of the Commonwealth School in Boston. We are all members of the North Dakota Study Group, a national (despite its name) network of political and child-centered progressives.

As products of the civil rights era and the 1960s revival of democratic, progressive education, we were committed to the elusive and lofty goal of democracy in education and the line of practice that runs from John Dewey and Leonard Covello to Lucy Sprague Mitchell and contemporary figures like Ted Sizer, Ann Cook, and Deborah Meier. We shared the old progressive dream of a society and a school system in which every individual can grow to full height. With Dewey, we believed that all learning is profoundly social, that conversation is not only the chief medium of learning but also—along with cooperative action—one of education's chief ends. We were convinced that in settings for good learning, the social and the intellectual intertwine.

Our friends and colleagues in the North Dakota Study Group had created wonderful progressive public schools in the decades following the 1970s. Such schools—with their emphasis on active learning and a demanding academic curriculum, their vision of teachers as thoughtful professionals and activists on behalf of children, and the profoundly caring communities they created—greatly influenced us. The image of teachers in such a school working together as a community of equals was a big inspiration. We wanted to create a teacher education program that would produce the kinds of artists, scientists, and activist-intellectuals we met among the school practitioners in the North Dakota Study Group (Engel & Martin, 2005).

For the better part of a decade, the five of us worked together to imagine, create, and run the Michigan State University Team One teacher education program. Besides teaching in the program, we each held a position of leadership. Sharon Feiman-Nemser and Jay Featherstone served as coleaders of the team from its beginnings in 1993 to 2000 and as faculty mentors of the internship year and the junior year respectively. David Carroll was the program coordinator responsible for day-to-day operations. Helen Featherstone and Dirck Roosevelt (at different times) provided leadership for instructors and students engaged with the senior-year course that focused on the challenges of teaching language arts, mathematics, science, and social studies to diverse learners. The five of us, along with Susan Donnelly and Margaret Malenka, formed a steering committee that met every two weeks to provide intellectual leadership and continuity and to deal with the full range of administrative, financial, educational, psychological, and institutional issues that arise in any enterprise focused on human improvement. In addition to addressing insistent problems, these meetings became a place to explore persistent dilemmas in the work of teacher education, to frame questions and provisional answers. In these meetings we laid the intellectual foundations of this book.

Authors of the individual chapters that follow all taught in the program. Several were PhD candidates when they worked with the team and have since taken the ideas that we developed together to other universities. Pat Norman does teacher education at Trinity University in Texas; Dirck Roosevelt directed the teacher education program at the University of Michigan for five years and now directs the elementary MAT program at Brandeis University; David Carroll is on the education faculty of Western Washington University. Thus the practices we developed and the lessons we learned are shaping and reshaping teacher education at Brandeis, Trinity, and Western Washington as well as Michigan State.

As a study of democratic, progressive change in a large and bureaucratic public setting, this book parallels a number of accounts of successful reform efforts in public schools and classrooms. One model for us in our practice as teacher educators and in our writing has been Deborah Meier and her powerful books about the creation of Central Park East Secondary School in New York (1995, 2002), and the Mission Hill School in Boston (two innovative and academically ambitious urban schools). Meier's volumes are intensely personal accounts; our story is a collective one told from many perspectives. As teacher educators we have felt keenly the lack of such stories in our field. Stories cannot take the place of analysis, but they embody complexity in ways that analysis often fails to do. If there is a document from the past that this book pays homage to it is Lucy Sprague Mitchell's *Our Children and Our Schools*, the account of Bank Street College's efforts to work with public schools in New York city in the 1930s and '40s. What would Mitchell's Bank Street look like if it took on the challenge of a big public university program in the 1990s?

In a polemic that blames the ills of U.S. education on egalitarians and progressive educators, conservative educator Diane Ravitch (2000) spares and praises a group she calls the "intellectual progressives" for their tradition of academic ambition and creative school practice. If she could wave a magic wand, she says, and have this kind of education for all children, she would do it in a flash, but she doubts it can succeed in ordinary, bureaucratic U.S. schools for most people's children. We on Team One are proud to call ourselves "intellectual progressives" in this long tradition; we dared to believe that public teacher education in our time deserved a shot at the ambitious package dreamed of by Dewey and Mitchell. Working in a land-grant college that is still a symbol of democratic aspirations, we wanted our students to get what the elites provide for their children: the very best.

From Boutique to Superstore:
History and Context of the Program

David Carroll, Helen Featherstone,
Joseph Featherstone, and Sharon Feiman-Nemser

As a field, we know very little about the struggle to create and sustain decent settings for learning to teach and the structures of support and thought such settings require. This chapter tells the story of the creation of Team One, a small group of colleagues who enacted an ambitious version of teacher education on a large scale in a big, bureaucratic state university. It is a quietly dramatic reform story of the sort often told about individual classrooms, and sometimes about schools, but rarely heard in the often dreary annals of U.S. teacher education. On the rare occasions when we do hear such a story, the case is apt to be a small program. The Team One story is about radical democratic change on a big scale; it parallels accounts of significant reform in large urban high schools. Just as we have learned from these tales of school reform, we hope the field of teacher education will learn from ours.

The Institutional Story

The story of Team One is partly a history of the College of Education at Michigan State University. In the 1980s and 1990s, the confluence of a visionary dean, a national center for research on teacher education, and a new initiative to create professional development schools resulted in the launching of a large-scale, ambitious, field-based teacher education program. In reconstructing the beginnings of this program, we draw on program archives, a published institutional history (Inzunza, 2002), and conversations with some of the central actors.

During the 1980s, Judy Lanier, dean of the College of Education, won national attention for her focus on the reform of teacher education. Since the late 1970s, Michigan State had been the home of the Institute for Research on Teaching (IRT), a federally funded center codirected by Lee Shulman and Judy Lanier. The IRT had begun to attract to the College of Education a cadre of research-oriented faculty who challenged the dominant view of teaching as a set of generic and easily learned skills and produced a body of research more attuned to teachers and their intentions. Building on this new research and a tradition of experimentation with alternative forms of teacher preparation, Lanier worked with new and veteran faculty to reform teacher education at Michigan State. She started the Holmes Group, an organization of education school deans committed to national reform of teacher education. With the faculty, she launched a series of small, experimental teacher education programs that were in many ways the forerunners of our own work on Team One.

Prior to this, teacher education at Michigan State looked a lot like it did at other large state universities. Students completed the familiar list of undergraduate courses in educational foundations and methods of teaching and ended their program with a ten-week student teaching experience, spread widely across a considerable stretch of Michigan in individual placements attended by occasional visits from far-flung university supervisors. Although experimental programs existed at MSU in the 1960s and 1970s, the so-called standard program still served the majority of students. Though most of us who later began Team One were new to Michigan State, there were plenty of veterans around (including Judy Lanier) to tell tales of large education lecture courses taught in the Kiva, a huge cavern on the ground floor of Erickson Hall.

While Lanier was attempting to make a land-grant giant into a crack research outfit, she was also trying to move the whole teacher education enterprise toward serious educational quality. The problem of scale was daunting: even with the drop in enrollments in the 1970s, the university had close to forty thousand students. The teacher certification program was still graduating large numbers of teachers a year, even though it was down from an all-time high in the 1960s when MSU certified around 850 elementary teachers and 1000 secondary teachers (Inzunza, 2002) each year.

Lanier's first step involved the creation of four small thematic teacher preparatory programs outside the large mainstream program. The names of the units signaled particular emphases favored by new clusters of faculty recruited to work with them: heterogeneous classrooms (focusing on issues related to student diversity); academic learning (focusing on subject matter pedagogy); learning community (focusing on the links among classroom culture, teaching, and learning); and multiple perspectives (focusing on teacher decisionmaking in the face of multiple and competing demands). Each of these four programs accepted one cohort (around thirty students) of elementary education majors each year; two also accepted thirty secondary education students.

The creation of these small thematic programs involved scaling down teacher education cohorts to manageable sizes while rethinking program purposes and curriculum to create academic depth and a sense of community. MSU was like a large high school that had developed a few high-quality alternative programs. There was a clear contrast between the intense academic and personal experiences students had in the four experimental units and the plain vanilla fare the mainstream program offered. Like special programs in a high school, these had the flair and dash of little boutiques. With their small size and webs of personal connection, they were able to invest in school sites with teachers who were known quantities, solving some of the big teacher education dilemmas of field placement.

As the College of Education experimented with alternative forms of teacher preparation and faculty engaged afresh with research on practice, Judy Lanier began meeting with deans of colleges of education in leading research universities to explore ways of making teacher education a new priority. These meetings evolved into the Holmes Group, a leading organization in the reform of teacher education during the 1980s and 1990s; initially the group had its headquarters at MSU. Around the same time, a national commission issued an influential report, A Nation at Risk, that pushed school reform to the top of the country's agenda. In addition to criticizing the "rising tide of mediocrity" in public schools, the report took teacher education to task for emphasizing methods courses instead of those that enhanced teachers' subject-matter knowledge. (Interestingly, Terrence Bell, then secretary of education, released A Nation at Risk at MSU, where he had come to give the IRT an award.)

The College of Education's growing national reputation in teacher education rested on the good work of the small thematic programs and on the body of research linking teacher education to school practice. MSU's central role in the Holmes Group also led it to inaugurate a network of professional development schools starting in the late 1980s and continuing through the

1990s. Plans for professional development schools outlined in the Holmes documents, especially the second Holmes Group report, *Tomorrow's Schools* (1990), called for new levels of cooperation between schools and teacher education. Deeply critical of mainstream thought and practice in major U.S. universities, *Tomorrow's Schools* presented a radically new conception of teacher education. This vision was framed in a rhetoric that combined an appeal to the values of democracy; intellectually ambitious teaching for all children; and a concern for schools as caring, democratic communities. This was a departure from the technical and professionalized rhetoric of the first Holmes report.

One scholar whose thinking influenced Lanier, the Holmes Group, and many MSU faculty was Harry Judge, a British educator who in 1982 had written a stinging and influential appraisal of U.S. teacher education in a report sponsored by the Ford Foundation. Judge, who had a joint appointment at Oxford and MSU for a time, attacked the values and priorities of the major research universities in relation to teacher education. The more ambitious was the research agenda, the more prestigious the institution, he argued, the greater the distance from schools, teachers, and issues of practice. Teacher education, which in Judge's view was central to the mission of schools of education, had become a U.S. Cinderella, subservient to other interests in schools of education.

Judge's analysis differed from many of the classic critiques (Bestor, 1955; Conant, 1964; Silberman, 1970) of U.S. teacher education. Judge himself was one of the faithful who believed that teachers could become intelligent practitioners through a reflective immersion in practice. Judge was a scholar who saw visionary potential in the kind of integration of theory, research, and practice that was already taking nascent form in certain patches of the MSU domain. He was taking the big research universities to task for embracing research specialties that had little to do with teaching and learning; not making the problems of teaching more central to their research agendas; marginalizing teacher education as a cash cow with little academic importance; and isolating research faculty from the problems of teaching in schools. He called for the creation of professional development schools loosely analogous to teaching hospitals for apprentice doctors, where teachers, researchers, and teacher educators could grapple in some long-term ongoing way with issues of theory and practice as they inducted a new generation of teachers. (For further discussion of Harry Judge's ideas and their impact on our work, see chapter 10.)

Judge's report, American Graduate Schools of Education: A View from Abroad, became for a time the bible of reformers inside teacher education, and helped shape the Holmes Group's first two reports, particularly *Tomorrow's Schools* (1990), a manifesto for teaching for understanding, equality in education, and professional development schools. Largely written by Lanier and a group of MSU faculty, including Jay Featherstone for the second report, *Tomorrow's Teachers* (1986) and *Tomorrow's Schools* (1990) helped to generate a small wave of teacher education reform across the country with much local variation but five common features: efforts to intellectualize the curriculum in teacher education; a fresh call for subject matter knowledge; the extension of student teaching into a thoughtful, yearlong apprenticeship; new partnerships between schools and universities; and more collaborative, practice-relevant educational scholarship.

This Holmes reform agenda was soon part of the discussions at MSU. In 1988, a College of Education task force argued for rethinking teacher education. In language reminiscent of the boutique thematic programs and compatible with the Holmes Group recommendations, the task force advocated a better integration of theory and practice, smarter teacher education and subject-matter courses, better field experience, and reflection on that experience in hopes of graduating teachers with

1. a deep understanding of subject matter and of pedagogies that "teach for understanding";
2. a democratic commitment to the education of everybody's children and to classrooms and schools that would embrace diversity;
3. the skills and commitment necessary to establish true learning communities in classrooms and schools;
4. the disposition and skills to participate in remaking the teaching profession, renewing schools, and making a better world.

Professional development schools, which MSU had inaugurated even before the publication of *Tomorrow's Schools*, symbolized an effort to move away from conventional teacher education with its lowly status and its education courses hermetically sealed off from schools. In the past, Michigan State, like other large public universities, had often separated the elements of the famous land-grant trinity—teaching, research, and service. With the success of the IRT, research had become more central to the mission of the College of Education. Now professional development schools began to take center stage in the vision of Michigan State as a premier institution for educational research and policy development directly related to school reform and teaching practice. In the air in East Lansing there was the hope of a new fusion of theory, research, and practice and a new set of partnerships with schools and teachers in the service of a new vision of teacher education.

MOVING TOWARD A FIVE-YEAR PROGRAM

In the early 1990s, Lanier and college faculty succeeded in pushing through a comprehensive shift in the design and structure of the teacher education program, moving to a five-year model that culminated in a yearlong, post-BA internship. Under the new design, students would begin teacher education coursework in the spring semester of their junior year, take a yearlong subject-matter pedagogy course with related practicums during their senior year, graduate with a BA, and then complete a two-semester internship while taking four graduate level courses. Instead of being scattered across the state, internships would be clustered in small groups in professional development schools or at least in a stable set of affiliated schools committed to long-term relationships with the university. Achieving this design required mounting and winning major institutional battles both within the college and across the university. Lanier succeeded in returning responsibility for subject-matter pedagogy to faculty in the Department of Teacher Education and in winning the adoption of the new fifth year internship.

The new MSU program design intended to blend teaching, inquiry, and service to schools in a unique and synergistic mix. The theory was that, mixed right, each element would strengthen the others. The new teacher education program, with its base in school partnerships, could help MSU become a crack research institution with intimate and ongoing ties to classrooms, teachers, and students. The resulting research would be a product of close-grained work in classrooms informed by scholarship that actually addressed practice.

The transition to the new five-year program was a process much like that of a big high school "de-tracking" its AP and honors courses and trying to sustain the old elite quality on a new, mass democratic scale for all students.

TABLE 1
Institutional Timeline

Date	Event
1976	Institute for Research on Teaching (IRT) funded by the National Institute of Education, with codirectors Lee Shulman and Judith Lanier (funded through 1986).
1980	Judith Lanier appointed dean of the College of Education.
1982	Four thematic teacher education programs established.
1983	*A Nation at Risk* released at news conference at MSU.
1984	The Holmes Group forms, with Judith Lanier as executive director.
1985	National Center for Research on Teacher Education established (funded through 1990).
1986	Holmes Group publishes *Tomorrow's Teachers.*
1988	MSU creates four professional development schools.
1989	Planning begins for new five-year teacher education program.
1990	Holmes Group publishes *Tomorrow's Schools;* National Center for Research on Teacher Learning established at MSU (funded through 1995).
1991	Michigan Board of Education approves new teacher education program at MSU.
1993	First cohort of students enters "new" teacher education program; Carole Ames appointed dean of the College of Education.
1995	MSU expands number of professional development schools to fourteen.
2000	Professional development schools disbanded in favor of a different model.

Within the institution, skeptics refused to believe that this goal was achievable. Indeed, whether MSU had the resources, energy, and vision to sustain quality teacher education on a large scale has remained a question.

The design of the new program called for structures of coordination and integration to support field-based learning and close intellectual and craft linkages between courses at MSU and teacher education in schools. The small, thematic programs at MSU had created such structures: clusters of faculty who taught courses and worked in a few schools with classroom teachers. Now MSU was proposing to take the entire teacher education program in these directions. It would now be divided into three teams of roughly equal numbers of students, distributed randomly. (In the initial years, all three teams worked with both elementary and secondary students. After several years and much debate, secondary students were pulled together into a new group, Team Four, leaving only elementary students on Teams One, Two, and Three. Team One fought hard to keep its secondary students, but it lost the battle.) Faculty were assigned to the original K–12 teams, with some attention to previous affiliations with the thematic programs and with the overall intention of providing each with a roughly equal number of senior teacher education faculty. Team leaders were recruited during this process, and Sharon Feiman-Nemser and Jay Featherstone became coleaders of Team One.

The new program had to develop school affiliations, which were determined on the basis of past affiliations to the thematic programs plus a new invitation process. Existing professional development schools were assigned evenly among the teams to preserve existing faculty-school relationships. New schools were invited to apply for affiliation with the program by submitting a brief description of their school and its potential as a site for teacher education work, and the teams negotiated among themselves about which districts and schools they would partner with. They divided up nearby suburban districts so that only one team worked with a given district, though since Lansing was the one local urban school district, each of the three teams partnered with a subset of its schools. Finally, each team took one larger urban site located forty to sixty minutes from the main campus in order to expand the number of urban opportunities for teacher education and to enable students living near those areas to intern close to home.

None of us understood at the time how complex would be the work of transforming the initial structural blueprint into an enacted program. At first we had only faculty and graduate students assigned to staff our team; course titles accompanied by vague descriptions; lists of students, which told us roughly how many sections of different courses to offer; and names of schools in which to begin working. Looking back, it seems clear that we were committing ourselves to the development of teams that would each create a collaborative culture and support a web of intricate and ongoing tasks: relating the field to the university, research to practice, reflection to doing—all the polarities that bedevil and challenge thoughtful teacher education programs everywhere. The teams would succeed if they could provide the experiences, ideas, and craft knowledge that students needed in order to become good teachers. They would do this by establishing a new ecology of relationships between the university and the field. MSU would have, in the three teacher education teams, a set of small, living laboratories for testing assumptions about teaching, learning, and learning to teach. "Small" is a relative word: each team would graduate about 125 interns a year, so each of them was as large as the biggest teacher education program in some states and much larger than MSU's own experimental boutique programs.

FORMING TEAM ONE

The core values and ideas around which we organized the work of Team One came from two sources. One was MSU and the history of reformist teacher education outlined in the previous section of this chapter. The ideas reflected in *Tomorrow's Schools* and in the MSU thematic programs—teaching for understanding, pedagogical content knowledge, classroom diversity, and learning community—were among the many on teaching and learning to teach that featured heavily in ongoing conversation and research at that time.

In particular, two key ideas stood out from this work and the body of local practice and thought that had grown up in the small experimental programs at MSU: one was the ambition to prepare a new generation of teachers and teacher educators capable of confronting the historic democratic challenge of educating all children to ambitious intellectual standards. For that reason, Team One put a special priority on developing partnerships with urban schools to enable us to engage our students with the greatest possible diversity of students. The other was the development of a body of thought and practice that would link university teacher education programs with public schools in a new kind of partnership.

A second source of values and ideas for Team One lay in the personal and collective biographies of the group of faculty and graduate students we assembled. One way or another, all of us were democrats and progressives who had shaped and been shaped by the educational opportunities and upheavals of the 1960s and '70s. We were all, in one way or another, products of open education and the civil rights movement. John Dewey, Leonard Covello, W. E. B. DuBois, and Lucy Sprague Mitchell were icons in a tradition of thought and practice and democratic activism we shared—one that was a blend of democracy; a concern for individual children; and a vision of teachers as a mix of artist, scientist, and activist. We sought to prepare teachers who would be practical intellectuals with the knowledge to teach the children of all the people. We would include ourselves among the allies of Theodore Sizer and Deborah Meier in their efforts to create schools and pedagogy that would, in Meier's words, give poor kids what the rich kids are getting, an education that respects their minds and develops them as intelligent citizens.

We shared two important beliefs: that classrooms ought to be places where children learn to use their minds and imaginations well, and that U.S. education must offer a much richer education to poor and working-class children. We were progressives in two familiar senses of the word: we believed in paying close attention to children and their thinking, and we hoped to create teachers and schools that could do democratic justice to everybody's children.

All of us drew heavily on the recent MSU experience with alternative teacher education programs, particularly the experience of the Learning Community Program, with its emphasis on the link between high intellectual standards and participation in a culture of ideas and conversation about experience in small community settings.

Another influence that shaped us, that had been noted by many scholars, including Christopher Jencks and David Riesman (1968), was the effort to take models of education developed in small and often exclusive private settings and democratize them in some new form in big public institutions. This had happened over the years with democratic progressive experiments in private schools, when ideas migrated into public school teaching. Since the 1960s, it was also a pattern for reform in higher education. It is no coincidence that some in our group had actually run small schools with big educational ambitions; such practitioners among us knew firsthand about having inhabited a unified small culture blending the social and the intellectual; the small-school democratic, progressive vision shaped our sense of how a team should operate. We were, in effect, trying to create on the university level the ethos of small schools like Prospect and Commonwealth and the progressive public school experiments that were such a dramatic piece of educational reform in the 1970s and 1980s—examples such as Deborah Meier's Central Park East and Central Park East Secondary School in New York and the many public and private high schools in Theodore Sizer's Coalition of Essential Schools.

Most of us, too, sensed that we were drawing on past and present work at the Bank Street College of Education from the time of its founder, Lucy Sprague Mitchell. We were attempting to create in a Big Ten public university a version of Bank Street's small and intense program, with its depth of intellectual life and personal commitment. We all drew in different ways from older models of decent and imaginative institutions: various school reforms of the 1960s, historic schools like the turn-of-the-century Dewey School in Chicago, experiments over the years in democratic progressive teacher education—varieties of intellectual progressivism, and the history of the democratic impulse in both schools and society.

Many of us had been influenced by work in particular curriculum areas that gave new subject-matter depth to the old democratic, progressive goal of paying close attention to children's thinking and the "having of wonderful ideas" and to connecting the child and the curriculum (Duckworth, 1987, p. 1). Two areas of the curriculum in particular had given tantalizing visions of the possibilities of engaging children intellectually: mathematics at MSU, with the pioneering work of Deborah Ball and Magdalene Lampert, and literacy, where the 1960s and '70s had broken new ground in having all children read and interpret ambitious texts and getting them all to write. All of us had some familiarity with teacher education—offering workshops, giving courses, running programs, but only Feiman-Nemser had a lot of concrete experience and a larger vision of the possibilities of a progressive version of teacher education involving intimate partnerships with teachers in the field.

Creating Team Structures

Basic to the work of the team was the understanding that good learning interweaves the social and the intellectual. Relationships and the cultivation of a good climate for human connections were central. This involved not only respecting people, but building structures in which respect could become manifest (Meier, 2002).

Coursework and Course Coordination

Course titles and credit allotments were built into the original program design that all three teams inherited. Within the constraints of a common program, each team developed its own identity and geographic base. Students entered as juniors, took two years of courses and fieldwork, and then did a yearlong internship in schools while taking four graduate-level courses and thus earning more than half of the credits required for certification during this fifth and final year. Over time, we learned that our students were entering the internship with insufficient knowledge of subject-matter pedagogy, so we began to focus the intern year seminars more on subject-matter teaching than we had under the original design.

In explaining the program to new Team One students, we often said that each year had a general theme. In the junior year, students begin learning to think like a teacher by enrolling in a course in which, among other things, they do a careful study of one child. In the senior year, students begin learning to know like a teacher—integrating subject-matter knowledge, curriculum, and pedagogy. In the intern year, students begin learning to act like a teacher—putting thinking, knowing, and doing together in supervised practice. Table 2 shows the sequence of courses taken by students in the program:

Because of the number of students on Team One, we typically offered four sections of each course. As is often the case in large university programs, instructors were a mix of tenured and adjunct faculty and doctoral students. While many instructors stuck with the team for a few years, there was also considerable turnover. Consequently, we struggled to find ways to sustain program continuity and ensure that key ideas in our "spiral curriculum" were being addressed in each course. Accordingly, we developed a team structure whereby we assigned a small amount of faculty load time to course coordinators. These people convened all the instructors for a particular course before the semester began to develop common plans and similar syllabi. Instructors continued to meet regularly across the duration of the course to adjust plans, discuss individual student issues, and support each other's teaching. In effect, each course in the program conducted a parallel seminar on itself, by and for its instructors. This structure was particularly helpful in mentoring doctoral students as they gained experience as teacher educators. Course coordinators also served on the Team One steering committee.

Steering Committee

From the beginning of the team in 1993, Jay Featherstone and Sharon Feiman-Nemser, as faculty coleaders, created a steering committee to deal with important issues and program business. Besides the two team leaders, the steering committee included David Carroll and Susan Donnelly as team coordinators, the coordinators for each of the main courses or components in the program, and Margaret Malenka, the coordinator of our distant site in Grand Rapids. Steering committee decisions were typically reached by consensus after informal discussion. An example of a meeting announcement from our first semester of work suggests the flavor of the group:

November 11, 1993

To: Team One Steering Committee
From: Sharon F.-N. and David C.
Re: Tomorrow's Meeting

Just a note to confirm the steering committee meeting tomorrow from 2:00–3:00 in Room 310. We want some advice about the following items: (1) "next steps" in our team-wide conversation about the emerging rationale of the program; (2) expanding to additional districts; (3) how to pursue the issue of "diversity" with interns and in the program overall. If you have other issues to raise, let us know.

The agenda often included problem-solving issues as well—how to resolve a concern about a particular student or instructor; how to stage a discussion at a school to get at conflicting understandings about a particular practicum experience; how to mount an argument at the department or college level about resources or staffing issues. At first we felt that the free range of the dialogue—moving from small topics and issues to profound questions—was a distraction; in time we came to prize the constant mix and connection of "high" and "low" and to value it as a way to develop ourselves as a group. Frequently the discussion would involve clarifying the issues or principles involved, outlining a tentative course of action, and delegating key individuals to carry out the plan. The snacks at the steering committee meetings were first-rate, and the spirit was raucous and egalitarian. From the start, graduate students, staff, and faculty weighed in as equals. Steering committee members developed the habit of asking who should handle a particular new problem, turning most of us into switch hitters. In addition to dealing with program administration, we all taught courses.

Team-Wide Meetings

Twice a year we arranged a team-wide retreat for all the instructors and other staff. The format of these changed as the program developed and new issues took center stage. An early format involved creating a talking tour of

TABLE 2   Courses in the New MSU Program

Year, Semester	Number	Credits	Title	Fieldwork	What Students Do
Junior, Fall latest	TE 150	3	Reflections on Learning	None	Study human learning, reflecting on one's own learning in college classes as example.
Junior, Fall latest	TE 250 or	3	Human Diversity, Power, and Opportunity in Social Institutions	None	Study processes that distribute opportunity in society, including the school; how human characteristics, including culture, affect those processes; issues of justice.
	CEP 240	3	Diverse Learners in Multicultural Perspective		
Admission to the Teacher Certification Program					
Junior, Spring	TE 301	4	Learners and Learning in Context: Thinking like a Teacher	Two hours per week child study	Consider relationship between teaching and learning, how teachers create learning opportunity, what it means to "know" students and build on their learning needs and interests. Teaching literacy.
Senior, Fall	TE 401	5	Teaching Subject Matter to Diverse Learners	Average four hours per week	Study and practice what it means to understand subject matters, subject-specific strategies to promote student understanding, forms of classroom organization consistent with those strategies. Conduct interviews with teacher and students about curriculum; planning and teaching content-oriented lessons to individuals and small groups.

Semester	Course	Credits	Course Title	Hours	Description
Senior, Spring	TE 402	6	Designing and Studying Practice	Average four hours per week	Same as above.
Fifth, Fall	TE 501	6	Internship in Teaching Diverse Learners, I	Average twenty-five hours per week	Coplan and coteach with collaborating teacher, with support from MSU liaison; continued work in curriculum and teaching in the areas of literacy and math; study of one's own teaching; exploration of teacher's roles and responsibilities in relation to the school and community.
	TE 801	3	Professional Roles and Teaching Practice, I		
	TE 802	3	Reflection and Inquiry in Teaching Practice, I		
Fifth, Spring	TE 502	6	Internship in Teaching Diverse Learners, II	Average twenty-five hour per week	Lead-teach and reflect with coaching from collaborating teacher and MSU liaison; curriculum and teaching work in science; continued study of one's own teaching through a personally designed inquiry project; preparation of professional portfolio.
	TE 803	3	Professional Roles and Teaching Practice, II		
	TE 804	3	Reflection and Inquiry in Teaching Practice, II		

each course. Instructors for each course would collaborate on the questions below and then choose a representative to present to the whole team:

+ What, in essence, is the course about?
+ How does the course connect with others in the program? To what extent does it build on what students already know or lay a foundation for what is to follow?
+ How does the course begin? What are key assignments?
+ How is student learning assessed?
+ What do students find particularly interesting or challenging?

Several years later, the team retreats focused on strengthening continuities across the curriculum. Groups of participants affiliated with core course clusters were asked to describe key tasks or assignments in their courses and then comment on how they related to the goals of the course and the standards of the program. On another occasion, we all looked at a set of teaching portfolios prepared by interns, refined the rubrics used to assess them, and considered how each course in the program prepared interns to create a professional portfolio.

Typically, each retreat would be followed by a sumptuous potluck dinner held at Jay's or Sharon's house. The care that went into preparing the food spoke of a deeper sense of community. The team often described itself as engaging in "serious play"; potlucks were heavily weighted toward the second word in the phrase.

School Relations and the Role of the Liaison

In previous MSU programs, people assigned to work with teacher candidates in the field were called field instructors. In developing the new program, each team formed partnerships with a network of districts and schools in which they placed interns in clusters of five or six per building. Department policy determined that working with this number would constitute a quarter-time load for a graduate student or adjunct faculty member. On Team One, we sought to construct this leadership role in new ways that reflected our understanding of the partnership with teachers and schools we wanted and the process of learning to teach. We named this position the "liaison," wanting to emphasize our intention of working with teachers and schools to help interns develop a professional teaching practice. A doctoral student who pioneered developing the role looked up "liaison" in the Oxford English Dictionary and discovered two meanings that were not only a source of amusement but also captured the complicated position we were seeking to invent: "(a) the binding element in a rich soup; (b) an illicit relationship."

Our program handbook listed the following responsibilities of the liaison:

- Help a group of interns in a school become a professional learning community;
- Observe individual interns in their classrooms, provide written feedback, and confer with them and their collaborating teachers about their planning and teaching (a minimum of two or three times a month for each intern);
- Plan and lead a weekly intern study group;
- Meet with collaborating teachers as a group periodically to discuss seminar assignments, clarify expectations, facilitate problem-solving, and provide support;
- Communicate with principals about interns' progress and program activities;
- Assist interns in developing and implementing personal learning goals;
- Convene midterm, end-of-semester, and end-of-year evaluation meetings with interns and collaborating teachers and assign final grades in consultation with them;
- Write descriptive summaries of interns' learning and accomplishments for placement files;
- Participate in staff seminars for MSU liaisons.

As this list of responsibilities suggests, we envisioned the liaison as having one foot in the university and the other in the school (a kind of illicit relationship in terms of past university-school relations) and playing a binding role between the two. By clustering interns and assigning one liaison to work with a particular school, we were able to develop a continuous and deepening relationship with most schools. Liaisons were to consult and meet with collaborating teachers, both individually and as a group, as well as work with interns individually and in a weekly intern study group held at the school.

To support the doctoral students and adjunct faculty who usually filled the liaison role, and to jointly develop the kind of school-based teacher education practice that the role required, we convened weekly or biweekly study group meetings for liaisons. Although these meetings also played an administrative function and enabled us to explain policy and procedures and communicate with interns via their liaisons, they were primarily a staff and program development opportunity. Here is how Jenny Denyer, liaison coordinator in 1998, announced the agenda for an upcoming liaison study group meeting:

> Just a quick note about our meting this week: Following our plan of looking at specific instances or problems from our practice, Pat Norman will present a case about helping new collaborating teachers learn to mentor their interns. First Pat will tell us a bit about her school context. Then she will describe how she has been working with two collaborating teachers, including a problem that she is encountering. At that point, we will think and talk together about Pat's case, drawing on our own work with CTs. The issue of how we work with CTs is one of the pivotal aspects of our role as liaisons. I'm looking forward to tomorrow's conversation to push my own thinking. See you at 9:00 in Room 310.

This example, in which a group used records of practice from one liaison to investigate broader issues and dilemmas, is typical of the study group's way of working. The study group also scaffolded the learning of teacher education doctoral students and adjunct faculty. The role of the liaison as we came to define it involved a complex reflective practice, and individuals playing that role greatly benefited from opportunities to develop it collaboratively with other liaisons.

Student Support

Intending to transform a large university teacher education program into a more responsive and intimate community, we asked Susan Donnelly to serve as student coordinator. Our awareness of this role's significance emerged gradually with the evolution of the team and of Donnelly's understanding of the position and its possibilities. At first we saw Donnelly and David Carroll as co-coordinators, together managing the administration and organization of course schedules, instructor support, student registration, school placements, and coordination of bureaucratic structures and requirements of the university. In the initial year or two of the program, as we made simultaneous transitions from student teaching to the new internship program and from a quarter system to a semester one, much of their work was devoted to putting out fires. Students and their parents challenged the wisdom of the new design, which required them to pay tuition—and forego a salary—for an extra year, and placed new restrictions on students' opportunities to request particular student-teaching placements. All of us struggled to invent and teach new courses, and many of us faced classroom mutinies and crises of confidence. Carroll and Donnelly spent a great deal of time visiting undergraduate classes, answering questions, and explaining the rationale for new structures and policies. In addition, they made a point of serving as ombudsmen for students and collaborating teachers in addressing particular concerns that arose in this transition period.

Donnelly gradually assumed a central role in assisting in situations requiring interpersonal problem-solving: conflicts between students and university instructors, difficulties between interns and their collaborating teachers, instances of unprofessional conduct by students. As she gained experience and insight into this work, Donnelly began to take a proactive role in helping Team One staff and collaborating teachers to anticipate problematic situations and find ways of dealing with them productively. She established routines that alerted her to emerging conflicts so she could intervene before they became intractable. She worked with others on the team to prepare students to share responsibility for forming collegial relationships with their mentor teachers. She articulated what became Team One dogma: it is far better to deal with trouble when it is small than to hope for the best until it becomes Big Trouble. She came to see her administrative and problem-solving role as an educational practice. In that sense, she deliberately began to shape her individual interactions as learning opportunities for the participants.

Donnelly succeeded in part because she came to know intimately both the content and aims of each course and the complex roles of the other players on the team, thus her advice rarely came across as generic. Her extraordinary capacity to listen made her a model of the team's difficult injunction to itself to pay attention to the individuals. Donnelly's work with students, instructors, teachers, and liaisons enabled her to play a large role in developing policy at the program level, defining appropriate professional conduct for students and a system of measures for dealing with difficulties.

Donnelly also attended to our students and collaborating teachers as individuals in the area of internship placements. Because we intentionally returned to the same schools each year for placements, we could give students only limited choice in the selection of their internship site. Similarly, our need to place all of our students—not just those with whom teachers wished to work—constrained teachers' choices. And within that closed universe of teachers and interns, we also tried to balance the clusters of students across our schools so that no school received only the most—or least—capable students. Astonishingly, Donnelly managed to design placement routines that offered both teachers and prospective teachers a measure of choice while also making use of the team's collective knowledge of all players.

In this system, prospective interns first stated their preference for type of school (urban/suburban or rural, elementary/middle), and schools identified teachers interested in hosting interns. All students were then sent out on two team-wide visiting days to two or three schools to participate in tours and group interviews with prospective mentor teachers there. Both teachers and students would then report to Donnelly, using placement request forms and listing a range of possible partnerships they could entertain. Donnelly reviewed the overall requests, consulted with other Team One staff who knew individual students or teachers, and talked further with many students about their requests. Next, she plotted potential clusters of intern placements and invited responses from teachers and students before finalizing plans. This kind of individualized attention to particular students' needs is more characteristic of small teacher education programs than large ones.

Donnelly also cultivated a small number of experienced mentor teachers who were willing to take on students with a troubled history in the program. She used her knowledge of individuals to make suggested matchups that seemed promising, and most students and teachers experienced at least a degree of choice in their final placements. (For a further discussion of Susan Donnelly's role, see chapter 2.)

Striving for Quality

The various ways of organizing and carrying out our work were all, in one way or another, ways of striving for quality in teaching and learning despite the demands of working with large masses of students. The challenge involved keeping in play several key relationships: the social and the intellectual, the academic and the personal—treating people as individuals while fostering a team sensibility, sustaining both individual and collective conversation. It also meant linking program standards to our efforts; managing crises, monitoring, and mentoring; personalizing learning; praising some people while critiquing others. In short, the central task was attending to all the ways that a group signals to its members and to the world that certain norms and practices and styles of thinking reign in this setting, and that each individual counts.

Quality also involved a constant effort at conversation—team members consistently reflected together on experience. And quality meant setting up institutional structures and social and intellectual practices that could help the team see itself and build connections. Susan Donnelly's practice of scanning students in need of special concern or attention—actively scouting out small trouble before it turned into big trouble—was one way that the team promoted quality. More often than not, her approach to a student of concern involved a conversation with the instructor and the student.

The work of liaisons in schools was another example: in addition to mentoring a group of interns in a school, liaisons served as bridges from the team to schools, getting to know important figures in the school community, building an ongoing and deepening connection. In the inevitable crisis, they usually knew whom to talk to. We realized after a time that we were building networks; that they were feeding each other to create a culture of conversation, reflection, and common action; and that we were learning as a collective, as well as individually.

The team tried to make problems and crises educational for the parties involved and for the organization as a whole. Here the constant focus on the individual came into play. Thus the problem of a failing intern could provoke a thoughtful exchange about standards and the nature of the mutual partnership between the classroom teacher and MSU, while the particular student remained the focus. Under such conditions, it was indeed possible to say at times that serious problems—shared, discussed, and overcome—made stronger partnerships and more reflective partners. And individuals were almost always far better served after such conversations.

Creating a Team Culture

These examples of team structures and the ways they helped us develop and sustain quality teaching and learning illustrate that Team One was much more than an administrative unit for delivering a program. We saw our work as fundamentally educational and value-laden in every facet. We were creating a culture, a community of conversation and practice, functioning much more like a school than an administrative unit in the university. Our school community as it emerged was guided by the following principles:

1. Attention to individuals and their experience lies at the heart of human endeavors of any kind. In our case it meant a steady attention to the individual MSU student, the individual child in a classroom, the individual teacher, the individual MSU doctoral student or instructor. Our work was both fundamentally informed by and responsive to the circumstances of individuals across the program. We were institutionalizing respectfulness and a faith in capacity and growth.

2. Our work was an ongoing process of inquiry, not the implementation of a program design. The intellectual work of deepening our understanding of teaching and learning to teach went hand in hand with opportunities for conversation and, more formally, social processes for collective inquiry and the public examination of ideas and practice. We were institutionalizing thoughtfulness. We were expecting to change as we went along, not to administer a fixed plan or implement policy.

3. Administration and coordination are acts of teaching and, ultimately, culture-building. The ways in which we communicated information, developed structures of organization, solved problems, and conducted business in general were occasions for enacting our educational purposes and values. Managing and teaching the program were not separate activities. We were a learning community.

Given the complexity and scale of what we faced, what allowed us to keep the big picture in sight and do the essential, ongoing work of relating small pieces to big? In our daily rounds, we were creating what Jerome Bruner (1996) calls "cultures of ideas and practice." Speaking of the role of schools in creating communities and cultures of ideas and practice, Bruner writes:

> I conceive of schools and preschools as serving a renewed function within our changing societies. This entails building school cultures that operate as mutual communities of learners, involved jointly in solving problems, with all contributing to the process of educating one another. Such groups provide

not only a locus for instruction, but a focus for identity and mutual work. Let these schools be a place for the praxis (rather than the proclamation) of cultural mutuality . . . which means an increase in the awareness that children have of what they are doing, how they are doing it, and why. . . . And since school cultures of mutual learners naturally form a division of labor within them, the balance between cultivating native talent and enabling all to move ahead gets expressed internally in the group in the more human form of "from each according to his or her ability." In such school cultures . . . being naively good at something implies, among other things, helping others get better at that something. (pp. 81–82)

Although Bruner is talking about schools, we always thought of Team One as, in effect, a small school. Our aim was to match this school spirit, with its emphasis on mutuality, teamwork, and the sharing and development of talent. Bruner's model applies well to the new reform-minded schools that were springing up in the 1980s and '90s in cities all over the country; the novelty of Team One was that it attempted something like it in teacher education. Like our school counterparts, we were struggling to construct a community capable of continuous reflection and self-development: a collaborative culture.

Each year at the start of the program, we extended to new students, staff, and collaborating teachers an invitation to collaborate with us. In the forward to our Team One handbook, we wrote:

We do not claim to have reached the promised land, but we have put in place a promising framework that blends contemporary research, the wisdom of practice, and our own experience with teacher education. Built into the very idea of teacher education with firm roots in the field is the notion that this program will evolve. Many as yet unknown features of this program will emerge from work in schools, the possibilities of which we are just beginning to glimpse. Teacher education students as well as teachers will take a hand in shaping this program as the partnership between MSU and the schools flourishes. . . . We are counting on you to work with us in making the program better.

2

Caring for Students
While Gatekeeping for the Profession:
The Student Coordinator Role[1]

David Carroll, with Susan Donnelly

As we launched Team One of the new teacher education program at Michigan State University in 1993, we had little prior experience with large-scale teacher education to guide ourselves. We were finding our way based on values and beliefs about teaching and a vague sense that we needed to remake the basic nature of the teacher education program as it had been known—something much more than simply reorganizing the program structure into teams of faculty and students. As teachers, we learned from our students and from paying attention to what they were experiencing and what sense they made of that experience. We also gained insight from each other and from important colleagues outside the team—particularly Joella Cogan, head of the student affairs office and a skilled counselor. Gradually, we began to understand larger patterns about the culture-building work of forming a team and a new program. Much in the way some middle school educators in that era were attempting to turn junior high schools into more developmentally sensitive and smaller-scale settings for meeting the educational needs of teens, we were trying to change the fundamental culture of the institution of teacher education in the university.

Before the reform efforts that began in many places during the 1980s, most students in large teacher education programs had to take personal responsibility for making coherent sense of a whole often made up of fragmented parts. At Michigan State, the standard program, which preceded the reforms of 1993, featured a laundry list of separate certification courses offered in multiple sections and taught by an array of tenured faculty, graduate students, and adjunct faculty assigned centrally by teacher education department administrators. What was taught in any particular section of a course depended largely upon who happened to be teaching it. There was seldom any conceptual linkage between courses and little in the way of a deliberate sequence building from one course to another. Student teaching arrangements were organized by a separate office responsible for hundreds of individual field placements in over one hundred school districts spread across Michigan. Each student teacher was essentially parachute-dropped into a ten-week placement and visited occasionally by a traveling field supervisor who might be responsible for up to a dozen students across several school districts. If students encountered difficulties with registration, or felt mistreated, or just needed advice of some kind, they had recourse to one central student affairs office serving over a thousand students.

One of our first moves in putting this legacy behind us was to assign the role of student coordinator to Susan Donnelly. She took on the lead responsibility for organizing the inevitable bureaucracy of the program related to registration, placements, and the interface with other university requirements, while also making students feel known and cared for in ways responsive to their individual concerns and needs. She also assumed a central role in assisting in situations where interpersonal problem-solving was required: conflicts between students and instructors; difficulties between interns and their collaborating teachers; and issues of unprofessional conduct by students.

The role Susan constructed for herself over time is reminiscent of the advisor's role in the Bank Street College of Education program, as described by Shapiro (1991):

> The advisor is counselor, supervisor, and a source of practical as well as theoretical information. He or she is also a trouble-shooter, a coordinator of the needs of different students, a support in times of difficulty, a challenge to perform at one's maximum. (p. 8)

This chapter describes Susan's work and the insights she developed around it by drawing on her own recollections of the experience as I collected them through interviews, augmented from my perspective as her colleague and fellow team coordinator.

In part 1, we describe getting started and our initial impulses to be responsive to our students in the same ways we had been guided as teachers. As we gained experience, we began to understand this as developing a culture of caring, in which our students would experience for themselves what we wanted them to create in classrooms for their students. Noddings (2001) has written extensively about this topic and the way that promoting caring requires attention not just to particular relations but to the overall institutional setting:

> The relational nature of caring . . . requires attention not only to the responses and reactions of students to their teachers' attempts to care but also to the settings in which teachers work. Relations between administrators and teachers can help provide a setting in which caring can flourish. (p. 103)

As program administrators, we were particularly conscious of the impact of our actions on this fragile culture we were attempting to build.

In part 2, we trace an underlying idea in our work—that our students were undergoing a significant transition in their lives from student to professional teacher—and discuss how that led us to create an informal curriculum for teaching professional behavior. Finally, in part 3, we examine the gatekeeping role that we enacted, with greater confidence and compassion, on the foundation of a culture of caring and professional mentoring.

GETTING STARTED: DEVELOPING A CULTURE OF CARING

Developing Systematic and Collective Approaches to Addressing Student Concerns

A major initial area of encounter with our students was introducing them to the program and addressing their questions and concerns. It was a new experience for students used to contending with the faceless bureaucracy of a forty-thousand-student university to be treated reasonably and responsively and to be provided with explanations for policies and procedures and multiple opportunities for raising questions. As Susan explained:

> One of the things that came through from the students was that they needed to feel they were communicated with and getting information. We tried to always be available and always respond to them—e-mails, phone calls. I never let a message sit for more than twenty-four hours before getting back to the student one way or another. I was trying to create an atmosphere of general responsiveness, by being available and being willing to talk, and by making information available.

Susan initiated the student advisory group, in which she regularly met with students from across the program to discuss their questions, hear their suggestions, and provide information. This was an important venue for her own learning, where Susan heard students' perspectives on the program directly. She attempted to recruit at least one student from each course section so that there would be maximum input and students would feel they had some part in their own program.

As Susan listened to students' concerns and worked with individual students around their difficulties and questions, she began to better understand how they were experiencing the program. She used these insights to organize systematic and proactive approaches to inform students and alleviate their anxieties, explaining:

> I realized that students needed information about the internship year much earlier than we had thought they would. Students often thought they would have to begin full-time teaching very soon after the beginning of the intern year, as had been the case with student teaching. They would get so anxious about the senior year because they didn't know what the expectations were for the internship. I went into all the classes in the beginning of the senior year to talk about it. It helped them enormously just to hear that in the internship they would build up toward teaching responsibilities gradually over several months.
>
> I also talked with them about the internship placement process. They needed to know how it was going to work and how they would be involved. I realized how reassuring it was to them to get more information and lots of opportunities to ask questions. I think that the more that we did that as administrators, the more the instructors did that, too. It became a team approach.

Problems Are Endemic

At any given moment, some of our students were experiencing a variety of personal-health or family-related problems that interfered with their ability to carry on as students. In a program of the scale on which we were operating, these kinds of problems are endemic. As Susan described:

> There were situations that came up that would interfere with their class work—a death in the family or a medical issue, for example. Usually I was alerted to those situations by instructors who would say, "Something's happened with this person. They started out the semester fine and partway

through obviously something changed." One girl was diagnosed with cancer. Somebody else had a grandmother whom she'd been very close to who had died. She'd gone to the funeral and tried to come back but been unable to keep up with the work.

We would make arrangements for them to take a break in their program and come back later. They wouldn't assume that they could do something like that and they would try to keep going until they'd be in really bad shape. If I talked to them and explained, "You know, if you can't finish this semester there are incompletes, there are ways to deal with this . . ." It would make quite a difference for them.

In addition to these typical life circumstances, which affected many students at one time or another, some students entered the program with acute medical or psychological conditions, which we only discovered as they surfaced in the course of their interactions with others in the program. Other kinds of serious issues emerged during the program with the onset of psychological troubles, reactions to personal assaults, relationship difficulties, et cetera. Susan described some typical situations:

When you have four or five hundred students admitted primarily on test scores with no interview process, some students get admitted who have serious psychological problems. With teaching, you have to be pretty emotionally and psychologically stable to deal with groups of kids because they're going to push your buttons. It's stressful and it can be very frustrating. If you've got buttons to be pushed, they'll find them.

Every semester there was somebody who disappeared from class. Almost invariably that turned out to be a student suffering from serious depression.

I would talk to people who knew them and see if anybody knew what was happening. If they lived in residences I would phone because there were residence advisors who would check on them. Sometimes we ended up being in contact with parents because something would happen that the parents were worried about. Several times we found people who were just not coming out of their rooms and needed attention.

By refusing to think generically or brush off the traumas of personal life or the inevitable snafus of institutional life as inconsequential, Susan treated our students to the kind of individualized attention that they might expect from a good teacher. By paying prompt and genuine attention to their challenges and difficulties as they navigated the life transition experiences they encountered, Susan began to convey the message that they were cared for.

Working with Team One Staff to Support the Culture of Caring

Susan also regularly attended course coordination meetings, where instructors met to plan and sustain their teaching around a particular course. In her responses to questions or concerns about students, she would model the kind of caring concern about students as individuals that we were attempting to embody as a team and relate that concern to our responsibilities as teachers. She explained, "I frequently talked with colleagues about how every interaction with students is a teaching opportunity—it isn't just in classes—all the time, in all the ways in which we interact with them, we teach them how to interact in professional ways." In those course meetings we also talked regularly about students of concern. These might be individuals struggling either academically or with the kinds of professional interactions we expected them to engage in. We also spoke about students who needed more challenge or whom we needed to watch because they were too quiet. Instructors shared observations about students, and often we advised ourselves to observe further or to arrange a particular conversation with the student, perhaps with Susan participating.

Susan also made herself available as a resource for instructors who experienced difficulties in their interactions with students. Often when she was facilitating conversations between a student and an instructor she realized that the faculty member or graduate student was feeling threatened. By working with individual instructors, she helped them avoid responding defensively, or from a power position—not necessarily giving in, but really hearing what the student was saying. With these beginnings, a new culture was being constructed in Team One.

BUILDING A CURRICULUM OF PROFESSIONAL BEHAVIOR FOR STUDENTS IN TRANSITION

Students in Transition

One of the things Susan came to see about her work was that our students were undergoing major life transitions—in terms of status, power, responsibility, and identity—as they moved from being students toward adulthood. Magnifying that process was the particular impact of becoming a teacher, an adult role that demands special emotional and psychological stability. Buchmann (1993) describes the transition that those who become teachers must make as assuming a role orientation, as opposed to a personal orientation. She identifies this orientation as crucial for teaching, and for which prior experience as a student in schools is not helpful:

> The teaching role entails a specific and difficult shift of concern from self to others for which the "apprenticeship of observation" provides no training. . . . In general, a shift of concern from self to others comes more from acknowledging, "This is the kind of work I am doing," than from stating, "This is how I feel" or "This is how I do things."(Buchmann 1993, p. 148)

With our new program, the yearlong classroom internship served as a pressure cooker for intensifying many of these transition issues. More generally, though, Susan came to understand the impact of this transition on students' interactions with each other, with their instructors, and with collaborating teachers in their practicum and internship placements. She also took steps to convey these understandings to students across the program:

> As I came to understand the transition they were going through I could talk about that with them and demystify it. We started when they were admitted by having an orientation that included talking about the stresses of the transition they were facing. They were embarking on two and a half years of very intense work. We let them know up front some of the potential pitfalls to watch out for and that if they ran into anything like that they could come and talk to me or they could talk to their instructors. I think that made a big difference right away.

By conceptualizing these transition issues as part of an identity transition, Susan helped the team see them as matters for teaching. Although Susan was effectively an administrator for the team, she brought her experience and orientation as a teacher and early childhood educator to the work. She viewed the business of the team as an array of opportunities for teaching students to move through these transitions in the most healthy and productive ways possible.

Building an Informal Curriculum for Developing Professional Responsibility

As Susan encountered these issues in the initial years of the program, she communicated to students, instructors, and steering committee her conviction that, while problems were inevitable, they could also be addressed through effort suited to each situation and the people involved in it. Susan came to see difficulties as opportunities to convey to students our sense of caring for and about them, to help them through the transition from student to adult/teacher, and to teach an informal professional curriculum. The curriculum helped our students learn how to interact respectfully and productively and how to balance their own needs with those of the larger learning community. She approached these challenges much as she would have as a classroom teacher; she linked her approach to her own experience as a teacher of young children:

> With young children, most difficulties they run into are in social situations that they didn't know how to deal with. I would treat it as a teaching opportunity—talking with them about what went wrong and what could be done differently. I might provide them with some language that they could use or teach them to negotiate situations where their needs were in conflict with somebody else's or where they had different expectations from somebody else or where something happened that they didn't intend.
>
> I think it's similar with teacher education students. To begin with, it means treating difficult situations as teaching opportunities. If they messed up in class or if they were not appearing in class but not letting anybody know, we needed to treat those as teaching opportunities to help them through that transition.

As our students encountered this transition experience, we realized there were things they needed to learn that were not part of the formal curriculum for the program. A critical element was inducting students into the kind of respectful, interactive classroom learning culture we wanted them to be able to provide for their future students. We also wanted them to develop a vision of teaching that included working reasonably and collaboratively with colleagues and peers.

Some students didn't understand or weren't concerned about the impact of their thoughtless remarks on their fellow students. Some also didn't know or care about how to raise critical questions with their instructors in reasonable and productive ways. They would sometimes confront an instructor in class rather than meeting with the instructor individually and saying what their concerns were and giving the instructor a chance to talk about addressing them. Susan viewed these occasions as the training ground for a kind of collaborative professional consciousness.

As fallout from these events would reach Susan through conversations with both students and instructors, she arranged meetings and facilitated conversations between the student and the instructor and helped the student learn different ways of approaching such difficulties:

> Students started to come to me if they had concerns about an instructor or about a course. I could talk to them about a good way to approach it and coach them through it. I could say, "Do you want me to facilitate a conversation or do you feel like you can do this?" If they wanted to go ahead and do it themselves, I'd say, "OK, pretend I'm the instructor. Try it out on me." I'd explain to them that if they felt angry and went to talk about this in that frame of mind, the instructor was going to respond to their anger, not to what their words were. So I'd say, "The first time there may be anger in there, the second time might sound better. Sometimes just when you're nervous about something it may not come across very well, so trying it out usually helps." Sometimes I would be in on the conversation with them because they felt pretty intimidated by the situation.

The Internship as a Challenge for Professional Communication

The yearlong internship represented a particular challenge for students, collaborating teachers, and faculty and graduate students working with them. It was fraught with potential landmines because the students and collaborating teachers were working so closely together, almost like a marriage. As Susan put it,

> For the teacher, it's their classroom and if this intern starts to mess up in their eyes, it's not like messing up an order form in a store. These are their kids and they're very very emotionally invested in them; it's very hard for teachers to give up control in the first place to a learner and then, if it doesn't seem to be going right, it can really upset the teacher. On top of that, the interns are so vulnerable because they are novices in other people's classrooms.

As Susan got more experience in intervening in such situations, she gradually developed a repertoire of insights and practices to guide her work:

> I would make sure I talked with both the intern and the teacher separately prior to any kind of joint conversation—so both of them would have a chance to give me their perspective on it. That was a lesson I learned early on. I made a mistake at first when I would just hear the teacher's side or the student's

side, and then the other one would feel that they were being attacked or that they hadn't had a chance to give their point of view. If I heard from each of them separately, that also gave me a chance to hear the different viewpoints.

Although sometimes there was a definite wrongdoer, I realized there was usually no one "right" side. In many situations the teacher and the intern had been somehow misinterpreting each other and they hadn't been communicating. They had been communicating about superficial things but not about the deeper things that were bothering them. They would get the feeling from the other person that something wasn't quite right. For example, if the teacher was not very comfortable with what the intern was doing but didn't say so, the intern would know something wasn't quite right but might think something like "the teacher doesn't like me." They would feel it, and then they would respond to the feeling in ways that would snowball.

When it worked well, I could help them identify, "Where did this get started?" and help them recognize that there was something that they weren't communicating about and get them to do that. Then, if we caught it before too much time had passed, problems could be mutually addressed.

However, sometimes the miscommunication had gotten to such a point that, even if we talked about it and identified it, they couldn't let go of the emotional baggage that had collected. Then we sometimes had to switch a placement and let the intern start someplace new. But quite often, and as people got to trust that there was a process that they could call on, they asked for help soon enough and we could sort it out.

Susan and the team also cultivated a small number of experienced mentor teachers who were willing to take on students who encountered such a breakdown in their placement, who were less sought after in the initial placement process, or who may have posed potential problems based upon their previous experience in the program. In this way, Susan was able to use her knowledge of individuals to make suggested matchups that seemed likely to provide these students with a fair opportunity to overcome our initial concerns. At first, most of the teachers she called upon for this role came from the professional development school we worked with most closely, Averill Elementary School:

I think it started at Averill because the principal had an attitude that, being a professional development school, they had responsibilities to the program that another school might not feel. Also, because of the work they had already done with Sharon Feiman-Nemser prior to the new program, they saw themselves more as teacher educators than teachers at some of the other schools did at first. They were beginning to assume that role. And sometimes we needed a teacher that we could really just talk "straight" with about an intern's prior difficulties and know that they would not be overly protective. I think it started with a couple of teachers at Averill, and then gradually, we could call on others elsewhere for the same kind of thing. Usually it was after we had already worked with a teacher on a difficult situation that just happened, and, because we had developed a relationship of trust, we could call on them again in the future. We tried not to do it too often to the same teachers.

In these ways, we gradually created a culture in which students, faculty, graduate students, and collaborating teachers felt some confidence that their concerns would be dealt with respectfully and responsively and they wouldn't be left to deal with difficulties on their own. Intertwined with this culture of caring, we developed an informal curriculum for scaffolding the development of professional roles and responsibilities and for helping our students begin to build a repertoire of skills for managing professional interactions.

GATEKEEPING

In tension with this array of efforts to respond to the professional growth of students and to create a culture of caring was the gatekeeping role we played in making sure the persons who graduated from our program were suitable for teaching. The kinds of increasingly systematic structures and practices described here for reviewing students' progress with both the formal and informal curricula, and for developing the capacity of Team One staff to respond to students' needs, provided an essential foundation for playing a responsible and effective gatekeeping role. We all felt more resolute in setting limits or taking steps to question a student's suitability for teaching when we knew that those steps were based upon a continuum of systematic and collective efforts to understand and support students' progress.

Students in Crisis

Susan's response to the gatekeeping responsibility evolved in tandem with her reaction to students' need for support in managing transition issues. The scale of the program and the absence of a very discriminating admission policy meant that there were some students in the program at any given time who were in crisis. In particular, various kinds of mental disturbance either became evident or emerged as students proceeded through the program:

> One woman had a sudden psychotic episode. She disappeared from campus and flew to a distant city. She was found on an intersection there directing traffic. Officials there found out who she was and they called her father and he had to go down and get her. At first she was terrified and didn't know what was going on. She felt it was just this acute episode that happened and she insisted, "I'm fine, I'm fine." She went back to school and her father didn't know what to do—she was an adult and was able to make her own decisions. She disappeared again about a week later and I started phoning. She was found in a cemetery this time. I talked with her dad a few times. He was very concerned about her. He was finally able to get her into treatment. She withdrew for the rest of that year and did get medication. She went and stayed at home, and then she came back the next year and she did finish the program.

Gatekeeping in the internship was particularly complex, as it involved interpreting situations through the filter of different school cultures and individual perceptions. In particular, it meant developing a joint assessment of an intern's progress and potential with the collaborating teacher, as the following example illustrates:

> With this particular intern there was no initial indication that there was a problem. He was in a classroom and the teacher called me a few weeks into the year and said, "There's something odd happening here." She described some really strange responses he gave to kids—they were out at lunch recess and he made weird faces at them through the window, sticking out his tongue. And there were some inappropriate responses in the classroom, she said. "I just don't know what's going on." So I asked, "What do you want to do about it?" She told me, "I guess I just want you to know." We decided that she would wait and see, but then she phoned in just a few more days and said, "Susan there's something really odd here" and described a couple of other things.
>
> I talked to him and he didn't seem to realize that he was doing odd things. Our conversation did not quite connect either. If he didn't realize he was doing odd things, there wasn't much we could do to help him stop. So we just decided he really needed to stop the internship, because things were becoming too inappropriate. I talked to him about it, and we said that he needed to stop this internship and if he wanted to try again he could come back and we

could see about it another semester or something, but that we couldn't continue this right now.

So he got upset about it and went to the student affairs office and talked with the director there. By then, it was another week or two later; she knew right away that this student needed psychological help of some type. His appearance was changing. He was getting gray and sunken eyes. His parents later came in to complain or to find out what was going on, and she suggested to them, "You need to get him psychological help right away."

They did take him to a doctor and they learned that he had developed bipolar disorder over the course of a few months, and we had just been seeing the beginnings of it. The parents got him into treatment.

Issues of Integrity

The assessment of interns' suitability for teaching was expected to be based upon the internship standards, which addressed the broad territories of planning, instruction, classroom learning community, and professional responsibilities. The wording of the professional responsibilities standard, in particular, provided some language that could be used to address areas of conduct and disposition not usually reflected in grades or course assignments—students were expected to "act in a dependable and ethical manner, react appropriately in stressful situations, and give and accept constructive feedback," among other things. Yet these phrases were sufficiently vague that they didn't provide definitive guidance. When issues of ethics or integrity emerged in the internship it often devastated everyone, and we felt sure such issues would have been evident sooner if we had been in a position to see them. One situation involved Susan in several months of extended problem-solving:

> One intern lied several times to her instructor about substitute teaching. She had stayed at school to sub and missed a class and lied about it and had talked to one of the other interns and wanted her to cover for her. We had a policy that you didn't miss class to substitute, and so we called her on that and she claimed she had misunderstood. But she had tried to recruit another intern to also lie on her behalf, and the other intern wouldn't do it. That's how she got caught eventually.
>
> I wanted to cut the cord right there. If somebody's going to lie, they do not belong in teaching, but I got overruled by the teacher education pro-

gram coordinator, who wanted us to give it another try. She felt it might have just been a postadolescent mistake and the student needed another chance. The student had brought her dad in on it, and she just seemed to me to be somebody who was not even facing the real fact of what she did and the real consequences.

Because the program coordinator said we needed to give her another chance, we found another placement for her with two teachers at a different school who only knew that it hadn't worked out at the first placement. She was given a legitimate second chance, but she totally bombed. The fourth and fifth graders in her classroom had no respect for her. I went in and observed, and it was painful. We ended up failing her.

Developing Professional Criteria

These kinds of challenging experiences with students in difficulty began to suggest gaps in program policies and procedures. For example, during the first several years of the program, the only criterion required for taking part in the internship was to have passing grades in program course work. It had become clear to Susan and others in similar roles, however, that many of the problems encountered by students in the intern year concerned professional interactions and matters of ethics or integrity. When such issues became evident only near the end of the program, it was extremely difficult either to address them or to decide they warranted dismissal of the student. There was a need for a systematic process for assuring students' readiness for the professional demands of the internship and later teaching. This began with establishing records that went beyond merely tracking students' academic progress. As Susan explained:

> We started to document because we had situations where at first we thought it was just a little incident that would go away. It was fine and we had solved it. Then we realized later on when an issue resurfaced that we had to have documentation of the earlier manifestations of the problem.

In working through a number of difficult cases with concerns about professionalism issues, Susan had frequent conversations with the ombudsman and the university lawyer:

> I learned a lot by working with the ombudsman's office and the university lawyer around situations where, clearly, we were headed toward deciding a person was just not suitable for teaching. Our responsibilities to them as

students meant that we had to give them a chance to succeed, but we had to make very clear to them what the standards were that they had to meet, what the consequences would be if they failed. We had to be very deliberate about it, documenting everything, making sure that due process was followed and that they really did have an opportunity to succeed.

Eventually we could fail someone in the internship based on the professionalism standard, but it was hard if they were meeting some of the other standards. And that's also where the relationships with the teachers made a huge difference. Because if the teacher was on the same page as we were, it was a lot clearer.

When Susan would attempt to explain to the ombudsman and lawyer the difficulties that resulted when students failed to communicate about absences in school placements or weren't honest in their explanations of events, they, in turn, would ask whether there were specific written requirements detailing such expectations. Building on these conversations, Susan played a primary role in establishing a program-wide set of criteria to be used for determining students' progress toward entering the internship. As Susan's comments indicate, it was a slow and complex process:

Because the professional standards for the internship weren't very specific, it became clear to me that we needed something more. I also knew that there were sometimes concerns about individuals before the internship, but they weren't documented because there were no criteria or requirements about professionalism at that point.

So I started to talk to the ombudsman and lawyer about some written criteria. They explained that it was very difficult to do in a way that would be acceptable in terms of due process but agreed that if those were important aspects of becoming a teacher then it was probably worth tackling. The ombudsman was from the nursing program originally, and she understood the necessity of those kinds of criteria, but she also knew the difficulty in articulating them.

By talking to them I started to get an idea of what would be required to have something that was useable. I began a draft about some of the things that we kept running into and sent it to them. They responded with wording changes and things like "you have to be more specific here, you have to have examples," or whatever. Then, after revising according to their suggestions, the next year I took it through a committee of the program governance structure with members from all the teams. Together we worked on it for another whole year, then sent it through the college review process, and through the associate dean for student affairs. Next, it went back through the lawyer, back through the ombudsman, and they each added things. But finally it was approved.[2]

Implementing the Professional Criteria

Once the professional criteria for proceeding to the internship were officially approved, steps had to be taken to implement them systematically. If criteria were to exist, they had to be implemented across the board, not merely brought out when there was a problem. A checklist was developed for instructors to fill out every semester for all students around the professional criteria. That also gave us a chance to have deliberate and systematic conversations about students' capacities and dispositions related to the criteria. Susan explained how the new process worked:

> When concerns were raised about particular students, we talked with them about what they needed to do to meet the criteria and put that in writing in a letter to them. The bottom line now was that they had to meet the criteria to go into the internship. If something was identified and communicated in the junior year or the beginning of the senior year, but still unresolved, we could refuse the internship. Or, if we decided to allow the student to enter the internship, at least there was prior documentation and if something happened in the internship, we could say, "We've talked about this before and this isn't changing."

Distinguishing Intern Difficulties from Placement Difficulties

As we became more clear about the demands of the internship and the balance between supporting our students and assuming the gatekeeping role, we became more clear about the role that collaborating teachers and principals needed to play as our partners in that effort. In some cases, what at first looked like a difficulty on the intern's part turned out to be caused by particular qualities of the collaborating teacher and her approach to mentoring. This wasn't always easy to determine, however, as the following example illustrates:

> At one point we had an experience with a teacher who complained about her intern but not so extremely that we removed him. The intern talked about it being hard and said that he'd barely made it through. And then, two years

later, we had another intern with the same teacher, and again it was barely working. She wasn't doing well. Although not at first, the intern eventually talked about this teacher cutting her down, and being very critical, and making her feel worthless. The teacher had another story that also sounded reasonable. I was wondering what had really happened with the previous intern and so I tracked him down by phone. He told me, "Oh I wish I had told you. You should have never put anybody else with her." He described a similar pattern of critical undermining by the teacher. We did then move the second intern.

In some cases of this kind, we came to the conclusion that we could not achieve the kind of partnership necessary for mentoring novices, and we terminated relations with particular teachers or with entire schools. This happened in a few instances where teachers would not collaborate reliably with program staff in addressing difficulties or where principals were unwilling to step into such situations on our behalf.

Counseling Students toward Other Professions

In extreme situations, where the gatekeeping process indicated that teaching was not a suitable occupation for a student, Susan tried to communicate that in as caring a way as possible:

What I tried to do was to talk to them about how teaching is hard and it isn't for everybody. Some people came to that on their own and called me and said, "I cannot do this. I cannot be this organized." For others who hadn't yet faced it themselves, I had to raise the issue for them. For example, one intern was much too timid for teaching, at least at that point in her life, so we talked to her about what her strengths were. She knew she wasn't being successful. We talked to her about other things that she could potentially be good at and about getting career counseling, reminding her of the facilities on campus for doing that. She did do something else for a while, but then she came back and did the internship a second time, with much more self-confidence.

It was never fun, counseling someone out. There were times when we did encourage people to get counseling and sometimes made it a kind of requirement for their return to the program. We couldn't require that they see a psychiatrist or pursue some specific therapy, but we could require that they see somebody—it could be their pastor or a counselor of some sort—about a particular issue.

CONCLUSION

Creating the atmosphere and impact of a small student-centered school culture in a large university is an ongoing challenge, as personnel and policies change, outside events intervene, and the endemic difficulties of lives in transition arise with little or no warning. Yet by developing systematic procedures for sharing information with students and responding to their concerns in the ways described here, we were able to establish a solid foundation for a culture of caring on Team One. With Susan's leadership, we created multiple opportunities to help Team One staff and collaborating teacher partners to see our students' inevitable difficult experiences as opportunities for teaching and learning. We were able to help those who joined us in this work to develop repertoires of practice for scaffolding our students' learning and supporting them in making the transition toward becoming caring and responsible teachers. We assumed greater responsibility for teaching them how to be responsible professionals. We were also able then to make the kinds of tough, evidence-based yet compassionate decisions necessary for gatekeeping the profession.

Ironically, however, the very success we had in bringing a degree of order and predictability to the kinds of situations described here made us vulnerable to budget cutting in lean times. In bureaucratic eyes, the coordinator role was an administrative expense that the department could cut as we got the program up and running. The kind of attentiveness to students' lives and concerns that was at the heart of the informal social curriculum we constructed was essentially hidden from institutional eyes. We knew it could not be sustained simply by establishing administrative procedures. Thus we had to steadily fight for the assignment of load time for coordinator roles and continually advocate to help others see this work as a form of teaching situated in and essential to sustaining a culture of caring.

3

Professional Standards as Interpretive Space

Sharon Feiman-Nemser,
with Cindy Hartzler-Miller

How can teacher educators engage prospective teachers in a genuine inquiry about good teaching and also promote allegiance to professional teaching standards? How can they keep standards alive and prevent them from becoming hollow rhetoric? Drawing on program artifacts and personal recollections, this chapter traces early efforts by Team One at Michigan State University to develop program standards and later work to sustain a fresh conversation about standards in the face of staff turnover, new cohorts of students, and pressure from some quarters to "get it right."

I begin with an extended story about learning to teach teachers in what was at the time a new five-year, field-based teacher education program. The narrator is Cindy Hartzler-Miller, a social studies teacher who came to the doctoral program in teacher education at Michigan State University in the mid-1990s and who worked as a liaison with Team One.[1] This story takes us beneath the smooth surface of talk about teaching standards to the lived experiences of a thoughtful beginning teacher educator struggling to make space for two seemingly incompatible values—honoring teacher candidates' personal conceptions of good teaching and being accountable to Team One and the teaching profession. It points to a way of managing the tension and introduces key ideas about the nature of standards and their use in teacher education and the improvement of teaching practice.

Rethinking the Nature and Use of Standards

Cindy came to MSU after teaching high school social studies for six years. As a doctoral student, her teaching assistantship involved working as a liaison with a group of six teacher candidates in a yearlong internship at a middle school affiliated with Team One.[2] Cindy describes the beliefs about standards that she brought to her doctoral studies in this way: "If I was aware of the existence of [teaching] standards at all, I interpreted them as rhetorical devices—deliberately written in vague but lofty language to inspire broad-based commitment to excellence" (p. 89).

Cindy first encountered the MSU program standards at a staff meeting in 1995 where they were distributed with the understanding that the standards should guide the assessment of interns. "There was nothing to disagree with," Cindy writes, "but nothing very concrete or useful either" (p. 90). As she prepared for the first of four assessment conferences with her interns and their collaborating teachers, Cindy was reluctant to use the standards as a basis for judging her interns' progress and performance. Rejecting what she calls the "Imperial Evaluator" role—"telling interns they have to meet the standards and grading them on definitions of good teaching that may not mean anything to them"—she preferred to have interns set their own professional goals based on their personal definitions of good teaching. "This approach fit my schema quite nicely. Interns' own ideas about good teaching . . . would drive their practice. The program standards could be consulted to be sure that no broad, general categories of teaching were ignored, but they would not be presented as performance criteria" (p. 92).

When Cindy reported her plan, the Team One liaison coordinator suggested that she consider taking a more educative role, modeling for interns and collaborating teachers how to connect standards to concrete teaching practices. Cindy rejected the advice, preferring instead a role she calls "Backstage Hand." In retrospect, she writes that she completely failed to grasp the coordinator's meaning because she was "imagining the program standards to be like stone tablets, fixed and frozen until some committee made revisions" (p. 93).

Throughout the year, Cindy met with her six interns in a weekly school-based seminar, but she did not use these occasions to discuss the program standards in any depth. Rather, she continued to invite interns to write about their goals, pushing for specificity but not challenging or critiquing their descriptions. In her self-assessment at the end of the year, Cindy expressed some disappointment with her interns' growth. "By and large," she said, "they have not developed a practice that models reflective thinking" (p. 94).

Cindy felt caught between two seemingly incompatible values: "my desire to respect my interns' personal conceptions and my accountability to the profession." She described her inner conflict to a Team One faculty member, who asked whether she thought it was possible for interns as a group to "construct *shared* understandings of teaching practice." Later, as she mused on the question, a new mental image began to form: "Instead of the solitary teacher writing her own standards, teachers could actually be talking to one another about what they thought good teaching practice looks like and modify their ideas based on the interaction" (p. 94).

A subsequent Team One faculty retreat enabled Cindy to take the next step. She heard team leaders talk about their intentions in creating the new teacher education program, how they wanted the school-based seminars to be places where interns experienced a professional "community of practice." She also looked at national standards documents that faculty had consulted and at earlier drafts of program standards, written in an effort to represent negotiated meanings among faculty from different teams. "With all these documents spread out before me," she wrote, "I could see that, although the final product was written in general terms, the conversations which created the program standards focused on specific priorities" (p. 95).

In memos and conversations, team leaders talked about the standards as a "work in progress." Rather than viewing their abstract nature as a limitation, we saw it as an invitation to fill out the meaning of the standards through interpretation and instantiation. The following memo, sent in October, 1996 to collaborating teachers, expresses this stance:

> Until we give [the standards] real meaning through our own interpretations and examples, they will not become part of our thinking and practice. . . . Too often teaching standards are laid on teachers by people outside the classroom. Because teachers do not have a hand in framing the particular standards, they do not accept them as integral to their thinking or practice. This is why everyone involved in the internship—interns, liaisons, collaborating teachers, seminar instructors—must participate in the process of recreating the standards. (Team One memo, October 1996)

Based on a new understanding of the socially constructed nature of teaching standards, Cindy began to envision new ways to use professional teaching standards in helping her interns learn to teach. Rather than presenting standards as "authoritative, unambiguous statements" far removed from teachers' experience, she could now use them as starting points for professional conversations within communities of practice. The following year Cindy experimented with treating standards as "vision statements" and with taking on the role of "instructional mediator." At the beginning of the year she asked interns to list five characteristics of a good teacher. Then she had them choose one and write about where the idea came from and what a visitor to a classroom would see if the teacher were enacting that standard in practice. They underlined significant words in their texts and looked up definitions in the *Oxford English Dictionary*. After sharing their ideas with one another, they looked at the program standards as a source for further categories and language to frame their statements. For each assessment conference, interns revised their goal statements, deciding what kind of progress they had made, selecting new goals to work on, checking with program standards to see which aspects of teaching they were neglecting. "Throughout the year," Cindy writes, "I tried to use both interns' goals statements and the program standards as dynamic points of reference, to elicit my students' definitions of good teaching and link those ideas to the broader public and professional discourse about standards through the medium of critical conversation" (pp. 96, 98).

Cindy's personal journey took place in the context of her work as a Team One liaison over a two-year period. It also unfolded in the liaison study group, where she was encouraged to study and write about her practice.[3] Cindy's struggle to reconcile her commitment to inquiry and professional accountability became an ongoing theme in our joint work. As we drafted and redrafted our program standards, we sought authentic ways to connect these abstract statements to teachers' practice so that they could become both personal possessions and collective tools for improving our work.

DRAFTING (AND REDRAFTING) PROGRAM STANDARDS

In framing a set of professional standards for our teacher education program, we were influenced by national efforts to develop learning and teaching standards. The National Council of Teachers of Mathematics (1989) had issued new standards for curriculum and teaching that projected a vision of reform-minded teaching. The National Board for Professional Teaching Standards had published a statement (1989) outlining what teachers should know and be able to do, and various national committees dominated by classroom teachers were translating those core principles into standards of accomplished practice for K–12 teachers of different subjects and age levels. The Interstate New Teacher Assessment and Support Consortium (IN-

TASC) had developed a set of principles compatible with the more advanced teaching standards to be used as the basis for licensing standards and performance assessments (1992). These documents shaped our images of what standards could look like and offered useful organizing frameworks.

Various MSU faculty had participated in these national standards-setting efforts and we drew on their experiences with the process. As a member of the middle childhood generalist committee of the National Board for Professional Teaching Standards (NBPTS), I knew firsthand the intellectual stimulation and challenges this task presented. Getting a group of educators from different backgrounds to delineate dimensions of good teaching is no small task. While most people have strong beliefs about what good teaching entails, few are accustomed to framing those beliefs in terms of what teachers should know or be able to do. Doing so involves eliciting rich, contextualized stories from classroom teachers and working together to draw out the guiding principles. Finding the right level of generality and specificity, what we came to call "grain size," is tricky, especially when standards need to apply across multiple teaching contexts. Determining when sufficient agreement has been reached or when wordsmithing ceases to be productive requires sensitivity and judgment.

The MSU faculty had been organized into three teams, each responsible for developing relationships with a set of school districts and for designing and delivering a version of the new five-year program to its assigned students.[4] In the early years of the program, each team engaged in K–12 teacher education. Officially, we had one program on the books, and the departmental leadership expected us to come up with one set of program standards. At the same time, each team wanted the standards to express its vision of good teaching. How were we going to develop a sense of ownership within our team while negotiating a standards framework and language with our colleagues on other teams?

Looking back, it is hard to remember the exact process we went through to achieve an initial draft of program standards at Michigan State. Most significant for Team One was the summer working group that we set up with collaborating teachers from our partner schools. I remember meeting several mornings with a group of teachers, MSU staff, and doctoral students to introduce the idea of teaching standards; share personal images of good teaching; and think together about what graduates of our five-year program should know, care about, and be able to do. We wanted to familiarize our school-based colleagues with national standards-setting efforts and create a sense that, by participating in this local work, they were joining a larger conversation about good teaching and helping to enhance the teaching profession.

We talked about national standards work, invited people to list qualities of good teaching, shared our ideas, grouped these ideas into categories, and compared our clusters to the core principles of the National Board. The writing went through many iterations, some with faculty on the other teams, some internal to our team. Eventually team leaders agreed on a formulation that laid out four broad standards broken into fifteen elements representing our view of good beginning teaching's core dimensions (Table 1).[5]

The first standard focuses on subject-matter knowledge for teaching. Various faculty members were studying and writing about this domain of teacher knowledge, helping to develop what Shulman (1986) calls the "missing paradigm" in research on teaching and teacher education. There was a widespread institutional belief that deep and flexible subject-matter knowledge is a foundation for powerful teaching and learning. On Team One, Dewey's (1902/1956) *The Child and the Curriculum* was a core text and we regularly taught an essay by David Hawkins (1974) called "I, Thou, and It," in which he argues that what makes teaching different from other dialogic relationships (e.g., parent/child) is the presence of a third element, an engaging curriculum. We frequently referred to the Hawkins triangle as a model of the instructional process. It is therefore not surprising that "knowing subject matters and how to teach them" appears at the top of the list and includes the phrase "teaching for understanding."

The second standard, "Working with Students," suggests in general terms a stance toward students that we wanted to foster and the kind of teaching we wanted to promote. We wanted our graduates to respect and care for all students in their charge and to affirm their capacity to learn. We wanted teacher candidates to promote active learning and to build on the cultural backgrounds and diverse interests of students. While the standards do not endorse a particular pedagogy, the first two standards present a broad vision of content-rich, learner-centered teaching.

The third standard, "Creating a Classroom Learning Community," also contains important code words and intended meanings. Rather than framing this standard in terms of classroom management and discipline, we focused on the kind of classroom community—safe, caring, productive, in-

TABLE 1
MSU Teacher Preparation Program Standards

1. Knowing subject matters and how to teach them
   + The intern understands the subject matter(s) as needed to teach (them).
   + The intern thoughtfully links subject matter and students, creating a responsive curriculum.
   + The intern plans and implements a curriculum of understanding.
   + The intern is thoughtful about assessment and its relationship to planning and teaching.

2. Working with students
   + The intern respects and cares for all students in his/her charge.
   + The intern promotes active learning and thoughtfulness.
   + The intern builds on students' interests, strengths, and cultural backgrounds.
   + The intern treats all students as capable of learning.

3. Creating a classroom learning community
   + The intern creates a safe, caring, productive environment in the classroom.
   + The intern makes the classroom an inclusive community.
   + The intern helps students develop personal and social responsibility.

4. Working and learning in a school and profession
   + The intern works well as a teacher in a school community.
   + The intern works productively with his or her MSU liaison, collaborating teacher, and seminar instructors in ways that support his or her learning to teach.
   + The intern reflects on his or her experiences and seeks opportunities for continued learning and improvement.
   + The intern is open to alternatives and constructive feedback.

clusive—we hoped students would create and on the goal of fostering social and personal responsibility for learning. While outcomes may be a priority, we wanted our graduates to know how to help students develop a sense of responsibility for their own learning and that of others. Team One pushed (unsuccessfully) for language about classrooms as democratic communities. Other teams pressed for language related to inclusion. We were only beginning to appreciate how much interpretation such standards would require to serve as meaningful and useful tools in learning to teach.

The fourth standard, "Learning and Working in a School and Profession," pulls together a variety of commitments associated with teachers as colleagues and students of teaching. Three of the four elements emphasize important dispositions—being reflective, open to constructive feedback from multiple sources, and active about one's own learning. We wanted interns to become contributing members of the school community and their professional learning community.

These standards served as an initial framework for the teacher education program across the three K–12 teams. Some years later, we reorganized into three elementary teams and one secondary team. Under the new arrangement, Team One took the opportunity to rewrite the standards, which had been a continuous focus of conversation with faculty, students, liaisons, and collaborating teachers. In particular, our work with interns had revealed a need for greater clarity and specificity. Certain aspects of teaching—such as instructional planning and creating clear expectations and consequences—had emerged as central foci in the internship curriculum but were not well represented in the standards. We also recognized the need to be more ex-

TABLE 2

Team One Professional Teaching Standards

1. **Planning**

In preparing for teaching, interns

a. evaluate their own understanding of subject matter and take appropriate steps to deepen and extend it.

b. identify "big ideas" and frame worthwhile goals based on knowledge of students, content standards, and curricular expectations.

c. consider a wide range of resources in the school and beyond, evaluating their appropriateness and making necessary adaptations.

d. take into account what students already know, how they learn, and what they may find difficult or confusing.

e. plan instruction and assessment together so that they support important goals for student learning.

f. design, adapt, and sequence learning activities that promote intellectual involvement with content and active construction of understanding.

g. think through the particulars involved in carrying out lessons (e.g., introduction, explanation, student grouping, discussion questions, directions, timing).

2. Instruction

In teaching and assessing students' learning, interns

a. communicate clearly and accurately.
b. help students make connections between what they already know and what they are studying.
c. elicit student thinking, listen carefully, and work to build on students' ideas.
d. use a variety of instructional strategies to make knowledge accessible and interesting to diverse learners.
e. adjust their instruction based on ongoing assessment (on the spot and over time).
f. provide students with informative feedback on their work.

3. Classroom Learning Community

In creating and maintaining an effective environment for learning, interns

a. foster shared responsibility and high expectations for student learning.
b. develop a culture of learning characterized by respect for diverse people and ideas, inquiry, and intellectual risk-taking.
c. develop procedures for the smooth operation of the classroom and the efficient use of time (e.g., routines and transitions).
d. establish norms for individual and group behavior and clear consequences that are consistently enforced.
e. use multiple strategies (e.g. nonverbal cues, proximity, voice) to manage student behavior and keep students engaged in learning.
f. arrange space and materials to achieve safety and accessibility and to promote learning.

4. Professional responsibilities

In developing as professional educators, interns

a. are punctual and rarely absent and communicate appropriately about absences.
b. act in a dependable and ethical manner; dress appropriately; and maintain student, parent, and teacher confidentiality.
c. react appropriately in stressful situations.
d. give and accept constructive feedback.
e. seek opportunities to observe and be observed and to discuss teaching and learning with their collaborating teacher, liaison, and fellow interns.
f. work on developing their practice by raising questions and investigating problems and issues that arise in their teaching and seminars.
g. use information about student learning to assess their own effectiveness.
h. work collaboratively with families to support student learning and keep them informed about students' academic and social progress.

plicit about forms of professional behavior to which we wanted to hold students accountable. New versions of elementary teaching standards were available to us and they informed the next iteration by suggesting language and formats.[6] Table 2 presents the version of program standards that appeared in the 1999 *Team One Handbook*.

Differences between the earlier and later versions of the program standards reveal important developments in our collective learning and practice. Two new standards—planning and instruction, with a total of thirteen elements, elaborate what was previously expressed in a single standard— "knowing subject matters and how to teach them," with its four elements. Other elaborations reflect our growing understanding of our students and the professional norms and expectations that needed to be spelled out— such as standards about professional dress, punctuality, and receptivity to constructive feedback. Finally, some of the changes were intended to help us communicate more clearly our vision of good teaching to principals and classroom teachers as the program expanded to new school sites.

Over the years we had worked hard with collaborating teachers to describe the invisible world of teacher planning and make clear what novices need to learn that experienced teachers often know and do without conscious thought. The new standards built on this joint work, expressing an approach to instructional planning that had become a major goal of the yearlong internship. New elements related to interactive teaching reflect our increased awareness of what teaching for understanding entails. From working in the field and from studying practice, we continually refined our understanding of the stance and moves that characterize such teaching in different subject areas. Adding elements eliciting student thinking, building on what students already know, and reengaging students were part of an ongoing effort to explicate that teaching so we would have a more developed language to use in our work with students.

As the program expanded into more schools, we needed ways to communicate the kind of classroom learning communities we wanted interns to observe and experience. The new standard of "instruction" and the elaborations of the classroom learning community standard express our values and understandings. Through our experiences in the field, we clarified what interns needed to work on in order to create and maintain effective environments for learning. Besides having smooth procedures and clear norms and consequences, we wanted to promote cultures of learning characterized by inquiry, respect for diverse viewpoints, and intellectual risk-taking. That language was an important tool for conversations with interns, liaisons, and collaborating teachers. If these were our program standards, then we needed to find and create opportunities for interns to observe and practice these aspects of planning, instruction, and assessment.

Finally, the elaboration of "professional responsibilities" reflected our growing understanding of who our students were and what they needed to learn, as well as some legal issues that had arisen in the course of the program's short history. Unless we wrote our expectations regarding professional behavior, we could not use the standards for gatekeeping purposes. On rare occasions, when we had to decide whether to remove someone from the program or to create a plan for reentry, we needed a clear statement of professional norms and standards.

Looking back, it seems that the impulse to expand and revise the standards came from developments in our thinking about teaching and learning to teach and in our practice as field-based teacher educators. The revised standards clearly reflect changes in our perception of what teaching for understanding entails and a need for more refined ways of talking about the practices we wanted to foster. The increased clarity and specification allowed us to pinpoint problems, develop plans, and determine whether needed learning was taking place. In a small number of cases, we needed language more specific than our initial standards offered. Over time, the standards increasingly came to represent our collective judgment and the fruits of our common experience.

STANDARDS AS INTERPRETIVE SPACES

Just as the Team One's standards emerged from conversations, so we continued to regard them as talking points across all levels of the program. Some of this talk took place on the steering committee, which consisted of the two faculty coleaders, the program coordinator, the student coordinator, and faculty responsible for each of the major components in the program (the introductory course, the senior year courses on subject matter pedagogy, and the internship) and the coordinator of our distant site.[7] Some of it occurred in a weekly seminar for the internship staff—doctoral students and retired teachers who worked with groups of interns and collaborating teachers in our partner schools. (We called these people "MSU liaisons" to avoid the more traditional label of "university supervisor.") It also took place in a monthly study group with MSU liaisons and teacher representatives from each partnership school, in weekly school-based seminars with interns, and in our courses where students were introduced to the program standards. These professional conversations were all part of an effort to connect abstract statements about good teaching to the concrete practices of teachers, to form an organic link between teachers' own experience and teaching standards framed outside that experience.

Reflections on Standards

One influential conversation occurred in a liaison meeting in the fall of 1996, when we did a "reflection" on the word "standard," following a protocol developed by Patricia Carini (2002) and her colleagues at the Prospect School in Vermont.[8] First, everyone wrote down images, phrases, associations to the word "standard." Next, each person read his or her list aloud while the facilitator took notes. Finally, the facilitator offered a summary of the various meanings, clustering some associations and phrases together to form a category and identifying a set of tensions inherent in the ideas people had presented.

Through our reflection, we realized that a standard can be a measurement of success or failure (or something in between). It can be a grade. It can be a floor (a level below which no one is allowed to fail) or a ceiling (something we all hope to rise to)—a basic starting point and something we aim for. A standard is a flag that leads people forward in a battle or a march. A standard performance can be in some sense guaranteed; in professional realms, standards of certification tell the world that a program and the people in it testify that graduates have shown basic professional competence.

A striking feature of our reflection was a growing sense that standards represent tensions within which all teachers, including teacher educators, work. All of the standards embody dilemmas that make up the daily labor of teaching. An intern and a collaborating teacher who struggle to transform a difficult class into a learning community must constantly balance the interests of the group and those of individual students. Teachers cannot definitively settle the question of how to do this. What works in one setting may not in another. A wise teacher knows how to keep shifting her stance. The same can be said of the tension between treating standards as uniform expectations for all students, which teachers sometimes invoke, and viewing them as a source of expectations and goals for individual students, which also figure in responsive teachers' practice. Partly because of these tensions, we came to think about standards as invitations to reflect on our collective and personal struggle over the dilemmas of teaching and learning to teach.

Following this conversation, Jay Featherstone, coleader of Team One, wrote an internal memo called "Creating Standards Together," which expresses some of our new understandings. The excerpt below comes from its concluding paragraph, which highlights the central role of values and judgment in the framing and use of professional standards:

> The liaison meeting decided that many common uses of the word "standard" are not helpful, because they take us away from the heart of teaching and learning which is the creation and enactment of values. The root of the word "evaluation," after all, is the word "value." A yardstick is not a value. The things measured against it are not values. Values are a result of human thought and caring. In classroom teaching and in teaching our interns, we need to develop our judgment so that we can help ourselves and our students come to stand for certain ways of teaching. . . . The judgments which we make together are qualitative which is not to say fuzzy. We will get more intelligent about these judgments as we move forward in our work together. The standards will help us see, and what we see will help us make better standards. The more we can see and be precise about what we are seeing, the more we can help each student and ourselves improve. But the root of this common work is value.

Filling in the Standards Again and Again

For program standards to acquire real meaning, they have to be filled in by the people who use them, not laid on by outside experts. This meant creating authentic occasions for people to talk about their teaching and their students' learning in relation to the standards and to get help making connections between idealized expectations and the thinking and practice of real faculty, students, and collaborating teachers in the program.

We created many different occasions for collaborating teachers, interns, liaisons, and program faculty to talk about the standards in relation to their role in the program and to scrutinize instances of standards-in-use. We developed standards-based observation guides, planning frameworks, and rubrics for analyzing interns' lesson plans and units. We designed a portfolio process around the program standards. Each year we held a faculty retreat where we examined course syllabi or student work in relation to the standards. We were always looking for ways to bring the standards alive, infuse them with personal meaning, and make them part of our shared vocabulary and collective agenda.

One such effort occurred in the spring of 1998, when we began outlining a clinical curriculum with teacher representatives and MSU liaisons in our monthly cross-school study group. We wanted to create a developmental framework of learning tasks and activities for interns related to specific standards that mapped onto the school year. We saw this as a chance to codify the experience of veteran collaborating teachers and liaisons while helping newcomers visualize more concretely what the yearlong process of helping interns learn to teach entailed.

We organized working groups around the three main standards (planning, instruction, and classroom learning community) and divided the internship into five main phases: late August–September, October, Guided Lead Teaching, December–January, Winter Lead Teaching. We asked each group to come up with specific learning experiences in each period that would help interns begin to understand and enact their standards and to specify what collaborating teachers and liaisons should be doing to support and guide the interns' learning.

The groups worked hard to devise concrete ways to help interns get inside the standards. In subsequent meetings we reviewed their work and tried to extract underlying principles about mentored learning to teach. For instance, it became clear that in the early phases of the internship (August–October) the collaborating teachers' practice is a primary site for interns' learning as they watch how their teachers begin the year with a new group of students. Thus, a major responsibility of liaisons and collaborating teachers at the beginning of the school year was to help interns see and understand how the collaborating teacher makes decisions about the setup of the classroom; learns about students; conveys expectations; puts in place norms, routines, and procedures; and engages in long-range planning. We wrote up the fruits of the discussion and assigned each school the task of adapting the framework to its academic calendar and building in opportunities for interns to observe and learn about unique aspects of the school's program.

In the end, we came to believe that the main value of this exercise lay not so much in standardizing the internship curriculum as in developing greater clarity about the central tasks of learning to teach and the role of liaisons and collaborating teachers in helping interns get inside these tasks. In later sessions, we addressed the matter of how to assess interns' learning by clarifying what to look for in their questions, actions, and responses at different phases of the internship. We had already framed and labeled four stages in interns' learning—observing, emerging, practicing and refining—and we used these labels to characterize their developing understanding and competence in relation to the standards. Through this kind of joint work we tried to make the standards a usable tool for interns, liaisons, and collaborating teachers.

WHAT ABOUT ACCOUNTABILITY?

In the context of the current standards movement, our approach to teaching standards may strike some as soft and subjective or at least too process oriented. Increasingly, teacher education programs are being judged by how well their students do on standardized tests, and there is a strong push to measure the impact of induction programs on how well the pupils of beginning teachers do on achievement tests. In this climate of accountability, with its emphasis on uniform standards and high-stakes testing, how can we defend our position that standards are both provisional and consequential?

Our efforts to create a standards-based teacher certification program were undertaken against the backdrop of national and state efforts to frame professional teaching standards. Such efforts reflected a shift in focus from a concern for the knowledge base in teaching to a concern for the uses of that knowledge in practice. They were conceived as ways to *professionalize*, not *standardize*, teaching. The decision to have a majority of classroom teachers on national standards committees meant that teachers, not outside experts, were defining good teaching and deciding how it should be assessed. The point was not to identify "one best system" but to explicate the best current thinking about good teaching that could apply to multiple contexts.

These national and state initiatives stimulated serious discussion about what good teaching entails. Mary Diez, dean of Alverno College and a major player in national standards-setting efforts, cites this as one of their most important contributions. In a published dialogue (1998) on standards organized by the American Association of Colleges of Teacher Education, she says:

One of the major impacts of the work of NCATE [National Council for the Accreditation of Teacher Education], INTASC and the National Board [for Professional Standards] as well as the work in states and learned societies has been the sparking of a serious dialogue about what constitutes good teaching. In fact, that may be the most important role of standards—to lay out a vision of teaching in a public way so that all in the profession can contribute to its critique and refinement.

We on Team One share this belief in the centrality of professional conversation as a central means of clarifying, interpreting, and revising professional teaching standards. Through discussion about the links between standards and practice, not increased standardization, teachers and teacher educators can develop shared understandings and maintain accountability. The program standards express our vision of good teaching. They are not fixed, authoritative assessment criteria. At the same time, we use the standards to document and describe interns' progress toward that kind of teaching and to determine whether they have successfully completed the internship. We rely on the professional judgment of several people—the liaison, intern, and collaborating teacher in most cases; these three plus the student coordinator and/or internship coordinator in more difficult cases—to determine whether interns are ready to be certified as beginning teachers. The standards are consequential because we hold interns to them and require them to produce evidence of their growing ability to teach for understanding and create classroom learning communities. At the same time, they are provisional, since we revise them as we learn more about teaching and learning to teach.

Clearly we have not reached the promised land. There is more work to be done on the standards themselves, on our curriculum, and on our ways of documenting and assessing interns' learning. For example, we have neither explicated specific subject-matter knowledge that beginning elementary teachers need nor figured out ways to assess that knowledge. Faculty in the subject-specific courses for seniors and interns have thought hard about this matter and made deliberate choices about what and how to teach; however, we have not yet codified their decisions. Nor have we created a forum where all the people who use the standards, collaborating teachers in particular, can participate in thinking about this aspect of teacher knowledge and teacher preparation and decide what this means for our collective responsibility.

We also need to attend seriously to the question of what can appropriately and realistically be taught and learned at the preservice level and what is best deferred until the induction phase of learning to teach. None of the national and state standards documents we consulted has adequately addressed this issue, either because they deal with accomplished practice or because they ignore the question. We know that beginning teachers are still learning to teach and that no preservice program, no matter how good, can teach them all they need to know. Should that insight lead us to formulate different standards for different stages in learning to teach, or do we need different expectations regarding the same standards?

Finally, how can we ensure that our judgments about interns' capacities are reliable and valid? In our view the answer lies not in creating more "objective" assessments, but in calibrating our judgments by talking about evidence in light of standards and identifying exemplars that represent our shared thinking. We did a small piece of this work in relation to the planning standard, which covers a complex set of understandings, skills, and dispositions that are difficult for novices to learn. Planning often seems quite mysterious to beginning teachers, especially because it is largely invisible. Over several months we investigated how collaborating teachers plan for teaching. We compared the work of planning from scratch with that of planning from prepared materials. We developed templates and criteria for the kind of written planning we wanted interns to do. Finally, we assembled video clips of coplanning sessions between interns and collaborating teachers illustrating a continuum in learning to plan, starting with an emerging stage, when interns are mostly learning about the mentor's plans, and moving on to the practicing and consolidating stages, when interns take increasing leadership in proposing and modifying instructional plans.[9]

Examining evidence in light of standards is an ongoing process. Moreover, it needs to go on locally with those persons who are responsible for making judgments and carrying out assessments of teacher learning and teaching competence. That puts us at odds with the dominant standards-and-testing paradigm, which presumes that a single definition of good teacher education can be used to measure and compare individuals and programs. More research will not determine which assumptions are right, though we continue to believe that standards should be set by the people who use them in dialogue with the broader profession and that prospective teachers should be assessed in ways that make evidence and reasoning public.

4

Preparing Teachers of Elementary Mathematics: Evangelism or Education?[1]

HELEN FEATHERSTONE

Many prospective teachers bring to their teacher preparation courses a history of negative experiences with school mathematics, deep doubts about their own ability to make sense of it, and considerable apprehension about teaching it. They see mathematics as a collection of rules for solving straightforward problems and teaching mathematics as explaining procedures and assigning homework that will give children practice using algorithms derived from the day's explanations. The vision of mathematics and of the teaching and learning of mathematics that they encounter in National Council of Teachers of Mathematics (NCTM) *Standards* publications (1989, 1991, 2000) surprises and confuses many of them. They worry that the reform teaching they read about and see on videos is an impractical invention of university-based teacher educators that would not prepare their future students for high-stakes standardized tests or for success in middle school and high school math classes. Outside the university classroom, a lively and polarized math version of the reading wars adds to the confusion, uncertainty, and mistrust.

In such a context, my early efforts as the teacher of an introductory math methods class (TE-401 or TE-402, depending on whether it is taught in the spring or the fall)[2] went into designing—and redesigning—learning experiences to convince prospective teachers that there were viable alternatives to the mathematics teaching they had experienced as children. More specifically, I was eager to persuade my students that teaching that takes children's ideas seriously, involves them in solving nonroutine problems, in explaining their ideas to classmates and the teacher, and in responding to one another's ideas would help their students to understand and to enjoy mathematics. Failing this, I wanted to convince them that listening seriously to children's ideas and "giving them reason," as Eleanor Duckworth (1987) puts it, was essential to the work of teaching mathematics.

I had, of course, other goals as well. I wanted my students to come to see inquiry as an essential part of teaching. I hoped that they would develop a new relationship to mathematics and even begin to see it as an intellectual playground for themselves and their students. I hoped that they would learn to interrogate their own experience as learners and come to see it, as Dewey (1904/1974) advises, as an invaluable resource in understanding learning. I hoped that they would learn a bit about how to make thoughtful use of commercially available mathematics curricula—both innovative programs like *Investigations in Number Data and Space* and the more conventional textbooks that they might very well find in their schools in a few years. And I hoped they would begin to think about creating a classroom culture for learning mathematics (Lampert, 2001; Lester, 1996). Although I certainly cared deeply about many of these goals, I was passionately committed to getting students to embrace a new vision of good mathematics teaching. I had become an evangelist.

There are some excellent reasons for missionary passion on the part of math educators. For one thing, they fight an uphill battle against current teaching and assessment practices in mathematics: although conservatives insist that a tsunami of ill-judged "reforms" followed the publication of the NCTM *Standards* volumes (1989, 1991, 2000), leaving American children unable to do long division or calculate a tip at a restaurant, in fact, most U.S. math teaching looks pretty much as it did a generation ago and many students—perhaps most of them—continue to arrive at college scared of math. Moreover, the anti-intellectualism that pervades both schools and the wider culture does demand a strong stand on the part of all teacher educators: we are in a position to influence prospective teachers' attitudes toward ideas and learning, and it seems important for us to respond.

Missionary work and education are not, however, identical, and there are real difficulties with teaching as evangelism. To begin with, educating should be about helping students to achieve purposes that are truly theirs. When we teach a child to read, we imagine her reaching for any book in the library, using this new power to answer questions we, her teachers, have not even asked. When we teach her teenaged sister calculus, we give her the power to choose a future as an engineer, a chemist, a research mathematician, an economist, or someone who enjoys college math. Real education opens new worlds and new possibilities and offers students the power to accomplish the goals they have set for themselves.

Second, we are trying to teach prospective teachers a questioning stance—we want them to understand that teaching is a journey and that they should be perpetually reflecting, trying to see new depths in their work. We want to teach them that problems are their friends—that working to teach in ways that help children to develop intellectual power, curiosity, and skill requires ongoing exploration and questioning. If we do not appear to be inquiring ourselves, if instead we seem certain that we have found the right way to teach math, we squander an important opportunity to teach the values of openness and curiosity. For as we all know, teachers can be powerful models.

Third, if we believe that all students bring a great deal to the educational transaction and that good teaching builds on what the students have to offer, then why is this not just as true of college students in a teacher education program as it is of young children?

Fourth, evangelism can kill—or at least maim—the instructor's curiosity. The more invested I am in getting my students to embrace certain beliefs, the harder it is for me to listen with genuine curiosity to the ideas they actually have—especially those that conflict with the ones I am trying to sell. The more I define my success as a teacher by my success in getting students to think about math teaching the way I think about it and to admire the teachers I admire, the less open I am to hearing their ideas about Saxon math.[3]

And fifth, evangelism can poison the teacher-student relationship. (Barbara Kingsolver, in *The Poisonwood Bible* [1999], paints a vivid and convincing portrait of the potentially curdling effects of such transactions when the evangelist is a Christian missionary and the objects of his determined proselytizing are villagers with strong beliefs of their own.) This may be particularly true in teacher education, where students arrive with a vision of the sorts of teachers they want to become; of how we, their professors, ought to help them become these teachers; and, in some cases, with a deep, even terrified appreciation of the magnitude of job ahead. They know that they need a lot of help in learning to teach. Although many of our students embrace our vision of math teaching, others find their frustration growing as we have them read chapters and watch videos that refer to a vision of teaching that seems to them out of touch with the realities of the schools that will ultimately employ them.

What follows is an examination of the first two weeks of one iteration of my math methods course that explores some of the complexities of the tension between teaching as education and teaching as evangelism. I have chosen to look closely at this particular semester for three reasons. First, that semester the course went far better than it had before, and the ways in which it went better seem especially relevant to the issue that concerns me here: the way in which the missionary stance widens the distance between a teacher educator and her students. Second, I am fortunately in a position to explore the reasons for this improvement, having kept detailed notes and journals and obtained permission from the students to use their words. Third, this iteration of the course differed from those that preceded it in ways that I believe made an important difference to my success as a teacher educator.

What follows is in five sections. First, I give some background on my efforts to re-imagine the course in the fall of 1999, followed by a whirlwind account of the first weeks of the course. Then, after a brief discussion of the data and my approach to analyzing it, I examine what I found when I looked closely at this data. The final section returns to the evangelism/education tension and attempts to make new sense of it in light of the present analysis.

BACKGROUND

During the fall of 1999 I became deeply engaged in thinking and writing about the role of play in mathematical discovery and in the teaching and learning of math (Featherstone, 2000). I hadn't been satisfied with the previous few iterations of the math methods course I had taught: although the class had definitely helped some students to believe that they were on the way to teaching math with interesting and effective methods, I did not think that it had worked very well for others. And it had not worked well for me, either. I had spent an unimaginably large number of evenings and weekends responding to students' written work, and it seemed that most of the students had not actually had the experience of listening with interest to a child who was explaining an idea. Their final teaching projects, in

which they planned and taught math lessons for a small group and then reported on what had gone well and badly, and on what they thought they
had learned, had been a little discouraging. In many cases I did not feel as
though I had managed to help students to plan lessons that revealed anything of children's thinking to them or even convinced them of the value of
doing this. Although there were a number of students who by the end of the
semester did seem to be excited about teaching math, many remained unen-
thusiastic. As a missionary, I did not think I was doing particularly well.

When I sat down to revise my syllabus, along with the questions I ask
myself every year (How can I help students to feel that teaching which takes
account of students' thinking is possible in the schools in which they are
planning to teach? How can I help them learn to listen to children's ideas
and to enjoy and celebrate them? How can I help them to get more out of
their efforts to teach lessons to small groups?) was a new one, which com-
manded my attention: How can I inject a spirit of play into students' experience of the course, and how can I help them to see possibilities for intellectual play in math and math teaching?

I did not face this question entirely alone. The steering committee of
Team One was a close-knit group that met twice a month to discuss problems large and small and to set directions for program improvement. One
of the eight members of this team, Dirck Roosevelt, had taught most of the
courses offered in the program and had, perhaps partly in consequence of
this, a deep understanding of our students and their needs. Moreover, Dirck
and I had been working together for the previous year on learning more
about the role of play in development; as I revised my syllabus we were preparing for an AERA symposium focused on extending the research on the
role of play in learning to an exploration of how intellectual play might contribute to teacher preparation. So it was natural for me to ask him to help
me rethink my math methods class.

In the semester that followed, I thought the course succeeded in ways it
had not in previous years: Students wrote better papers, class discussions
probed ideas more deeply, and I enjoyed myself far more than I had in the
past. The same appeared true for my students: their end-of-semester evalu-
ations of the course and of their own learning were far more positive than
they had been in past years; their final lessons were more satisfying both to
themselves and to me; and they seemed to finish the course more excited
about teaching math and more confident about their ability to continue

learning. Although I have examined my own extensive journal notes and e-mails and students' written work, I cannot say with what Einstein termed "savage certainty" which of the changes I made were crucial to the success of this revision. I have some conjectures, based on analysis of the data documenting the early part of the course; this chapter explores the factors that I now think were most responsible for the changes.

I will look closely at the first two weeks of the semester because, even though much of importance happened throughout the semester, it was in those first two weeks, I think, that we laid the foundation for a better course.

Two Weeks Together: A Whirlwind Tour

TE-402 meets four times a week for fifteen weeks and begins preparing prospective elementary school teachers to teach mathematics and literacy. Each section of the course has two instructors—one for math, one for literacy—and in an ordinary week the students meet for seminars on two days, one day for each subject area, and they spend the other two mornings in elementary school classrooms, observing math and literacy instruction and working with small groups and individual children. Since we want to have some time with the students before they begin their work in schools, the literacy instructor and I meet with the students all four days during the first week. This strong start provides quite a bit of momentum and means that by the end of the second week we have had six of the twenty-eight classes we will spend together.

Briefly: the students, the literacy instructor, and I met together in our on-campus classroom on Monday, January 10—when we all explored some children's books, introduced ourselves, and discussed what the students had learned in earlier education courses that might be relevant to teaching math and literacy—and on Tuesday—when, among other things, we worked on our first math problem. On Wednesday we visited the second-third grade classroom of Patricia Pricco in a nearby urban district. (I scheduled this visit because we had been assigned to a suburban school for our regular field placement, so I knew that unless we visited an urban classroom this first week, most students would get no chance to see poor or minority children reasoning about math.) The college students observed the math lesson and talked to the children as they worked on the math problems, and the teacher talked to the TE-402 students about her teaching both before and after the lesson. The next day we met again in seminar at the university. We discussed what we had seen the previous day and how the students were connecting this teaching to the pages of the NCTM *Teaching Standards* everyone had read for homework. We also continued to work on the math problem.

The following week we began our regular schedule. The students met with the literacy teacher on Monday and on Tuesday went to their field placement (in a suburban school about fifteen miles from campus) to observe a literacy lesson. Wednesday I met with them in seminar, and Thursday I accompanied them to their field placement in the suburban elementary school, spending about half an hour in each of the five classrooms to which they had been assigned for math.

A Word on Data and Method

To understand what happened and why during the first weeks of 402, I needed to learn both about my own state of mind and intentions—how I had seen what was happening and what I needed to do differently—and also how the students were thinking and feeling during the same period.

With these goals in mind, I divided my data into two piles. In one, I put the journal entries and e-mails *I* had written during the week I was putting together my syllabus and planning the class and during the first two weeks of course meetings; in the other, I put the data documenting the 402 students' perspectives. I had documented my own thinking pretty extensively; I had far less on my students, but I did have the in-class writing they had done after visiting Ms. Pricco's class and some of the journal entries they had written about that event, as well as my own class notes on our discussion of the visit during class the following day. To deepen my understanding of my own state of mind and pedagogical reasoning, I read through all of my the e-mails and journal entries, looking for themes; once I had identified key themes, I made several more passes through the data, coding for these ideas and looking for others I might have missed. I then wrote memos to myself about them. As I looked at what I had written about the first two themes I uncovered a third theme—one so obvious, that I had missed it entirely for some weeks. And then, to learn more about the students' thinking, I engaged in a parallel process with the data I had from them.

MAKING SENSE OF WHAT HAPPENED

I have divided my report on these analyses into three parts. The first discusses the three themes that emerge from analysis of my e-mails and journal entries, written during the week I was putting together the syllabus and planning class activities and during the first two days of the course. The second part examines my students' responses to the visit to Pat Pricco's class: what they paid attention to, what they felt, and how they connected what they saw to what they had done before in the teacher education program. Finally, in the third part of this section I return to my own writing, tracing the development of the three major themes through the next week and a half of the course.

Looking at the Course through Helen's Eyes: Getting Started

Three themes emerge from my analysis of the journal entries, notes, and e-mails I wrote documenting my planning efforts and the early weeks of the course: first, my wish to introduce intellectual play into students' experience of the course, which was quickly transformed into a resolve to nurture my own curiosity about the teacher education students' ideas; second, my determination to think well of my students; third, my growing enjoyment of the students and their ideas.

Play and Curiosity

The role of play in learning had been a central focus of the reading and writing I had done during a yearlong leave that ended just a few days before the semester began. Although I had focused at first on the play and learning of children, in the summer I had begun to think more about the learning of adults. I wondered whether there were ways play might become a part of teacher education and professional development. It seemed that if we wanted children to play with ideas in academic areas like mathematics, we needed to help their future teachers engage in intellectual play themselves. My wish to do this, together with a puzzlement about how it might be accomplished, are visible in my writings during that first week in January, as I planned for the course and wrote my syllabus:

> To think about: How to put more Play (for tchr and for students) into TE-402 math? (January 4)

I am Determined . . . to build in play. (January 5)

Lovely to . . . get several good thoughts about generating play. The image of the piles of books to look through, remember, etc. was tremendously generative, helping me to remember that talk about stuff is one of the essential features of the play I want. (January 9)

However, this focus on play underwent a rather rapid transformation in the days just before the first meeting of the course. This seems to have been largely—or at least visibly—a result of Dirck's influence. Although he responded supportively—and with suggestions—to my requests for help in thinking about how to generate "play," his responses sometimes suggested a shift in emphasis. The night before the first meeting of the class, I seem to have picked up on this idea in what apparently felt like a powerful insight:

> But the most important thing Dirck said today, the most profoundly helpful to my efforts to figure out where I go wrong, where I might do better at this TE thing, was that one thing he had learned . . . was that when . . . he did not feel at all like teaching, he found it helpful to remind himself that he really was curious about how these students thought about things, that it was really true—not just something one said—that literacy (etc.) was to empower them for their own purposes. I thought (and said) that I thought that my attitude had often been less open and interested—[more of] a missionary impulse to convert them to a better way of teaching math. And D. talked about the balance, having purposes, etc. but also curiosity. I'm not getting this right (as far as what D. said), but it is true that I think I haven't truly been curious and open (often not even close) although I have tried to seem that way, to make the classroom safe for all ideas.
>
> I think if I want people to play with ideas I do need to cultivate this genuine curiosity, and a genuine commitment to *their purposes.* (January 9)

The realization that I had been almost without curiosity about my teacher education students' thinking came as a particular shock because I had, from the first time I taught TE-401, explicitly emphasized both with the students and in my own thinking, that a major goal of the math methods course was to help students to learn the skills and pleasures of listening to and exploring children's mathematical ideas. Vivian Paley's wonderful essay (1986) on the central role of curiosity—curiosity about children's ideas—in teaching had been a cornerstone of my thinking, so I was more than chagrined to discover that curiosity was not much in evidence in my own teaching of undergraduates. Paley—and Deborah Meier (1995, 2002)—cautions that we cannot really respect someone unless we have made an effort to understand how they think. In the weeks after writing this journal entry, I focused on nurturing my own curiosity about my students' thinking. The journal entries and e-mails that follow indicate that I was able to keep attending to this goal and make it a part of my attitude. In quite a few of them I refer directly to my curiosity. The next day, for example, after my first meeting with the 402 class, I concluded an account of the morning's events by noting, with apparent satisfaction:

> I did feel [today] much more open and curious and even affectionate [toward the students]—annoyed, for example, at the [various departments involved], and not at all at the students, for putting those who are student teaching in the position of having to get out of my class early in order to get to their ST placement.[4] It felt good. (January 10)

The next day, though I do not explicitly mention curiosity in my journal or e-mail, I describe the class discussion with careful attention to what each student had said, suggesting that I had indeed taken a strong interest in their ideas.

Attending to My Own Attitude toward My Students

The idea of fostering my own curiosity, though it comes initially from Dirck, falls on receptive ears: I am already thinking that my own attitude is critical to improving the course. The first sign of this conscious attention to my own attitude toward students comes in an e-mail written almost a week before the first meeting of the class and is closely tied to my focus on play:

> I don't teach until next Monday, which is good as I am quite a ways, still, from a syllabus, but my mood is pretty good about the whole thing and I am determined not to blame students for the difficulties that I'll surely encounter. (January 4)

Perhaps this resolution is responsible for the positive tone of the e-mails and journal entries documenting the first meetings of the class. Although I record disappointment with the introductory activities that occupied the first hour of the first class, there is no suggestion in my journal that I think less of the students in consequence; I seem to attribute the lackluster response to these activities to my own inadequate investigation of other instructors' practices:

> [A]nd then (catastrophe!) we did the introductions/passions thing I did last year with Paula and it turned out they had done it in Every course!!! (January 10)

And my summary of the third event of the morning notes the students' insight—and my resolution to focus on these good moments:

> After the break, though, they were quite animated and often insightful in making potential connections between what they had learned about teaching science [the previous semester] and the math segment to come. So, I guess I need to try to focus there. (January 10)

This Day 1 report ends with my observation (see above) about feeling "more open and curious and even affectionate" toward the students.

Pleasure in the Students and Their Ideas

The third theme in these early entries, pleasure in the students, their ideas, and their attitudes, was invisible to me on initial passes through the data. Though linked to the first two themes, it differs from them in two important ways. First, there is no sign of any *resolution* to enjoy the students or the teaching (though interest in play might suggest I was hoping to achieve this, in fact my interest was more in getting the students to engage in intellectual play than to see the course as a place where I might play). Second, and more obviously, there is no mention of hoping to enjoy the students or their ideas before the first meeting of the course. However, after the first class, I noted that I had enjoyed the feeling of being on the students' side as we addressed the problem of their having to leave my class early to meet another obligation. My account of the second meeting of the class is saturated with pleasure—in the students and in all they had done with the activity I had planned. I have emphasized passages that particularly catch my attention (and I note that exclamation points, rare even in my informal writing, are scattered like confetti):

> We did the horse-trading problem ["A man bought a horse for $50, sold it for $60, bought it back for $70, and sold it again for $80. What was the financial result of these transactions? He lost $30, lost $20, lost $10, broke even, made

$10, made $20?"] and the participation was very animated and cheerful, *and a quite lovely thing happened*: for the first time ever (and I have done this problem on the first day [of TE-401/2] quite a few times), all those who reported answers/ways of doing the problem had the right answer. I was astonished. Two people explained what they did and others said they had done pretty much the same. Both solutions were simple and straightforward. I asked if anyone did anything different and no one said they had.

So I said "This is the first time I have ever had a class agree on an answer, and if you use this problem in your 4th grade you will probably not have everyone agree. So what I would like you to do is try to imagine how someone might get a different answer . . ." And Miranda raised her hand and said, "Well, I know how they might get a different answer, because I did!!!" And she explained her way and it sounded very reasonable, and then others said that they had done what she did but when they heard Cheryl's solution it made so much sense that they decided it must be right. *(And I got to point out that we should all be really grateful to Miranda for being brave and saying this because it was a vivid demonstration of how hard it is to create a culture/ environment where people feel comfortable having a way of thinking about the problem that they think is probably wrong.)* And then 4 other people explained how they got $10 (wrong answer) and why it made sense to them and one student really grilled one of them while he was at the board on his thinking and she was kneeling on her chair leaning towards him (her chair was facing away from him and the board) she was so intent (but he seemed to take this completely in stride) and then after he answered about her 5th question she almost shrieked "Oh, ok, *now* I get it. It makes perfect sense!" and it seemed that although most of the 4–5 dissenters had decided that $20 was right because it made sense (and probably because so many people had gotten it), none could see any logical or mathematical flaw in their earlier solution. I sent everyone off to write a few sentences on how they solved the problem and how someone who got a different solution solved it and how they would convince the person who got the different solution that their solution was right. *I was (obviously) very pleased.* (January 11)

Looking through the TE-402 Students' Eyes

I have far less information about how the TE-402 students experienced these first weeks of the course than I do about the sequence of events and about my own thoughts and feelings. However, I've got their Thursday in-class writings about what they noticed during their Wednesday-morning school visit, some of the journal entries they wrote at home the night before, and my handwritten notes on Thursday's class discussion. Analysis of what students wrote at the beginning of that seminar class about the visit to Pat Pricco's math lesson reveals four themes: the college students' deep appreciation of the way the children listened to and respected their classmates; their feeling that the visit to the third grade had contributed greatly—and in multiple ways—to their own learning; astonishment at the variety of ways children solved the math problems; and the children's pleasure and excitement during the math lesson.

More than three quarters of the students wrote with appreciation about the learning community that appeared to exist in the classroom, the respect students showed their classmates, and the interest and attention with which they listened to one another's ideas. Children, the college students said, seemed to feel safe both to present their ideas before their classmates (and even before the twenty-six strangers from the university)—even when they were unsure about being right—and to explain their strategies even when these might be seen by others as babyish. Several MSU students were astonished that children would admit publicly to counting on their fingers (they noted that they would *never* have let others see them using their fingers after first grade). It was the quality of the children's interest in one another's ideas that my students mentioned most often: the visible attention, the kinds of questions they asked the child who was at the board presenting his or her ideas. For example, one student noted in the conversation that instead of asking, "What do you mean?" students had, on several occasions, tried to articulate what they *thought* the presenter had said, asking, "Do you mean . . . ?"

The second major theme—visible in the comments of well over half of the college students—was that the visit had contributed in important ways to their own learning as prospective teachers. "My entire paradigm of mathematics teaching shifted as a result of our visit," asserted James. And Randi wrote, "Seeing [Ms. Pricco and her intern] teach made me excited for my internship next year and has opened my eyes to different ways of teaching math." Several noted that they had read about teaching this way, "but it was much more useful to see it in action," as Robert put it. Here are a few typical comments:

I see now that textbooks are not necessary.

It was wonderful to see all the things we've been reading about in action. It really helped the concept to sink in and make me believe I could do the same thing.

To see teachers experimenting and exploring new teaching methods is exactly what I want to be a part of. Ms Pricco's class was absolutely wonderful; I have yet to see a classroom environment in which children were so engaged in a lesson.

Students also noted with apparent pleasure how much the second and third graders seemed to enjoy the math lesson: "It was exciting to see students so energetic about math and working so hard to communicate their ideas." "I was surrounded with evidence that proved how dedicated and excited the students were," wrote Louise. Cheryl said that the student she worked with had told her, "I really like this. I have my parents make up problems for me at home." And several of the college students noted, delightedly, that when the discussion had gotten to the last and most difficult problem the children had cheered; one had exclaimed (apparently expressing the general view), "That was the *bestest* problem!"

A number of the TE-402 students also commented on the intellectual achievements of the seven- and eight-year-olds. "The students' ability to conceptualize the hundreds chart in mentally formulating answers during the arrow math session was amazing!" wrote James. "I was amazed by the variety of ways students answered the question," commented Lisa.

Looking at the Course through Helen's Eyes—Redux

After the visit to Pat Pricco's class, the themes of curiosity, affection, and pleasure thread through all my writing about the course. It seems clear that the students' response to the math class visit delighted me and supported my impulse to see the issues that came up in class through my students' eyes. My journal from the day that followed our visit to Averill is typical in savoring the twists and turns of the class discussions—curiosity now required no self-prompting—students' ingenious *explaining* strategies and their unexpected insights and connections. My pleasure in the play of their thinking is so pervasive that it would be hard to choose particular sentences to highlight:

We all came to today's class fresh from the visit to Pat Pricco's room—a visit that seemed, both at the time and from what was said today, to have been hugely successful. Carolyn [who was teaching the literacy part of the course] started us off today on the debriefing by asking what people had noticed about classroom culture and every comment—and there were many, from all parts of the room and a variety of students—was favorable. They also (not, of course, unconnectedly) seem quite perceptive to me. We talked for quite a while about Pat's class . . . and then segued into the horse problem. . . .

Everyone seemed very much engaged by the problem, once again. Ruth (the student who had all but toppled her chair on Tuesday in her relentless pursuit of Mark's reasoning) was eager to go to the board immediately (only one person had gone to the board Tuesday—others had explained their solutions from their seats) saying that she had done it again and gotten an answer different from any we had had so far, and that it was probably wrong (something about being bad at math), but that she just couldn't find any flaw in it. She seemed very genuinely to want the help of the class in thinking about her idea. She wrote the numbers in a column,

50
60
70
80

and said, "he made $10 on the first transaction, then, when he bought the horse for $70 he was in the hole $10, and then he sold it for $80 so he came out of the hole and broke even." Miranda said, "Makes perfect sense." (It was Miranda who had changed everything on Tuesday by saying that she could tell us how someone could get something other than $20 because she had gotten $10.) There was more conversation about how Caitlin's explanation of $20 made perfect sense to everyone, but that no one was able to identify and explain any error in the solutions (like Ruth's, Miranda's, and Mark's) that led to other numbers. Someone else came to the board and showed that if you add together the amounts the man paid for the horse and then subtracted that sum from the amount he sold it for, the result was $20 profit. No one disagreed, but the problem seemed to be no closer to being solved. Then Barb (who is a little older, I think) said she had created a game that showed what happened. She came up (at my urging) and dealt out to herself and Connemara pieces of paper representing ten dollar bills—so she and C. each had $80, but Barb also had a paper marked HORSE. They enacted the transactions, at the end of which Connemara had $100 and no horse. There seemed to be general relief: This proved that $20 was right. But then there was more conversation about how these other solutions also made sense (I must say that they do not make sense to me, but . . .), and Barb's "game" made assumptions and that maybe it would be different if you did not assume that the man started with $80. An impasse?

Then Jennifer said that she could show that you do not need to assume that the man has $80. She would, she said, enact this with Mark and Cheryl. She would start with $50 of her own, buy the horse and have no money, (this is all enacted), and then sell the horse back to B for $60 and have $60 ($10 more than she had at the outset). She would then decide she needed the horse after all and borrow $10 from Cheryl and give the whole $70 to Mark for the horse. Now broke and owing her friend $10, she would resell the horse for $80. After paying Cheryl the $10 she owed her she now had $70, $20 more than she had started with. $20 profit. People pondered this (no one seemed bored). However, a little bit after this Louise . . . said that she felt frustrated and confused and that I needed to tell them the answer. Several others seemed to agree. I agreed that it was frustrating (I was also thinking about Don Finkel's argument [2000] that the teacher needs to provide closure—emotional as well as intellectual—after a long joint investigation). Still, I was curious (YES!) about how the group would think about this frustration. I proposed that we think about what would be gained and lost, in their 4th grade class, if they said, at such a moment, what *they thought the answer was* (I had told them that the problem was from Marilyn Burns and that she doesn't say what the answer is so I could only give them my opinion and my reasoning). A number of people spoke about the ill effects of frustration, that it was valuable to hear the many ideas, but at a certain point. . . . Then a student on the right hand side of the room who hadn't given a solution yet said she had been talking to the students near her and they were all struck by something: "We all say we need to be told the answer. But yesterday in Ms. Pricco's room, not one child asked what the answer was. They were all focused on the reasoning. [pregnant pause] But I think we have been programmed to need to know the answer. . . ." Silence as we thought about this. I was amazed—and in fact I thought, "Yes, she's right, and I should respect that: they have been programmed to need answers, and they have been patient and now (or soon) it will be time [to tell them my answer]." I did not say this, though, because others were clearly pondering this point. No one disagreed. So I summarized where I thought we were: Most people thought the answer $20 made sense several ways and thought it was the answer but that they were frustrated and confused about why a plausible line of argument led to $10. Some people thought it was $10 (this was only really Miranda, I thought, but did not say) but couldn't see why a plausible line of argument led to $20. I asked whether there was anyone whose current thinking did not fall into one of these groups. No, there wasn't. We returned to the question of whether my telling my opinion would be useful. The third person I called on said, well, I just want to say one more thing about the problem. . . . And we were off again. Now I was beginning to get a bit frustrated [it was long past time for break], although I was also delighted by the intensity of people's interest both in the problem and the ideas of others. But then I think it was Jennifer who said that she had figured out how you could show that you did not have to make any particular assumptions about how much money the man started with, and then provided an explanation that convinced almost everyone and seemed to lead to general satisfaction. And then Miranda said, "Wait I just did it again and I got that He *lost* $30!!!" and she came to the board and explained, and then Jennifer said, "You are right that someone loses $30, but it is the *other* man and need not concern us!" and she showed Miranda where the illogic was, and Miranda saw!! And then I asked whether there was anyone who was not sure that they already knew what I would say if I said what I thought the answer was. And no one seemed to be in doubt, so we had a break. Whew. (And during the break Miranda, Angelica (who had been frustrated), Louise, and several others continued to work on figuring out, at the board (so, publicly) what the logical flaw was in one of the other $10 solutions. And succeeded.

What a long blow-by-blow description of a class. But I really wanted to get it down. How does this all connect to play? Well, one thing is that it seemed as though it was completely safe for people to be invested and involved in the discussion: by the end of the period I think everyone except maybe George had spoken at least once (not all of them in the horse-trading part—but most of them then) and had done so without being asked. And everyone seemed to be listening to and considering every idea. It also seemed to be safe (no danger of adverse consequences) to offer wrong ideas: indeed, Connemara and Miranda at least, and others as well, I think, seemed to be asking for help in identifying the logical flaw in their thinking. Isn't this what we mean by "playing with ideas"? That you are putting the idea out—outside of yourself—for others to look at with you, and examine? Play with?

So, what made all of this possible? Certainly it wouldn't have happened if Miranda hadn't come out of the closet on Tuesday with her $10 solution. I think the example of Pat P.'s students loving doing math together and listening so thoughtfully to one another's ideas played a part. Barb's game. Jennifer's enactment. All of these moved us forward when we could have gotten stuck. Genuine curiosity is surely central: people really wanted to figure this out—whatever "this" was for them. And what about my curiosity?

My journal entry of the following Wednesday continues in a similar vein, but I will not try the reader's patience with another long excerpt. I note, however, that I used the word "delight" four times, twice to refer to my own reactions to the students' contributions to the discussion and twice to refer to the students' responses to what they saw in Pat Pricco's class. My reflections near the end of the entry are of particular interest:

> I need to stop, but there was a point I wanted to remember to write down: The students' enthusiasm for Pat Pricco's class, and the depth of their understanding of and valuing of the *Standards* [NCTM, 1989, 1991] and the vision behind the *Standards* makes me feel much more bonded with them than I have to other classes at this point in the semester. I am, for a variety of reasons, disposed to see things their way (illustrated by the fact that I was pretty much convinced that I should tell them what I thought was the answer to the Horsetrading problem, which I have never felt an impulse to do before).[5] In other words, the success of one effort (the trip to Pat's class, the horse-trading problem, and Molly's saying that she got $10) leads *my attitude* toward the students and the students' ideas to shift somewhat (and of course there is the conscious effort I am making to be more playful, to look for signs of play, and as a part of that my conscious effort to nurture my own curiosity about the students). Because the bond of affection I feel becomes a bond of curiosity very quickly: I am curious about those I like and love, and not so curious about those I do not like or love. (Isn't curiosity a kind of love almost?)

DISCUSSION

Now let us return to the issue of purposes, evangelism, and education, and whether we are trying to convert our students to particular ways of thinking about mathematics teaching or trying to help them develop in their own ways. If we take the students' notes on the visit to Pat Pricco's classroom and their comments during the class discussion as indications of what is on their minds and in their hearts as they begin their math methods class, we learn that they want to feel that they are learning to teach math, that in a classroom they attend carefully to children's treatment of one another, to mutual respect and human relationships, that they are happy to see children thinking about and doing math in ways more flexible than those they remember and that they are delighted to see children excited by a math lesson.

Teacher educators and prospective teachers may share far more common ground than we teacher educators see when, for example, we show videos featuring children grappling with and discussing their strategies, effective and otherwise, for solving a challenging mathematics problem. When our students tell us that "There just isn't time for all this talking. There is too much to cover, and there are all these tests… and the children's invented strategies are not as quick as the real way," we may need to pause and wonder more about what they are reacting to. The comments my students made in their journals, in-class writings, and class discussions suggest that their concerns were not so different from mine: like me, they wanted to create a classroom culture in which the *feeling* in the room was positive, students seemed genuinely curious about the ideas of others, and students were clearly learning and were excited about doing challenging math (and math really did seem to be play in this elementary classroom). Moreover, what they wrote about this classroom visit as an occasion for their own learning has helped me see differently what we in the university sometimes call "resistance." These comments suggest to me that in the past I have failed to provide prospective teachers with the kinds of field experiences that could help them connect the teaching they read about to the work of real teachers and children in real schools. Would it not be reasonable to guess, given these data, that students' skepticism about "teaching for understanding" or "*Standards*-based mathematics teaching" may be based less in the anti-intellectualism and conservatism of which Dan Lortie (1975) has made us so aware than in a strong commitment to values we, their teachers, may share but talk less about. Our students tell us that they are going into teaching because they love children (and we sigh inwardly that they say nothing about loving subject matter); they know that relationships are at the center of teaching, that the feelings of children matter immensely. When my students visited a classroom where children were kind to one another, supportive of their classmates' thinking, and excited about learning, many immediately fell in love with what they saw. They announced that they now knew how they wanted to teach math. An hour working with and observing children who are talking animatedly about math accomplished more of my goals for students than a semester of evangelism.

Probably all teaching—or all passionate teaching anyway—contains an element of missionary work: we become educators because we want to open new worlds to students. In teacher education, the impulse to proselytize may be especially strong. The teaching in most American public schools is pedestrian at best; in some places it is actually harmful. In mathematics education, the scene is especially bleak. Most of today's prospective teachers experienced or endured mathematics teaching that focused almost exclusively on accuracy and speed in computation. Those who remember elementary school math warmly enjoyed the lack of ambiguity it offered and their own skill at completing sheets of computations—"mad minutes"—quickly and accurately. They were "good at math," which meant that they had memorized their multiplication tables and were able to do tedious computations without becoming distracted. Most prospective teachers, however, were less lucky: they were bored or confused—perhaps both—by math and decided that they were not good at it. Most math educators lament this heritage and hope to convince their students that there are better ways to teach math than the ones that left them feeling incompetent. We are math educators because we enjoy math and we hope to teach prospective teachers more satisfying and empowering ways to teach it.

We come—I came—to the teaching of math methods courses with images of good math teaching that are very different from those our students bring to their first math methods classes. We offer them our images, and we work hard to convince them that these represent the work of real teachers in real schools—that they too can teach in ways very different from the ways in which they were taught and that in doing so they will find deep satisfaction as well as much challenge.

This effort at persuasion is surely part of what it means to educate, to "lead out": we are leading students out into a wider pedagogical landscape, one that includes far more than the one to which they became accustomed in thirteen years of public schooling. Our missionary stance can, however, put a distance between us and our students at a time when we could accomplish more by standing near them. Students come to us with some fairly durable images of what it means to teach mathematics, ones formed through their apprenticeship of observation and then reinforced in conversations with friends and relatives who teach elementary school. They hope and expect that we will teach them how to do what elementary math teachers do, help them to develop the skills they think they will need to provide children in large groups with skills to succeed on standardized tests, in the next grade in school, and in the wider world. When we show them images that are very different from the ones they know and suggest that *this* is what we mean by "teaching mathematics," we set off complex responses. Some students, remembering how much they hated math in school, are delighted to think that there may be another way to teach and learn it. Others worry that our visions of math teaching are unrealistic—however humane and attractive they may look—that they will not play in real classrooms, that they would not prepare children for the inevitable standardized tests, that they would not be acceptable to principals, parents, or colleagues. They fear that we will not equip them to "really" teach math, and they feel angry, scared, or sad, depending on their temperaments.

When we send our students into the classrooms where they are expected to observe math teaching and to work with small groups of children, often what they see looks very much like what they experienced as elementary school students. These field experiences can confirm their suspicion that real teachers in real schools have little to do with the reform-minded pedagogical practices about which we talk so much. In consequence, the visits to schools can widen the breach between us and our students—their sense that we either cannot or will not help them learn how to teach math as it must be taught in the schools in which they intend to work.

These problems had, I think, created distance between me and my students for a number of years. I labored to persuade them of the merits of an approach to mathematics teaching that they saw as counterintuitive. Even though I worked hard at being open to their ideas and misgivings and at creating a learning community in which all ideas were considered respectfully, the readings I assigned, the videos I showed, and the activities we did in class all spoke of teaching mathematics in ways very different from those they knew. My efforts to persuade were clear even as I tried to model openness and interest in their ideas. Moreover, in many cases the students' weekly visits to their field placements confirmed suspicions that real teachers in real schools did not teach math in the way that the teachers described in the course readings and shown on videotape did.

The philosopher David Hawkins (1974), in a now-classic essay, explained that teaching can usefully be looked at as a triangular relationship between I, Thou, and It: the teacher, the student, and the curriculum. Hawkins worried that many conscientious teachers of young children saw the central relationship in the classroom as essentially dyadic—a relationship between I (the teacher) and Thou (the student).

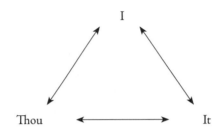

The teaching relationship only develops well, Hawkins argued, if there was some It—perhaps a set of batteries and bulbs, or Maurice Sendak's drawings of "Wild Things," or maybe a Shakespeare sonnet—in which both student and teacher were interested. As I reflected on earlier iterations of TE-402, it seemed to me that the pedagogical triangle had looked more like this:

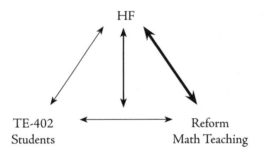

I had directed most of my attention at the reform mathematics teaching that I was hoping to interest my students in learning about, at the skills I thought that they would need in order to teach in ways consistent with the NCTM *Standards* volumes (1989, 1991), and at their attitudes toward this kind of teaching. I was also, of course, concerned about the students themselves, but I do not think that they were my primary focus. Although some of my students took an interest in the sort of math teaching I was hoping to teach them, many remained skeptical that this kind of instruction was actually practical or desirable with real children in real schools facing real demands for accountability. To them, the articles we read and the videos we watched represented a kind of teaching that made sense to people in universities, but had little to do with what happened, and could happen, in schools.

In 2000, Dirck Roosevelt's successful effort to shift the emphasis of my efforts and attention from getting students to "play" in mathematics to nurturing my own curiosity about their thinking seems to have launched a series of changes in my attitude and in those of the TE-402 students. Apparently in consequence, the focus of our interchanges changed. The instructional triangle now looked more like this:

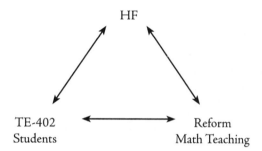

The relationships among the parts of the triangle were far more balanced—and closer to what Hawkins had had in mind. Perhaps we could say the attention I had previously directed to the relationship between the students and the It—reform math teaching—was now refocused on my students and their ideas. My determination to nurture my curiosity about their ideas suggested a new focus.

In his effort to articulate and explicate the basis of moral behavior, Immanuel Kant (1785/1964), in his *Fundamental Principles of the Metaphysics of Morals*, argued that it was never moral to treat (or regard) another human being as a "means." Human beings must be seen and treated as ends in themselves. This is a rule that good K–12 teachers instinctively obey: their work with their students, whether first-graders or high school seniors, is undertaken for the good of the students and not to accomplish a goal external to these students' well-being. As I have worked with the data we have just been examining, construing and reconstruing the meanings of this story, I have come to believe that there is a pitfall in the work of teacher education. Like me, most of my colleagues became teacher educators because they were dissatisfied with U.S. schools and hoped to have some positive impact on at least a few of them. Because we no longer teach in public schools ourselves, the prospective teachers we teach represent our best hope of having a positive impact on the lives of schoolchildren. While the impulse to improve the lives of children is surely a laudable one, we nonetheless may find ourselves in a position Kant has advised us to see as problematic: our students have become, at least partly, a means to an end—the improved educational opportunities for *their* future students—rather than an end in themselves. This difficulty was at the heart of the problem I was facing in January 2000.

Kant implicitly asks us to think hard about how our purposes as teacher educators connect to the prospective teachers who are actually in our classrooms. Hawkins reminds us to ask ourselves whether we have listened hard enough to these prospective teachers. This story is about what happened when I took multiple steps that closed the distance between me and my students, putting myself in a position to see their point of view. My new location allowed me to do a better job of connecting my students' purposes to our work together. When this happened, I looked and felt more like an educator and less like an evangelist. I also made more converts.

5

"What Gives You the Right?" Earning Moral and Intellectual Authority to Teach[1]

DIRCK ROOSEVELT,
WITH JULIE HANSON-EGLITE AND GRETA McHANEY-TRICE

Some fourth graders, black children, complain to their teacher that they can hardly set foot in the convenience store near their school before they are told to hurry up and make up their minds about which chips or pop or candy to buy—demanded, too, to explain why they are not in school—and they feel closely watched the whole time. Their white friends and classmates do not have the same experience. Their teacher, herself black, in her second year, though with appreciable life experience, works with them to design an experimental inquiry, sending first some white students, and then some black, into the store, on the same day, the same clerks on duty; the trips are all timed and observed from a discreet distance outside the store. The class repeats the experiment a few times, varying the sequence. Each time, the white students get bored and leave the store after five minutes or more without having been questioned or followed; the black students are always accosted within two minutes. The students carry out the experiments during school hours. They make an ad hoc field trip, leaving the school grounds and negotiating heavy traffic. They depart as well from the prescribed curriculum: Actively testing for bias in the practices of one's community is not in the state standards or district benchmarks.

To me, this is a story of imaginative, admirable, indeed exciting teaching, the more so on account of its spontaneous nature, modest size (of course, an ambitious, weeks-long unit similar in method and meaning would also be entirely admirable), and yet representative character. Turning it over in my mind and sharing it with others, I want to understand it in terms other than those of personal courage, initiative, imagination, and passion. I respect these qualities hugely, of course, but for purposes of teacher education they give me limited analytic purchase. And I do want to learn from the story.

So begins the inquiry of which this chapter is one result, an inquiry that began to take form when *authority* came to mind as a way of discussing the qualities of the pedagogy I found compelling in this story. I began to formulate the idea that an aim of teacher education, perhaps a central one, should be to enable the prospective teacher to achieve *a sense of earned intellectual and moral authority to teach*. If this formulation is slightly awkward, it is because I mean "sense of" (as in the prospective teacher's own feeling that) and "earned" (in the sense of warranted) with equal force; while the second *may* seem obvious, the first appears less so. There is much to be said about the concept or concepts of "authority" and their relevance for teaching and learning to teach; here, however, I can only do some of that work, as I want to devote the bulk of my available space to two teachers who represent and question their own practice and purposes in ways that go some way toward illustrating and making the case—entailing political, moral, practical, and theoretical elements—for the composition of authority I mean. One reason for this decision is that these teachers, Greta McHaney-Trice and Julie Hanson-Eglite, speak distinctively and with power to the question "What gives you the right to teach other people's children?" (which I think of as the "authority" question when it's in the trenches, borrowing Delpit's [1998] well-known phrase). Another reason is that Greta and Julie are Team One graduates from whom we think there is much to learn about the work of democratic teacher education. Their voices are the moving force of this chapter.

I will then be drastically parsimonious, here, about theories of authority, whether within or without school contexts. When I began thinking about this there was not, as far as I could discover, much that was fresh in the way of theoretical or theoretically well-informed discussion of authority issues in teacher education. The classic work of Weber (see Gerth & Mills, 1946) and Durkheim (1956), and some basic reference works (e.g., "Authority," 1996, 2002; Krieger, 1973), gave good initial bearings, however. From these I took "the legitimate exercise of power" as a basic working definition of authority. Weber's typology of "traditional," "charismatic," and "rational-legal" provided a useful analytic lever; Durkheim's stress on moral bases for the authority of the teacher, in particular—although founded on an assumption of consensus, whose *absence* is, in my view, a major reason why a self-conscious conception of legitimacy as a question, not a given, is imperative for teachers today—is also very valuable. That emphasis is prominent in the essential work of Metz (1978). In her analysis of authority as its structure becomes evident in conditions of crisis in schools, she employs an elegant and powerful definition:

> Authority is the right of a person in a specified role to give commands to which a person in another specified role has a duty to render obedience. This right and duty rest upon the superordinate's recognized status as the legitimate representative of a moral order to which both superordinate and subordinate owe allegiance. (p. 27)

The concept of "moral order" is something I am particularly glad to be able to borrow from Metz. Finally, there *has* now been, over the past few years, some very fresh, strong, knowledgeable work on authority in teaching and learning to teach. I have learned a lot from the work of Judith Pace in particular (e.g., Pace & Hemmings, 2006a). Pace and Hemmings argue usefully for an understanding of authority "as a complex social relationship . . . a *social construction*" (2006b, p. 1).

Speaking to one half of the basic definition, then, teaching is an exercise of power, one intended to have deep and far-reaching consequences. Indeed, its social justification rests on the *expectation* that it will influence students' thought and conduct in the long run, while in the daily activities of schooling, teaching routinely and necessarily seeks some control over students' behavior and attitudes. Of the various points that could be made about "legitimacy," half of the basic definition, one will have to suffice: In a system of mass compulsory education operating as an agent of democracy, the question of the basis and nature of the teacher's right to teach is obviously a political one, one that cannot be taken for granted. And "they told me to" is not a sufficient justification for the exercise of teacherly (or other) power over "other people's children."

My interest is in how such a right *might* be properly earned and how it and its earning might usefully be understood by teachers, prospective teachers, and teacher educators.

An Orientation for Professional Practice: The Demand for Real Experience; or, Greta Reconstructs Teaching and Learning to Teach

Greta McHaney-Trice is an African American woman who returned to school as a nontraditional student for her BA and teaching certificate. She had been a student of mine for five semesters; at the time of the long conversation from which much of the following discussion is drawn, she was close to the end of her third year of teaching fourth grade in a Lansing public school sometimes euphemistically referred to as "in transition," which means that it has recently come to serve students of color predominantly, many of them living in circumstances of high poverty. Greta identifies her priorities and commitments as a teacher in terms of social justice; it is she who directed the impromptu bias investigation. She and I have stayed in close communication since her graduation; we exchange classroom visits (I to her fourth grade, she to my teacher education classes) annually:

> It was on a game show, "What's a *cicada*?" and I thought *cricket*. I flashed to—
> it had to have been fourth grade when I first came in contact with that word,
> "cicada," and I thought, now why would you remember that of all the things
> in fourth grade? Why would you remember "cicada"? I can almost remember
> the lesson. I can remember the day. I can remember the teacher talking about
> the difference between the cricket and the cicada—and I couldn't tell you,
> but I remember knowing that there was one, and that it's an insect and it's in
> the cricket family if it's not indeed a cricket. That word took me back to an
> experience in school. A clear vivid experience in school, a real experience that
> won't dissipate over time. That nobody can tap into. To me that's it.[2]

We do not know from this recollection what exactly to say about the specifics of Greta's learning on that day in fourth grade. We do see that "school" here is associated with intensity, with a moment of life in concentration, an experience of such value that it exemplifies the *real*, where "real" means desirable and precious: a moment of such personal significance that it has apparently become an integral part of the self, the self that endures and perhaps sustains, resisting the trespasses of time and persons.

As we will also see, this experience comes to symbolize for Greta the purpose that matters most to her as a teacher: for students to learn to "push" for "more"—to push back, to push Greta herself, to push their future teachers, by extension, to push the society they come into, for more: for "real experience that won't dissipate over time," that no one can take away.[3]

This is a bold credo, a Deweyan conception of educational justice. It is not a purpose of schooling that can be supplied or specified by state standards or district mandates—with which, indeed, it is likely to be in tension, if not outright conflict. The contrarian nature, political import, and costs of "pushing back" as a purpose are crucial to this story. Greta's work as a teacher and the authority she establishes, in both its strength and its vulnerability, cannot be understood without recognition of the challenging character and central position of that purpose. But the difficulties of this avowed purpose bring into focus the underlying and fundamental fact, of broader implication, that Greta claims responsibility for the purposes of her teaching in the first place. To do so is an act of rectitude with consequences. One necessity in being accorded legitimacy—in being constituted *as* a person "in authority"—is said to be a well-founded presumption of efficacy (Metz, 1978). In exercising the authority for her purposes, Greta will need to make effective decisions about curriculum and pedagogy, for these are among the means by which educational purposes are to be realized. Claiming and articulating responsibility is, then, both to assert moral authority and to work at earning it.

Deciding what is to be studied and how it is to be taught is a fundamental expression of power in teaching, as well as one of its inescapable responsibilities. This is to state both what is obvious and what is exceptional: obvious because little could be more self-evidently germane to the professional activity of teaching than content; exceptional because teachers in fact have constrained freedom to make such decisions—hence, compromised authority. Thus, while it may be familiar, it is not trivial to say that moral authority can be earned by taking responsibility for one's own conduct, for better, that is, and worse. Greta's teaching encompasses both a sense of high purpose and a robust, complex reality principle, existing in what is for her, frequently, a relationship in conflict. Managing this battle, which threatens her sense of her own integrity, can also be understood to constitute a process of earning the intellectual and moral authority to teach.

These issues are all visible in Greta's account, deep in our long conversation, of what becomes in the telling a touchstone experience in her education as a teacher, a teacher who acts as if she has the kinds of rights and responsibilities I indicate, one who declares that she teaches to foster in her students the wish and the will to "push back." We have been discussing instances of unplanned teaching. This topic has come up by way of Greta's recollection of a thought she describes as having "jumped out and bit [her]" during her first semester in Team One, in TE-301, "that teaching isn't a 1, 2, 3, A, B, C . . . do right, do wrong kind of a thing—that teachers have *choices.*" Asked how she came to this thought, she had said, "it's going to sound like a pat answer, but it really came to light during the Huck Finn thing, you know, and studying Dewey. . . . I can remember it very vividly . . . 'cause I was really struggling." *Tom Sawyer* (Twain, 1876/1981) had been on my syllabus for that course; *Huckleberry Finn* (Twain, 1885/1961) had not been. However, I had been moved to suggest that we take up *Huck*, which, after some discussion, we did. Greta now recalls the last of the *Huck* sessions. Students had been given the assignment of making multimedia representations of their understanding of some aspect of the book.

"I remember," Greta says, "what struck me in a very profound way [was] when people presented and came up with some of the most far-from-my-thinking, never-had-even-thought-about-it things about the book." She continues, "I thought I was smart enough and [had] learned everything, and I remember struggling to do something right for the project." To her surprise, I had in class that evening accepted many different representations of the book's contents and meanings as valid. There was no clear or single "right" way to do what I had called for. A number of these unexpected responses to the assignment had proven compelling for Greta. "What was *right?*" she remembers thinking. "So," she says, these six years later,

> that was kind of when things started to really go wow, you know, there is not a lot of right and wrong here when you come to teaching and how kids can kind of really get to some very astute things without having to know the right and wrong—whether or definitely because I didn't plan it or teachers didn't plan it.

"And," Greta continues, "that just felt good." The idea that being "right" is not the only criterion for learning has come to the fore, in tandem with the realization that teaching does not consist only of moves and "outcomes" selected in advance: indeed, discoveries not foreseen by the teacher can be the richest of all, for both student and teacher, as multiplicity of interpretation can surpass singular correctness in value. "This is what learning and teaching really is all about," she recalls feeling; and, "It felt good as a student, it felt good as a prospective teacher . . . it felt like, oh, *now I can begin to learn how to teach.*"

As Greta revises her conception of learning and teaching, she quite logically reconceives *learning to teach* as well. When she decides, "Now I can begin to learn how to teach," she constitutes herself as an agent. The reconstruction brings to the surface and to some extent resolves a felt conflict. On the one hand was her "desire to be . . . a good student . . . and obviously at some point in time a good teacher—whatever that 'good' means," an expectant stance of "show me how to teach, show me what to do, show me the A, B, C, 1, 2, 3." She was, she recalls, "waiting to feel *comfortable* that I would learn how to teach." She continues, "A lot of kids [i.e., the eighteen- to twenty-one-year-olds who make up most of the class] have that frustration: 'Teach me, show me, when [are] you going to show me?'" On the other hand, this feeling was mitigated for Greta by the pleasures of novelty and of learning more generally: "I was learning so much and enjoying that . . ." Nonetheless, she also "didn't feel that [she] was *learning how to teach*" (emphasis added). These recognizable conflicts—between learning as being told and learning as finding out and between teaching as the transmission of authoritative knowledge and teaching as dialectic, as provocation into inquiry—are to a great extent resolved by reconstruction or repositioning herself, signaled by a feeling of relief: "I got a chance to really feel that 'oh yes you are,' kind of, 'this is what teaching really is about.'"

The surprising experience with Tom Sawyer and Huck Finn in TE-301 gave Greta a new perspective on teaching, or an image, cathected and complex, through which to think about it. The salient elements of the episode apparently are, jointly, being disconcerted as a *student* (unable to navigate by the beacon of the single right answer), being surprised and pleased as a *learner* (realizing that quite a few responses to this text, including several that are startling, have merit and appeal), and feeling stalled as a *prospective teacher* (wondering and hearing others worry, "when will someone *show us how?*"). This seems to be a catalytic intersection. A different light is cast on learning, which reflects back an image of teaching, and Greta's attention completes the circuit with a reconceptualization of learning to teach as a project over which she has some power, some responsibility. She begins, in effect, to engage the problem of authority.

However, while Greta as a student of teaching was able to resolve the feeling of conflict—between different conceptions of *learning* and of *teach-*

ing—which thus freed more energy and will for that very task, it persists or recurs, not surprisingly, when she is herself a teacher. At this point, the tension or conflict is aggravated by the sense of duty. *Its* claims are multiple and discordant—and it is precisely the sense of earned authority that offers a way not exactly to resolve or dissolve them but to cut through them.

"The conflict," she continues, "is still in my practice . . . when I stand before my students on a daily basis. It's still in my practice when I find myself going rote and [teaching to the] tests." She "feel[s] pressured" to devote more time to the state tests, to place a premium on recall and speed, to behave as if there was almost nothing but right and wrong to teaching and learning—pressed by school and district administration and the relentless pace of the tests, by social pressure and the climate of the times. Sometimes "for a . . . moment I think that it makes sense"—to teach in a highly directive way, to drive the students to learn to "do school," above all, to score passably well on the tests. The persistence of racism and her urgent desire, communicated explicitly to them, that the African American boys who comprise a majority of her class succeed by the conventional measures and defy the expectation of their failure prompts her to play devil's advocate for the tests, to remember "that it is not always black and white and clear cut. Sometimes it involves me going, 'OK, what value do these tests have? . . . How can I make them work for me?'" Keeping the conflict alive, keeping open to the perspective that challenges you, allowing doubt entry, is surely one way of earning moral authority—if the doubt is an adjunct to, not a substitute for, continued principled and purposeful action, protected to a degree by reason but not by certainty.

This is costly, though. Greta explains bitterly that often, when she does teach to the test, "I know I've cheated myself and I know I've cheated the students. I can do the rote," she says—in fact "probably *better* . . . in a sense, than I can the other things that I want to do. . . . It's not hard to think through, 'open the page, copy the problems down, write the answers, and move on.' It's not hard to say that and call it teaching." Demoralizing and unsatisfying though that is as a substitute for teaching, however, it is not where the conflict cuts most sharply. That comes "when I . . . take that approach and try to get something out of it that I still deem as *meaningful* . . . for the kids." *That* is a fraud, a cheat. The education the children are *not* getting when they are doing "the rote" is sufficiently precious that not to provide it constitutes an affirmative deprivation. The analogy is to an inalienable right. To prevent someone from enjoying such a right, whether or not they are aware of its existence, is an outright theft, in this view:

> If that's what I do and that's all that I do, I *know* that I'm taking something away from them. . . . It goes back to . . . the beginning of the conversation . . . letting the kids choose, letting the kids explore, and have experiences that are valid for them like *Huck Finn* is valid for me. That's learning. That's also teaching, because a worthwhile product resulted. A worthwhile awareness resulted. . . . You know . . . who was the protagonist, who was the antagonist . . . what century was it and where's the setting, the where, when, what, why, how: You know, I probably couldn't tell you. . . . But I know I loved the book. I know that it's worthwhile literature on a lot of levels. That people can learn about people. People can learn about humanity, people can learn about decisions, people can learn about influences, people can learn about peers and friendships and relationships, people can learn about abandonment, people can learn about democracy and right and wrong and sometimes having to do something wrong for the right reasons. And that's rich as opposed to "write a paragraph about what happened in chapter 2." So it's similar to. . ."I sold the shadow to support the substance." You know that really was a very small minute part of *Sojourner Truth*.

Greta has in fact named major themes of *Huck*—but as "themes" of life or "real experience," not decontextualized topics for formal analysis. "Learning," as she represents it here, is something done with, not to, the text. She also knows that I know she is deeply attached to the phrase (appearing in a biography she'd read to the previous year's class) associated with Sojourner Truth. Its placement here signals that we are at the moral heart of the matter—and it is at this point that she tells the cicada story presented earlier, the memory that, paired with the surprising *Huck Finn* episode, provides a touchstone, a way to think about and explain what school experience could and should be. The positive value at issue—the thing that students, and Greta herself, are in danger of being "cheated" out of, the element that has the moral and affective upper hand in the conflict within Greta's practice—is "real experience," "clear and vivid," "that won't dissipate": the quality of enduring life.

We talk about other books that have been important for the class, that seem to have occasioned some moments in which education has that quality of a life worth living, *Number the Stars* (Lowry, 1989) and *Bud, Not Buddy* (Curtis, 1999) among them. We glance, too, at an artifact from TE-301, the same course in which we had tackled *Huck Finn*: a "bibliography card" on which Greta had selected and annotated a quote from *The Child and the Curriculum* (Dewey, 1902/1956). "What concerns him as [a] teacher .. is the ways in which [the] subject may become a part of experience; what there is in the child's present that is usable with reference to it." On her card Greta has also made reference to "the logical and the psychological," glossing this with the comment, "continuum." Now, she reconstructs her ideas about *The Child and the Curriculum* and connects them to what is on her mind as we speak. Curriculum, now looked at more as something developed in context than as external mandate, becomes an additional way for developing her ideas about "clear, vivid experience." "These words," she says, convey

> a lot about things that I grappled with . . . in trying to work my way through a decision or a place in mapping out my own curriculum and becoming a teacher. . . . I continue to do that . . . because I think it had been understood by myself as being drastically two ends of a spectrum . . . rote memorization versus experiencing and touching and feeling . . . different dialogues when it comes to literature. Having kids experience .. the literature, have a sense of relating to the literature either vicariously or intimately, their own sense of "I can relate, I can't relate, what the hell's wrong with Bud. . . . I would never have gone and stood in the soup line. I'd a died first." Or, "I've been there before. . . . I know exactly how he's feeling." . . . [To] make those experiences real so that they can say "yeah, that makes sense . . ." and talk about it in those terms I think is a reason that kids should learn how to read and write. . . . *It justifies a need to be able to read and then write or write and then read*, as opposed to just having it be a skill that has no meaning [emphasis added]. You know, I can do it, but why? You know, what's the purpose, why do I need to put these arbitrary letters in front of themselves, to do what? To convey what? To say what?

A certain kind of robust encounter with literature—one in which readers "relate"; make social and intellectual connections; affirm, challenge, or reject meanings and ways of being, for example—can, then, constitute "real experience that won't dissipate over time," which is what "curriculum," as planned or plotted by a teacher but lived by students and teacher together in the classroom, can be. For the students, this is to be positioned as people who are entitled to *reason*—to justification. For the teacher, it is a matter of pleasure, of course—the enthusiasm with which Greta recalls the students' engagement with *Bud, Not Buddy* will be recognizable to any teacher—but it is also a matter of doubt and uncertainty. For if a *justification* for learning to read and write is due to students, if they have a right to feel that they are not being held accountable for learning something entirely arbitrary, then *teaching* requires justification. It has no automatic nor unassailable legitimacy. This, in fact, is the question of authority.

If the quality of children's experience both in the lived moment of school and in the afterlife of memory is the standard of value, the measure of justification, it is clear that authority is unstable and must be continually in the process of being remade. A teacher can be aided or impeded in that construction, but it cannot be done for her. It is true that the scope of students' assent—the range of experience they find "vital," the qualities that elicit their allegiance—is, itself, educable. This is one meaning of Dewey's demand for an "education of, by, and for experience" (1938/1963, p. 29). That would be a somewhat demanding responsibility under most circumstances, and it is far more so when the quality of experience the teacher seeks feels antithetical not only to what is required of her by the imperative to standardize, measure, and control—to determine a uniform "pace"— but also, and more urgently, to the implacable need she sees for her students, her African American boys in particular, to learn to comport themselves well and "measure up" to the tests. Success of this sort seems essential to their survival, and yet it comes at the cost of experiences that justify and enable real learning. We return, inevitably, to a sense of binary choices, to conflict—not only the conflict Greta experiences as a teacher, but also that which she believes she subjects her students to. She worries that it is wrong to place them in that position, and yet her whole educational aim may be said to be to place them—equipped as well as she is able—in that position. She speaks with growing anger:

> I've felt [conflict] very strongly this year. I've felt that for some reason I'm going to be forced to choose. . . .I'm [angry that] I have to choose. I don't know that even when I choose . . . that I'm doing what I say I've chosen. I've chosen, chosen verbally and mentally, to say I want these kid[s] to have these real experiences. . . . Am I helping a problem or making the problem worse in some sense? . . . How can I put that pressure on fourth graders, nine and ten years old? . . . Maybe that's helpful, maybe that's harmful conflict. . . . I think on one hand that it's helpful, because it might alert them to be kind of pious, help them deal with people that won't give them that experience because they won't even *try* to get beyond the dilemma or *recognize* the dilemma. [I want to say to the kids,] "When you run into teachers that say, 'Sit down, be quiet,

open your books and this is it,' *will you expect more, will you want more . . . will you push them to do more?"* And I *want* to push them to do more. I want them to push *me* to do more.

Education is in conflict with schooling. For students to learn to push for more is the point of Greta's teaching. In being purposeful along these lines, she conceives of the students as persons of legitimate desires and righteous purposes. This is a stipulation of the standards by which we should, in a democracy, judge our societal provision of education. It is to invoke an "education of, by, and for experience." It is, in the spirit of Dewey and DuBois and others, an education that raises children to desire and to demand full participation in the making and remaking of culture.

With respect, then, to Greta's earned intellectual and moral authority for her teaching, a number of points emerge. The sources of her legitimacy include her insistence on taking responsibility for educational purposes and for attendant means. In the construct, brought forward by Metz, of a "shared moral order" to which both teacher and students feel allegiance, we can see another source of her legitimacy, if we regard the "real experience" to which she repeatedly appeals as a kind of moral order. In her account, we see her having students assenting to that order, one aspect of legitimacy— and we see her having some success in realizing it (e.g., in discussion of *Bud, Not Buddy*), another aspect.

At the same time, that educational experience, that "vital" and moral climate, is in felt conflict with schooling—with the order of "rote," "pacing guides," "sit down and open your book to page 339." Whereas education courts surprise, schooling loves only the predetermined goal. The experiences schooling affords do not achieve validity. But they are backed by force, which contributes to some fear on Greta's part that the conflict to which students are exposed by her pursuit of ambitious purposes will *not* prove educational. Thus, her endeavor entails moral hazard, a possible threat to her legitimacy. Keeping the conflicts alive, exposing herself to doubt, and recognizing risk, mitigate the risk and in themselves constitute some of the work of earning moral authority.

It is a tenuous business. No wonder, then, that Greta wonders urgently, "will you expect more, will you want more, will you push ... [for] more?" Educating students to hunger for and demand "experience...that arouses curiosity, strengthens initiative, and sets up desires and purposes sufficiently intense to carry a person over dead places in the future" (Dewey, 1938/1963, pp. 37–38) is, as aim and as accomplishment, the ambitious and risky source of her authority to teach.

Julie and the Energies of Commitment: "I Want to Be What That Parent Envisions for Their Kids"

Julie Hanson-Eglite is a white woman who grew up in a small town in Michigan, in her late twenties at the time of the interview upon which I draw heavily in what follows. She received her BS from and did her teacher preparation (with Team One) at MSU; she had been a student of mine for each of the five semesters of the program. On the hot, still, midsummer afternoon of our conversation, she manifests the confidence, and a certain invigorating restlessness or edginess, some version of the old academic pleasure in disputation, that I remember. She has just, a few weeks earlier, completed her fourth year of teaching chemistry in a public middle school in a suburb (neither the wealthiest nor the whitest) of Chicago. She had also just earned a master's degree in science education; in the fall she begins a new teaching position, in a high school that will, she hopes, be a less "toxic" environment.[4] She identifies herself as Christian, conservative in her politics, and, at this point in her life and career, "empowered." Professionally, she sees herself as someone who goes "kind of against the grain," in that she is a "Republican conservative teacher," whereas "most . . . are liberal . . . Democrat[s]." Upon a moment's further consideration, a more nuanced description of herself as a teacher emerges: She is "conservative" in her emphasis "on education" and on "preparing them for the next level." "But I'm really liberal in *how* I teach," she says; "I really want the kids to learn from experience. . . . I love doing labs with them." She takes an "inquiry" approach to science teaching, not uncritically, and with a clear and articulate rationale in which disciplinary considerations come first and pedagogical ones, while clearly important, second. Some meanings of earned moral and intellectual authority for teaching become clearer on consideration of Julie's testimony.

Julie demonstrates, as she puts it, a "stubborn" streak, and perhaps that sense of "empowerment," on an array of issues: by asserting her right to make explicit references to her faith (e.g., by speaking of "Christmas vacation," not "winter break," which feels unfamiliar to her) in a school with many Jewish, Indian, and Arabic students—though she goes on to say that personal religious beliefs seldom come up in her conversations with students; by defending the appropriateness of her frequent use of an avowedly "sarcastic" humor with her students—not that her humor always deserves that description. And she reports vigorously challenging the legitimacy of her principal's decision to permanently remove gas jets from the chemistry lab. "She doesn't know anything about science. . . . [She has] *no* experience in science classrooms"; (and later, on a different dispute: "I don't think [she] . . . has the *authority* to tell me. . . . She's not a scientist"). Julie and a colleague, by contrast, looked into "what the research says," and learned the practices of other schools, in support of their contention that the jets should stay. She also reports that neither this principal nor any of four administrators she has worked with have ever given her advice about how to improve her practice:

> I know there are things that I could do better. But they don't know enough to be able to suggest those, so . . . they lose credibility with me. . . . And they don't support [me] when I tell them I need things, and I feel like I'm in a pretty good position to know. I do my homework, I know what I need, and I know what I think is good. And I trust my judgment.

In fact, she says, she is the only (self-assigned) mentor to new teachers in her school. It's a good thing she "trusts her judgment," reasonably, it appears, as there is little else to rely on.[5]

These glimpses into Julie's narrative suggest that her willingness to challenge her principal stems largely from two sources: her sense of professional authority, funded to a significant extent by confidence in her disciplinary knowledge, and her personal qualities of stubbornness, feistiness, appetite for a challenge. Many more examples of each resource could be adduced, and the suggestion is so far correct. It is, however, incomplete. Julie's construction of professional expertise and warrant for judgment is nuanced and multifaceted; and expertise is not the only root from which her authority grows. There is a pronounced moral element and, what could be considered a property of that element, there is in her account the character of a live and open-ended process.

The speed with which Julie takes up my question, "What gives you the right to teach other people's children?" and the persistence with which she reverts to it are themselves striking. She calls it a "great question," one she seems surprised to find unfamiliar: "I don't even know how to answer what gives me the right to teach other people's kids." I offer to narrow the question, but she ignores me: "I don't know what gives me the right." I again offer to refocus the question or make it more concrete and am again ignored: "I never even thought about it." Far more than I had anticipated, the critical problem at the heart of "authority"—the question of legitimacy—becomes the explicit theme of our conversation.

Over the course of that quite long talk, with a good deal of catching up and a degree of sometimes probing recollection of our time together as teacher and student interspersed, Julie brings up for consideration a number of possible sources of legitimation, never, at least on this afternoon, finding any one of them sufficient. Included in the catalog are: her personal qualities (e.g., "morals," independence); her own investigations ("I've done my research, I've done my homework"); her own "struggles" with subject matter; her analysis of her own experiences of learning and teaching (see Richardson & Roosevelt, 2005); her disciplinary knowledge; her pedagogical content knowledge; her formal preparation, as a substantive matter; her official license to teach; her "intrinsic motivation." She also says, partly with reference to her professional education, first at MSU's Team One (about which she is far from uncritical), more recently at Northwestern, recognizing that its substance—in particular, its stress on "inquiry science" and complementary expectations or opportunities to conduct structured inquiry into one's own practice and to "kind of build your own . . . philosophy"—reflected a particular time as well as a particular place, "I was lucky. I feel . . . God was on my side."

In one direct attack on my question, Julie considers a notion of authority consistent with the "rational-legal" form in Weber's typology (Gerth & Mills, 1946). She supposes that the authority to teach is to be found in—or perhaps more accurately, managed by—systems: "What gives me the right? . . . Well, [my students'] parents choose the school, their parents move to communities. . . . I don't know if it's a right, but their parents have to trust school systems." Julie's invocation of community or parental "trust," as part of the same thought that refers her individual authority as a teacher to the "school system," is noteworthy. It suggests that the system is basically a conduit for authority conferred by persons who will be directly affected by its exercise. This is an understanding that at least one scholar finds foundational for the concept (and present throughout its unsettled history): "The idea of authority," Leonard Krieger argues, "arose when men freely chose final human depositories for their trust," as one vital move in addressing "the crucial problem of establishing a basis for government beyond the specific punishments [it] . . . could impose . . . [or] the specific benefits it could deliver" (1973, p. 146). In a nice set of distinctions that jointly illuminate why recourse to the idea of authority is so frequent in efforts to analyze social matters and why appeals to it are so often doomed to failure on the very occasions—occasions of conflict—when they are particularly likely to be made, he continues, "authority was essentially fiduciary: where the correlative of reason was *conviction* and the correlative of power was *obedience*, the correlative of authority was *trust*" (p. 146, emphasis added). A question for the rational-legal, bureaucratic, or technocratic system as a source of authority is: Is that system in fact a repository of trust, an authentic expression of familial and communal trust, or not? An affirmative answer would not settle the question, but it would certainly bear on it; a negative answer further exposes the challenges for Julie, or any teacher.

"*Do your students learn?*" is a question that might be asked by someone challenging a teacher's authority or by someone seeking to understand it. I am prompted to ask it in the course of Julie's strongly felt and interestingly skeptical discussion of the inquiry approach to science that she describes as her practice—in a balanced way, with conviction, without the fervor of a convert. "True inquiry," she says, is about educative experience and real investigation, not experience for its own sake:

> Teachers can spend six weeks out in the rivers but the kids could learn nothing but how to splash around. . . . It's how do you do it. . . . People [say], "Oh I do inquiry." And then you watch what they do and, "You're not doing inquiry, honey, you're just letting them play back in the lab."
>
> I know I'm right. . . . I feel like I'm [doing what] make[s] sense . . . but other [people] feel they make sense too, so who knows? . . . I think I'm much better off balancing what I do than trying to be a gung ho, all we do is inquiry, because nobody's shown that—in fact I've seen studies saying that kids are not necessarily learning—and there's nothing proven that inquiry kids are learning more than by reading textbooks. But who am I to be teaching this way if my kids aren't necessarily learning any more?

"Well," I ask Julie, "*are* your kids learning, do you know?" "That's a great question," she instantly replies. "I hope so. I think they are." She has ready at hand a recent example that appears to signal genuine learning. It seems to please her; I know I am taken with it. As part of her application for the job that she has since been offered and will be taking in September, members of the hiring committee came to observe her teach:

> It was really cool. We were doing a lab where the kids are doing exothermic and endothermic reactions. . . . And they were talking about solubility and temperature change and . . . the [visiting] teacher just said "Are you studying that?" I said "Oh no, we did that back in the fall," so it was . . . just cool because they're using the vocabulary but I don't give, I've never given a vocabulary test in my life. But you know I *talk* it, we *teach* it, we *use* it.

At various other points, Julie makes it clear that she has, in fact, seen support for the inquiry approach, in published reports of research conducted by science educators. But the metaphor she several times uses, for her philosophy as a science teacher, and for her students' conceptual understanding, is "build." The totality of her account strongly suggests that, while "what the research says" is certainly *one* form of justification for her pedagogy, neither it nor any other single source can stand alone. No one plank suffices. Authority cannot reside in expert pronouncements. Verification procedures are needed. Intellectual and moral authority for her teaching is earned by them, by triangulation, and, underlying these, by keeping the question of justification open—by entertaining doubt, as Greta also does. Although for Greta management of the doubt is anguished, for Julie it seems positively energizing; and it makes it difficult for others to pigeonhole her, a fact I surmise is in itself satisfying to her.

Struggle plays a part in Julie's self-construction as a teacher, yielding both sympathy and insight. "I think I am such a good math tutor because I struggled with math," she says, "and it's a lot easier to teach kids because I know what it's like to struggle . . . where people that just *get* stuff don't understand why you don't get it." Specifically, "As I've tutored more . . . I started to realize that . . . what really helps those kids is . . . [when I] tell them, 'Watch me and listen as I work through a problem. Now you do it and you talk me through it.' And it just became . . . one of those 'aha!' strategies." This is but one of several times she cites "struggle" as a resource for her teaching. After the interview is over and the tape recorder off, as we leave, I propose that it is not hard work and struggle alone that enables her to sympathize with and help children who also struggle, "but also, you watched your self, you observed, and you analyzed what you saw. Somehow you learned to analyze" (field notes, July 13, 2002). To this comment, so unfortunately open to the charge of being self-serving, she replies, more or less, "I did that in [TE] 301, wasn't that what we learned to do in 301?" (field notes, July 13, 2002) Though pleased, I am (rightly) inclined to discredit my hearing, and to discount her response in any case as perhaps more cordial than considered. However, subsequent review of the audio tape shows that Julie has already described what she has learned in tutoring as an example of "things that you develop as you think about your own practice."

She has also fleshed out her reasoning a little, with a clarity she attributes in part to study of her own practice in the course of her master's program:

> The way I teach is . . . I verbalize how I would solve that problem to the kids so that . . . they're hearing how I'm thinking. I'm not just *showing* them how to do it but I'm talking them through my process. And I think . . . I see . . . a huge difference because they're hearing their teacher talk their process through and so then *they're* going to develop the process. They're not just seeing me do numbers. And so I . . . have caught on to how I do that and I've made myself do it a lot more.

And the statement with which she concludes this account of the value of the tutoring could not be, all on its own, finer:

> The more I tutor the more I learn how to learn. And I think that makes me such a better teacher. . . . That's why I like tutoring, because I love those kids.

Intellectual authority in and from "learning how to learn," is here directly connected with "love," with the force of affection and commitment. Indeed "learning how to learn" and "loving those kids" are offered as parallel or reciprocal constructions, almost as two aspects of one phenomenon. In tutoring, Julie sees more clearly both her own learning and her students' learning—as *they* are able to make use of what *she* has learned from observing and making sense of her own learning. Some degree of valid generalization from her own experience is thus going on—a useful way of legitimating pedagogical decisions (Richardson & Roosevelt, 2005), made far more potent, as an ingredient in moral authority, by its association with the fundamental assertion of commitment and care for the students.

Julie makes more than one stab at the construct, less reassuring than may be wished, of legal-rational authority:

> You know then it's a state given right . . . if you look at it that way . . . they give certificates because they feel we're competent. Do we believe in that? Abso-

lutely not but . . . I feel I'm lucky because yes, I think I'm competent, apparently schools think I'm competent, and most parents think . . . maybe some don't, but if you looked into most teachers, I feel like I'm just so different . . . because of my education [at MSU and because] . . . I have such a motivation intrinsically. . . . I would've taken a pay cut to be in a better school. . . . If I wanted to make money I'd leave. I can do a lot of things but that's not what it's about. I like these kids and it's almost like, *I feel like, somebody's got to do it. You know, why not me? If somebody's got to teach them.* I don't want my kids with crummy teachers any more than . . . any other parent does. So *I want to be what that parent envisions for their kids,* you know what I mean? [emphasis added]

When Julie, not at the time a parent, speaks of what "any other parent . . . envisions," I hear John Dewey's ghost insisting that "what the best and wisest parent wants for his own child, that must the community want for all of its children" (1900/1956, p. 7) when she says, blending modesty with unmistakable seriousness, "somebody's got to do it . . . why not me," I hear an echo of the injunction, "Whatsoever thy hand findeth to do, do with all thy might," drawn to my attention by Julie many years ago, in the course of an independent study, in its appearance in *Composing a Life* (Bateson, 1989). Dewey holds the whole community up to the standard of its "best and wisest" parent-member and perhaps also encourages all of its members to imagine themselves acting (insofar as their actions impinge on schools) behind a Rawlsian veil of ignorance. In a reciprocal gesture, Julie, in addition to projecting herself into the parental position she does not yet occupy, wishes as a teacher to represent and, in a sense, realize the community's best hopes. The gesture is saved from any tint of grandiosity by the plain simplicity of her words, corresponding to the dailiness of teaching, and by the familiarity of the admonition to "do unto others." It is nonetheless a heroic ambition, one that finds the right to teach embedded in the transactions of trust and hope that characterize a family's gradual release of a child into the care of others and, through them, the larger world. Even if the state were qualified to certify competence, such distant assurance could play only a small part in legitimating the exercise of teacherly power over other people's children. That authority is earned more immediately and precariously by the movement of sympathy and affection, the effective exercise of care, the work of the moral imagination in putting oneself in another's shoes—by proposing to be the object of the *other's* legitimate hopes.

Julie relies on a sturdy sense of disciplinary and pedagogical knowledge, commitment to a well-understood and examined conception of good (inquiry-oriented) practice, developed habits of disciplined inquiry into her own practice, respect for her own professional education, and a vigorous sense of professional autonomy ("I did not want to be told what to teach.... [That's] not going to happen," she says at one point; "You've got to trust the teachers," at another). All of this may be said to amount to robust professional authority for her teaching. But her quality of self-interrogation—her tussling with the question of what gives her the right, for instance, or her several statements that the educational value of the method to which she tries to take a balanced, judicious, approach is not proven beyond doubt—and the role she assigns to luck, to God, to her own struggle—most of all, the place of personal responsibility and moral imagination in the structure of her authority suggest that legitimacy is not a *deposit*, nor is authority an accomplishment, so much as it is a process over time, an ongoing engagement of the self with the meanings of the work and its human situatedness, those others without whom it is nothing.

Conclusion

Julie Hanson-Eglite and Greta McHaney-Trice take up questions of legitimacy as if such questions are themselves legitimate. They don't appear to take "the right" to teach for granted; they neither reify it nor depend upon distant powers to guarantee it. They treat it more as a work in progress, a function in part of an ongoing dialogue (literal and metaphorical, internal and public), maintained by doubt far more than by certainty. The earning and the exercise of authority are reciprocal, partaking equally of necessity and of risk. Warranted confidence in one's own judgment—not an expression of certainty but a necessity in, precisely, its absence—is one ingredient; participation in a generative and transparent sense of educational purpose to which one holds oneself morally and practically accountable is another. Moral and intellectual authority to teach is earned, not given; dynamic, not static; problematic, not certain—open to question, as it should be. Getting an education in teaching is in part a matter of making that question one's own. The democratic paradox is that, to make the question of pedagogical authority one's own is to recognize it as others'—while also knowing that one is never at liberty to surrender it.

6

Keeping Real Children at the Center of Teacher Education: Child Study and the Local Construction of Knowledge in Teaching[1]

DIRCK ROOSEVELT

The . . . institutes were organized to follow methods that had been used in the physical sciences, that is, to take exact measurements of children. What could not be measured was simply left out. They began with physical measurements since these seemed the simplest to make. Even here they ran into difficulty. . . . When the research institute in Iowa wanted to measure children's physical growth, the children wiggled and they would appear to grow one day and shrink the next—so the research staff put the children into casts in order to measure them. They knew the children wiggled, but wiggling seemed unimportant because it couldn't be measured. And they knew that it was an emotional strain for the children, but you couldn't measure that, so that was disregarded. Science ought to be obeyed, and science has measurements. Now, *we* cared, really, more about the wiggle.

LUCY SPRAGUE MITCHELL, quoted in Antler (1982, p. 575)

The argument between cast imposers and wiggle favorers goes back to the start of the last century—indeed, to the beginning of the modern era. The imperial stipulation of uniformity, flatness, and standardization stands in contrast and, I argue, in opposition to, a democratic preference for variety, difference, change, and changeableness. A child cannot grow in a cast.

Education is threatened today—as it has been often in the past—by a reductive educational discourse in which test scores serve as proxies for children. At the policy level, and too often even in schools and classrooms, children are seen not as ends in themselves but as means toward ends, higher test scores and economic productivity being two of the most popular. The quality of the child's educational experience itself is not, within such an orientation, a standard of value, while alignment of the child's use-value as a product of schooling with the purported needs of the economy becomes the overarching consideration and, indeed, justification of the enterprise. These pressures are real in the day-to-day work of teacher education. They exacerbate the understandable and well-documented (e.g., Kagan, 1992) tendency of prospective teachers, themselves subject to evaluative scrutiny of various sorts, to focus less on children than on self—on *my* skill, *my* performance, *my* lesson plans, *my* instructions . . . above all, *my* management practices. In this context, concerns in teacher education for democracy and social justice may, for the teacher candidate, take on a somewhat ritualized character and tend to vaporize when he sits down to figure out what to do in math on Tuesday morning with Darius, who is struggling. Although some teacher educators cope superbly with this challenge, almost all of us, I wager, find it tough at times to locate the big ideas and values of justice and democracy in the daily particulars and moment to moment lived experience of teaching teachers.

I argue here that democracy, and what I will call "democratic teaching," rests on assumptions about the capacities of all individuals, foremost among these the supposition of "widely distributed human capacity to add worth to the world," in Carini's words (2001, p. 52). I argue that as teacher educators we have a corresponding obligation to foster prospective teachers' belief in such capacities by helping them to, in fact, perceive them in all children. Democratic teaching attends, concretely and as a stance, to the particular strengths (and, in their light, naturally, particular needs) of the specific children being taught.

Keeping real children (who wiggle, are ends in themselves, have agency, and are the justification for and limit conditions of just and decent pedagogy) in sight and at the center of practice poses moral, political, and pedagogical challenges with which we must contend. We likewise face the challenge of making "democracy" mean something in the vision, practice, and daily conduct of our students and in our own day-to-day practices of teacher education.

The current tendency is once again to privilege authoritative and standardized systems of knowledge (knowledge deemed expert and research-based, produced at several or many removes from the classroom, designed for purposes of classification, comparison, and control). Adopting Wenger's distinction between the "production and adoption of meaning" (1998, e.g., p. 203), we readily see that this disregards local knowledge made in context, positions teachers as adopters, and marginalizes these teachers in what ought to be, professionally, the *core activity of understanding children as learners.* "Child Study," the subject of this chapter, is, by contrast, necessarily local. It presumes that worthwhile knowledge about children and their learning can be generated and shared by teachers—that this in its way is also a "widely distributed capacity." It can thus, in its assumptions about sources of knowledge in teaching and about children, be thought of as a democratic epistemology.

As teacher education, Child Study is a contextualized practice that seeks to foster teachers' capacity and inclination—wiggles, after all, are *interesting* as well as significant—to produce generative understanding about children's learning (and in doing so to counter the growing tendency of centralized, standardized systems to delegitimize local knowledge). While teachers' capacity for independent judgment and action is under attack, Child Study can support democratic schooling, both by helping prospective teachers to see capacities in each child and by helping them to see themselves as makers as well as consumers of knowledge about teaching.

Overview

This chapter undertakes a conceptual analysis, with empirical referents, of Child Study. As I use the term, "Child Study" refers to a particular historically and philosophically situated project, a well-specified, substantially theorized practice of teacher education with which I have long experience both as a designer and as a practitioner. It is a prospective teacher's semester-long guided inquiry into the strengths, educational needs, and worldview of an individual child. Acknowledging that "Child Study" carries various associations and meanings in different contexts, I will use the term here to refer specifically to this project, as designed and developed by myself and Team One colleagues Jay Featherstone and Susan Donnelly, with contributions by numerous others, drawing deeply on the work of Pat Carini at Prospect School (as discussed shortly), repeatedly revised and adapted over the years. This is the Child Study as it has been undertaken by my students, and all other Team One students since 1994, in TE-301, "Learners and Learning in Context," the first course they take after admission to the Team One program in the junior year.[2] The study engages prospective teachers in the creation of data and in sustained, grounded contention with the problem of what constitutes adequate and useful evidence for claims made about a child's knowledge, skills, or needs as a learner. It aims to keep the attention of prospective teachers and teacher educators on "real children" and to educate that attention.

In making the case that Child Study can be a consequential element in the totality of responses to the standardization pressures which seem always to be with us, but which have been immeasurably strengthened by current educational policies, including the 2001 No Child Left Behind Act (NCLB, 2002), I draw on Deweyan conceptions of democracy (Dewey, 1916/1966, 1938/1963, 1939/1988) and on concepts of teaching as a particular form of human relationship (Hawkins, 1967/1974; Lampert, 2001; Steiner, 2003).

Dewey, in brief, sees democracy as a set of propositions about human capability and community and conditions of worthwhile human experience, not merely a set of procedures for governing. Practices of schooling for democracy, in turn, are predicated on assumptions about human capability. In this frame, I connect the kind of careful and attentive knowing of students as individuals, and as contributors to shared experience that is promoted by conducting a Child Study, to the idea of democracy.

Lampert (2001) formulates an elegant and powerful model of teaching as "working in relationships." These relationships are purposeful, which is not so usefully said of all relationships, and center on "stuff," which is a way of talking about both their ends and their means. Lampert's formulation joins the most innocent of prospective elementary teachers, all parents, and the wisest of philosophers in a common and elemental understanding. Socrates, one archetype for teaching, educates by drawing his interlocutors into a force field of human relationship. Absent his *engagement* of them, they learn nothing from him. With him, what they learn is a product of that distinctive engagement; indeed, one thing they learn is how to have that relationship. Very similar things can be said of a first grade child, as parents and guardians feel in their bones. As a human relationship, teaching can be assessed not only in terms of its efficacy but also, like any other human relationship, in its moral qualities, in how it positions the parties vis-à-vis each other and the world they jointly inhabit. A fundamental criterion for assessment of any human relationship is the treatment of persons as ends in themselves (see Kant, 1785/1959; also see Buber, 1958/1987). A venerable tradition says that treating others as *means* degrades, dehumanizes, and is finally indefensible as a human practice.

Of specific interest here is the thought that painstaking attention to the particulars of an individual child's strengths and tendencies as a thinker and a maker is a way of valuing the child as she or he makes him- or herself known and present—that is to say, in the here and now, not as a condition of who she or he could become. In this suggestion, the necessary democratic presumption of capacity and the morally required acceptance of the other as an end converge.

In what follows I briefly locate Child Study in a historical and contemporary context, give an overview of the project's aims and what it entails procedurally, and then use examples of student work to give a sense of what it asks of prospective teachers and what opportunities it affords them, and to make my analysis of its larger meaning and potential concrete.

Sources and Contexts of Child Study

"Child study" as a term and an activity has been around since the turn of the last century, when it was for a while prominent. However, it has meant quite different things to different people and has served conservative as well as progressive agendas (see Antler, 1982, 1987; Cremin, 1961; Mintz, 2004; Perrone, 1989). G. Stanley Hall's child study movement enlisted mothers in gathering data; the aim was generalizable, "scientific" knowledge and specification of developmental stages. Like Hall, Lucy Sprague Mitchell and Harriet Johnson, founders of Bank Street College, were interested in using child study data to construct norms for child development and to develop curricula for early childhood education. Unlike Hall, they considered that teachers' observations of real children in their classrooms were well used as a check on theory. They expected ongoing observations to contribute to continuing and situated curricular revisions, not for curriculum and pedagogy to simply reflect or apply positive knowledge (Antler, 1987, pp. 285-286).

By far the most salient and proximate source of Child Study as I discuss it here is the "Descriptive Review of the Child" developed by Patricia Carini and colleagues at the Prospect School (where it originated and where I was, as a young teacher, first introduced to it) and elsewhere (Carini, 2000, 2001; Himley, 2000; Kanevsky, 1993; Roosevelt, 1998). In TE-301 at MSU and in current courses, I assign the framework of Carini's (2000) Descriptive Review to prospective teachers. It is a foundational resource, one that provides a partial vocabulary and guide for their observations and for the avowedly interpretive moves they will make later.

For Carini and her colleagues, a primary impetus for the original development of the Descriptive Review was to make space in schools for discussion of individual students that is substantial, detailed, collective, and (in contrast to conventional staffings) explicitly not deficit focused but, rather, capacity presuming and capacity seeking. In addition to framing consideration of the child around strengths and interests rather than inadequacies, the Descriptive Review framework rejected developmental norms as either the initial or final terms of discussion. In the teacher-education Child Study, this legacy can be seen in the firmly inductive posture and in the injunction to "choose for your study child someone who *catches your curiosity in some way*," rather than a child believed to be "difficult" or "a problem."

A variety of practices, similar in design and intention to the Child Study work I report, often drawing on other traditions and at home in other contexts, deserve mention. A vibrant tradition continues at Bank Street, where a meticulously designed Child Study continues to be part of learning to teach (Haberman, 2000). At the University of Pennsylvania, influenced in part by the Prospect Descriptive Review, prospective teachers conduct a well-integrated Child Study organized around "a central question about teaching," incorporating explicit attention to the study children as students of mathematics and literacy (Schultz, 2003, p. 150). At Project Zero, Steve Seidel and colleagues do remarkable work both similar and distinct in form and spirit (see Featherstone, 1998; Reggio Children & Project Zero, 2001). These and kindred projects can all, of course, be understood as major currents in what has seemed until recently a burgeoning tradition of practitioner research at both preservice and in-service levels (see Cochran-Smith & Lytle, 1993, 1999; Zeichner & Nofke, 2001).

The political import of an emphasis on capacity is usefully and rightly, I argue, salient for some observers. Abu El-Haj (2003), for example, in her study of the Teachers Learning Cooperative (TLC), a grassroots group that has met weekly since the 1970s to support and study participants' teaching and has made substantial use and aided in the development of Carini's descriptive processes, argues that the study of individual children may lead to significant ideas about and enhanced commitments to equity and social justice: "This *commitment to the recognition of the person* contains within it the belief that one root of academic inequality lies in the educational imperative to evaluate children in narrow and comparative terms" (Abu El-Haj, 2003, p. 827, emphasis added). Indeed, the capacity-oriented work of Child Study will sometimes be a beginning teacher's first step toward a practice that is equipped to deal with racism and inequality. For this to occur and to acquire solidity, however, it is necessary for the course—in our case, TE-301—to take responsibility for drawing students' attention to the ways the particular is always situated within larger political and cultural contexts.

In authorizing teachers as *creators* of knowledge, and in constructing children's capacity as both a premise and, in part, a product of educators' attention, Child Study traditions differ in epistemologically and politically consequential ways from currently dominant modes of perceiving children and positioning teachers, as these are instantiated and contested, for example, in practices and paradigms of assessment (see, e.g., Bryk & Hermanson, 1993; Moss, 2004; Wilson, 2004).

OVERVIEW, CONTEXT, AND AIMS OF THE CHILD STUDY

As a sustained, structured investigation of a child's modes of thought, expression, and action as these are manifested amid the particular affordances and constraints of a classroom and a school, the Child Study, as we conceived it in Team One, is guided and supported from within a class, TE-301, the first course prospective teachers take after being admitted to the program. The observations and interactions take place in the classroom serving as that semester's field placement.

TE-301 is a core course. Child Study is its central project but by no means its sole preoccupation. Thus, in addition to providing necessary space for instructor guidance and collegial work on the Child Study itself, the course is also a site for engaging other ways of representing children, childhood, and teachers' work. My students, for example, are likely to read Dewey's *The Child and the Curriculum* (1902/1956), a teacher narrative thick with description of children (e.g., Gallas, 1994; or Paley, 1979), perhaps a fictional rendering of childhood like *Tom Sawyer* (Twain, 1876/1981) or *The Bluest Eye* (Morrison, 1970), as well as products of markedly different discourses (Vygotsky, 1933/1976, perhaps, or an account of NCLB in historical perspective, e.g., Jennings, 2003). The power of the individual case is enhanced by readings that feature the inquiries of teachers who, in the context of whole-class teaching, study individual children in order to mediate race and class lines. In this way the profoundly individual orientation of the Child Study is tempered with a steady attention to the social. TE-301 is not an educational psychology class, and the Child Study, though obviously not atheoretical, seeks to engage the student in a highly inductive, situated, local process of theory-*making*, rather than in illuminating, qualifying, or refuting a theory being studied, as is often the case in a psychology class.

The method of inquiry in the Child Study is participant observation. The process is naturalistic: No intrusive measures are taken, everything that is required may legitimately be undertaken by teachers in the normal course of their professional work. While profoundly inductive, it is also systematic and structured. Its one essential theoretical premise is that human behavior is meaningful and, as a corollary, legible, up to some point.

Three convictions critically inform and focus the project: (1) all children bring educationally and socially potent strengths and interests to school; (2) careful attention to the specifics of children's strengths and interests, as well as to needs and vulnerabilities, is a basis for powerful teaching of all children; and (3) observation is an ethic, a habit, and a discipline that improves with practice. The immediate goals of the project are for the prospective teachers to

1. learn and develop skills and a stance of observation and description of children, with particular attention to children's strengths and interests as these are manifested in school;
2. develop skills and standards of judicious interpretation of what they observe; in particular, to develop defensible hypotheses about the study children's modes and strengths and emergent prospects as learners, on the basis of their observations and interpretations;
3. begin to under stand the concept, the practical requirements, and the educative possibilities of a responsive, capacity-oriented pedagogy by putting their observations and hypotheses to concrete instructional use on behalf of the study children.

Specific products and performances, described in more detail below, are associated with each of these goals. In field logs, memos, and formal reports, students make visible their learning with respect to observation, description, and interpretation. By designing, justifying, enacting, and appraising a learning occasion for study children, they demonstrate and further develop their practical pedagogical understanding of their own observations and hypotheses about study children's specific interests, strengths, and intellectual inclinations.

A different aim is to influence the discursive practices of the prospective teachers *and* their professors such that "real children" are habitually referenced as living standards to which all generalizations and theories can be held accountable. The idiosyncrasies, the nongeneric characters—the particular wiggles—of the study children become, ideally, presences in the seminar room and in the imaginations of the prospective teachers.

The aims of the Child Study project for the students' eventual teaching practice, then, embrace not only skills and practices but values, orientations, and dispositions. Thus, the project aims

1. to evoke in prospective teachers a feeling and a stance of *advocacy* for their individual study children, and for children generally;
2. to foster prospective teachers' moral and intellectual habits of observation as embodying qualities of attention and care, discipline and respect, as carrying entailments of responsiveness;
3. to incline prospective teachers toward a capacity-oriented, responsive view of instruction aimed at furthering "children's ability and inclination to think and act with purpose, power, responsibility, and pleasure" (Appendix); to develop a practice of teaching based on reading a child's capacities, needs, and interests; to read the child fairly and uniquely despite the racism and inequality of U.S. society and a particular school setting;
4. to instill in prospective teachers habits and expectations of grounded, data-based, or evidentiary discourse and decisionmaking, which requires persuading them to understand what they are doing in Child Study as, in part, the generation of data and consideration of evidence, which in turn implies or entails framing Child Study as a legitimate and effective form of assessment and research;[3]
5. to persuade prospective teachers to understand themselves as *creators* of knowledge in and for teaching;
6. to help prospective teachers develop skills that will support "plain," authentically interested, confident, and respectful talk with families;
7. to contribute to the prospective teachers' earning moral and intellectual authority for their own teaching (see chapter 5).

THE CHILD STUDY IN ACTION

A minimum of one field visit per week for the length of the semester is necessary.[4] In many respects the Child Study is a one-to-one affair: Each teacher-education student selects a single child "whose particular strengths and interests, manner of connecting and communicating, modes of thinking and learning [he or she] will take special care to learn" (Appendix). In the class (e.g., TE-301) that serves as the project's home, there must be regular whole-class discussion not only of the requirements of the project but of the specific children whose thoughts and actions the students are asked to appreciate. Students also work frequently in small groups on interpretation of their descriptive data and on planning next steps in the project. In the field placement, on at least one occasion students deliberately engage the study child and several classmates in a "learning occasion." Conversely, students should occasionally be relieved of immediate instructional responsibility in order to observe and take field notes in a more sustained, focused, and deliberative manner.

This is a ten- to fourteen-week project that often appears to be experienced in phases: Students' initial curiosity, interest, or good will rises, as they find themselves noticing more and more about the study child, to enthusiasm and an air of knowledgeability, followed by a lull and perhaps a feeling of impatience, when they may think (and indeed say) that there is nothing new for them to see in the child—followed in turn by uncertainty, and renewed energy and attention, as they are pushed to make sense of their (continuing) observations as windows into the child's patterns and tendencies of *thinking* and *learning*. What often comes next—when the project goes reasonably well, and stipulating that the enunciation of "phases" is too linear and neat—is a markedly sturdier and more nuanced approach to the child and a certain air of authority (as befits one who has worked hard to create new knowledge). A good deal of articulated structure is helpful if developments of this sort are to occur, largely because the learning involved is indeed somewhat complicated and at times challenging, and also and not incidentally because that articulated structure sends the message "this is real work." The constituent elements of the project that give it some of its structure both procedurally and substantively follow.

Selection of the study child. Minimal criteria are provided, for example, "a child who catches your curiosity in some way" is appropriate; a child already positioned as an extreme outlier is not. This is to forestall bracketing everything learned from or about the study child as having no relevance to other children.

Consultation with responsible others. The student must explain the project to the cooperating teacher, get her or his approval, and find out if school or district policy requires familial consent for it. Since the Child Study ordinarily entails nothing that a teacher might not appropriately do in the course of good professional practice, consent is not usually needed.

Introduction to practices of "observation, description, and interpretation." This frequently repeated phrase provides a simple schema for the essential work of Child Study and discursively situates that work as skilled and in some sense specialized. An initial exercise in these practices can demonstrate that these are indeed disciplined methods, and gives occasion for use and explication of the terms. I have sometimes, for example, required students, in small groups, to select, examine, and describe to their classmates a public space—a nearby classroom or student lounge for example—and then to begin to develop some inferences and hypotheses (i.e., interpretations) about how users might experience this space.

Guided observation. I expect students to make entries in their field logs at least once weekly. One standing directive for their observation is broadly inclusive: "make note of anything that catches your eye."

Additionally, I often provide specific foci, sometimes drawing these from the Descriptive Review of the Child (Carini, 2000), which is organized around five or six headings, for example, "physical presence and gesture," "disposition and temperament," "modes of thinking and learning." Some of these headings make useful guides for observation; others help students organize data already collected. Carini's "Letter to Parents and Teachers" (2000) is an irreplaceably good resource for students. In it, Carini fleshes out the headings with prompts both useful in themselves and suggestive of other possibilities, for instance:

> Thinking of a child's *Physical Presence and Gesture*, be attentive to what stands out to you immediately. Then, take note of size and build. . . . Visualize how the child moves, with attention to pace, characteristic rhythm and gestures, and how they may vary. For example, you might think about how the child tends to enter the classroom. . . . You might think, too, of how much space a

child occupies, where the child tends to position him- or herself in a group, and so forth. . . .

. . . Think about where the child seems most at ease and how you can tell that is so; then take it other side round and think of where the child seems least comfortable or most constrained.

Other slants you might take . . . include the voice, its inflection, volume, and rhythm; characteristic phrases and ways of speaking; the expressiveness of the eyes, hands, and mouth . . . where and when energy flows most easily . . . where energy seems to be concentrated; how tension shows itself; and so forth.

Attending to expression makes a natural bridge to the child's *Disposition and Temperament*. You might start by reflecting on how the child usually greets the world. (p. 58)

These prompts, and the letter in its entirety, are enormously helpful in making the observational work and stance feel concrete and attainable.

I also support observation, description, and interpretation by reviewing and responding to students' field logs. In-class review of selections from the logs, especially, provides opportunity for articulating a *continuum* from description to interpretation and for distinguishing between entries at one end of this continuum or the other—high inference and low inference suppositions is a familiar way of putting it—and for giving directions, in context, that help students take on the discipline and see these distinctions as tools for understanding rather than simply puritanical injunctions. For example, it is often helpful to assure students, as they are beginning this work, that it is absolutely fine to record an impression (a kind of interpretation)—"the classroom is cold and unwelcoming," "the child was angry"—but that they should then seek out evidence (creating descriptions) that may vivify and substantiate the impression, qualify it ("the room is extremely orderly; precision is valued in this space"), or contradict it ("the human tone is such that this room in fact, when inhabited, feels warm and inviting, the somewhat Spartan material setting notwithstanding").

Finally, as the semester progresses, I expect students to search explicitly—in the course of their observations, and as they review their logs—for study children's *interests* and *strengths*. This part of the inquiry necessitates in-class support as well, to help students think expansively—"Barbies" can be a way of naming an interest, but so can "social complexity and intrigue"—and in order to help students figure out how they might, by observation in school, *learn* a child's interests and strengths.

Collaboration with peers. In small working groups, students enjoy exchanging stories; with guidance they can also help each other develop richer and more nuanced descriptions, entertain competing interpretations, and otherwise advance their study.

Exploratory memos. As with any research project, it can be helpful to step back and make provisional review and organization of one's data with respect to emerging hypotheses. For example, to affirm that a central intent of the Child Study project is to develop potentially fruitful understandings of the child as a *thinker* and a *learner*, while also nurturing curiosity and comfort with uncertainty (and discouraging undue reliance on constructs like "kinesthetic learner"), I often have students write a memo about the child's "mind activity."[5]

Learning occasion. Approximately two thirds of the way through the semester, I ask students to use their developing ideas about the study child as a thinker, as a person of strengths and interests, to design a "learning occasion." I want to help the prospective teachers appreciate how and why to build on learners' existing capabilities and use their interests and strengths as assets for further learning—and to use their own self-created knowledge and understanding of specific, actual learners as a basis for planning, teaching, and assessment. I stipulate that the learning occasion must

- span two sessions,
- involve two to four children, including the study child,
- be approved by the cooperating teacher,
- build on an observation-based estimation of a generative interest and/or an appreciable learning strength of the study child's,
- be conceptualized as creation of an educative experience,
- incorporate a question or hypothesis about the study child as a person of mind and purpose, and
- include some form of data collection.

I advise them that the occasion has two aims: it should constitute an educationally worthwhile experience for the child and her/his peers, and it should further the teacher candidate's understanding of the child as a learner, thus increasing his or her ability and warrant to serve as the child's teacher.

Reports. The exploratory memos and the learning occasions entail both analysis, digging further into an observation or hunch, and synthesis, taking account of observations and thoughts to date and formulating them so as to surface possible implications and broader meanings. Students also prepare one or two formal written reports. The interim report, typically framed by the Descriptive Review headings, is a portrait of the study child as she/ he has become visible to the student at midsemester. It generally concludes with one or more questions, posed by the student, for pursuit over the remainder of the semester, and may include an attempt to articulate the study child's "world view." The final report is usually either a narrative description and analysis of the learning occasion or a memo for the study child's teacher, focused on instructional implications of the prospective teacher's observations. (Though if a student has struggled with the Child Study, a substantially revised and improved portrait of the study child may be an appropriate final report.) Students usually make an oral presentation toward the end of the semester. Ideally, this stimulates rich discussion in class and assists the student in writing a final report.

As a piece of work by a prospective teacher, the Child Study project can be thought of as the construction of an idea, both warranted and provisional, of an individual child as a learner with particular strengths, interests, and tendencies, based on observational data created by the prospective teacher, formulated so as to contribute, actually or potentially, to the child's education.

And so, in the actual Child Study work we hope to see palpably real, vital, and particular children as learners; prospective teachers' enthusiasm for and pleasure in the study children, sense of continuity between themselves and study children, and growing commitment to them; substantive perceptions of capacity; and evidence of theory-making, warranted, and suggestive of the prospective teacher's capacity to produce relevant knowledge about children's learning.

GLIMPSES INTO CHILD STUDY IN PRACTICE

This excerpt on "physical presence and gesture" from the transcript of Efrat's final oral report on Marquis provides a first glimpse of what this can look like.[6]

Well, everyone remembers that a month ago when we were writing up our posters about our child study project, I'm at a bit of a loss on who my child study subject was . . . in terms of his personality, . . . his interests, . . . his strengths. I knew he likes basketball, because I had seen him playing on the playground, and I knew that he was a good listener—no, maybe I didn't know that yet. But I knew that he was very good at focusing on the person who was speaking in the class. So, when I sat down to do my portrait of Marquis, I was really pleased and excited to see how much I had learned in the past five weeks. I started off just making a list of descriptive words or phrases that came to mind, and I went stream of consciousness for a little bit, until I hit upon the word that I want to start with, which is "observer."

I chose Marquis as my child study subject in September [conscious that we were different not only, obviously, in race, age, and background, but also in style and manner—he with his faux alligator-skin, patent leather loafers, and . . . neatly-knotted tie.] And after three months of observation, I find it somewhat ironic that the child I chose to observe quietly and discreetly, often times from more of a distance than up close, on many occasions displays the same approach to his own academic studies that I took to study[ing] him.

In terms of motion and occupying space, Marquis has a way of coming into the room in the morning, and just *appearing* at his desk. There are so many times when he walks in, and I don't even notice that he's made it to the closet, deposited his bag, hung up his coat, and gone up to his seat, until he's sitting there working. The only times I really notice that he comes into the room [are] when he comes in late from breakfast, and he does that at least once a week. But his strides are unrushed, and although he carries himself with purpose and steadily, he does so without being obtrusive.

At his seat Marquis is constantly moving about, his legs swing forward and backward; he is either flopping his head on his elbows, sometimes his hands are fidgeting with something on the table, playing with his tie when he wore a uniform—he stopped wearing his uniform a few weeks ago—moving his lips, twirling a pencil, but any of these motions are silent motions in the sense that they're not noticeable unless you're looking to notice them. And it's almost uncanny: when I am in front of the class teaching a lesson, I have no sense of him moving about at his desk. But when I'm observing him, I fixate on these little things he does. He has this special technique of twirling his tie up on his two thumbs, and unfurling it back down, and twirling it back up, and unfurling it, or balancing a pencil between his nose and his upper lip, or kind of sliding his leg to the back of his chair, and reaching and reaching and reaching, until he's kind of found that just right—*hug*.

The other thing that I've noticed about him is that his voice is kind of like a hoarse whisper, or a shouted whisper. It's hoarse, but it's pronounced. And another way—another part of him that's exceptionally communicative is—are his eyes. He has very wide—a very wide-eyed look to him, and his eyes are also very focused on wherever speaking is coming from, or outside noise is coming from. He's very aware of the things that are going on around him, *and that's why I think of him as an observer* [emphasis added]. Only when he is exceptionally tired, or feeling sick do his eyes look cloudy or unfocused, and when he is sick or tired—which is rare—they look really different, like he can't focus on anything. They just—they go from being extremely sharp to being kind of cloudy. I think you'd almost have to see it to imagine it. (Transcript, December 15, 2005)

There is much to notice here. First, some of the hoped-for and hypothesized results of such study—in Efrat's comment, for example, that although in choosing Marquis she was conscious of her sense of difference, she learned by observation, and by analysis of those observations, that he approached classroom learning in much the same way she approached the task of learning about him. In her description, we see her growing sense of continuity with her study child; we also see her commitment to this child, her delighted perception of his capacities and distinctiveness as a learner. Here, certainly, we see a discourse of capacity as well as clear evidence of Efrat's skills and insight as an observer. The child she describes could not be anyone but Marquis.

Here, too, we can begin to see an almost imperceptible process by which description—as close attention to detail and disciplined effort to capture it, while curtailing, deferring, or at least separating out inference and judgment—*becomes* interpretation. We can see interpretation as layering, as finding as exact a word as you can, as the occurrence of abstract language— apt, economical, not necessarily deliberate—in the midst of description so concrete and "thick" it feels natural, is not altogether experienced *as* abstract, survives scrutiny, is acceptable as logical upon (re)inspection of the more concrete description. At the same time, we sense the way this work is supporting the development of Efrat's intellectual and moral authority as a teacher. The construction of understanding here, and of knowledge, is her labor, fruits of her attentive engagement. She has tools and is disciplined in their use, but she is not applying ready-made categories, constructs, or interpretations. She is producing—it feels almost like eliciting—meaning.

Such intellectual agency, unique in its particulars, widespread and reliably available as human, teacherly, capacity is part of what I mean by "democratic epistemologies."

In her final report, Efrat explains how she designed a learning occasion around a quality, a strength, that she thinks she has discerned in this particular child: he is an "observer" and a particular kind of observer, too: a listener. The learning occasion is a lesson on interviewing. After some demonstration by her, the children will interview each other. The interview protocol consists of some questions prepared in advance—and a space in which it is incumbent on the interviewer to improvise, to craft a question on the spot, responsive to something the interview subject has said. This is a key pedagogical move on Efrat's part: If her hypothesis is correct, Marquis will be in a position to apprehend that his capability as a listener is something he can use as a learner. She, at any rate, will not only have further confirmation of that strength; she will have possession of an idea about how to turn it to Marquis's advantage. The results appear to support her interpretation:

> Marquis was as engaged as I've seen him all year. This was evidenced by his excitement and participation every step of the way ... he kept track of all the questions, he contributed to our question writing, he wanted extra cards for extra questions. I have *never* seen or heard Marquis ask to do work above and beyond what's required of him. Marquis volunteered to interview me impulsively, without considering that he might feel shy about it. [When Efrat first explained that they were going to be interviewing each other, Marquis confided that he was shy and not sure about doing this.] He was the first to pack his bag away in his backpack after the lesson was over. (Kussell, 2005, np)

Now we turn to a shorter excerpt from another prospective teacher's— J.L.'s—careful description of a younger child, Matt, as he works on an art project of his own devising. Again we see attentive looking of a high order, the "palpable reality of the child," the prospective teacher's perception of capacity, of continuity between herself and the child, her *commitment* to this real actual child. And we see J.L. and Matt in dialogue, evidently educational if not instructional, structured around his desire, commitment, and purposefulness:

> After half a minute or so [Matt] seems to come to the conclusion that he will keep working on his art project. He grabs a bottle of glue, two ... wire-like craft supplies ... a small piece of white construction paper. He proceeds back

to his table, stopping for a moment to look over the shoulder of two boys who are ... doing a ... large floor puzzle. Matt sits back down. . . . He sets the glue bottle immediately in front of his drawing. . . He puts the wire-like materials to the right of his drawing, just far enough away so that they are not in the way while he is working. The piece of white construction paper gets put on top of his drawing and he is again looking for a marker (with both hands). He searches for a few seconds and, looking confused, gets out of his chair and proceeds to walk over to me.

In observing Matt, I have not considered myself a part of the classroom. I am so absorbed . . . that I am startled when Matt walks right up to me and says "What color are birds?" (Levi [1998], pp. 31–32)

It *is* startling. By getting up and walking straight to her, Matt has reminded us—and J.L.—that this is real time, a real place. *We* are voyeurs of a sort, but *she* is present in the room, she is familiar to him, and she is paying attention, becoming absorbed in his doings, to the point almost of co-participating in them. He is surely aware of her nearness; he probably feels the quality of stillness.

But when he actually speaks, he goes further. He interrupts the stillness, the almost-silence that has been enveloping him, J.L., and the reader. His question is both direct and somewhat mysterious—because, as he will shortly demonstrate, he must know that birds come in more than one color. Asking the question in the singular, after having been silent for some time, and after much evident deliberation about his materials (including magic markers of several different colors), gives it a certain gravity. It also confirms that he has been thinking all this time. He has been going somewhere with this piece of work (whether or not that destination has evolved or been revised), he has been deciding which materials to use, and he has some idea in his mind of what the requirements (standards) are for the piece of work (some form of accuracy, it appears).

This is what thinking can look like: care, patience, deliberation. His capacity for these qualities is on display, discernible to the patient and attentive observer. These are qualities that emerge in the context of activity that matters for the actor. Matt is working with "purpose" in Dewey's (1938/1963) sense: He has something he wants to accomplish, he has opportunity to consider and select means appropriate to that purpose (markers, white construction paper, "wire-like" things), he is acting to effect that purpose. "It is," Dewey argues, a sound instinct which identifies freedom with power to frame purposes and to execute or carry into effect purposes so framed. Such freedom is in turn identical with self-control; for the formation of purposes and the organization of means to execute them are the work of intelligence. . . . A slave [is a] person who executes the purposes of another; and . . . a person is also a slave who is enslaved to his own blind desires. (p. 67)

Matt is alive to J.L. as a purposeful, deliberate, thinking being. His drawing is a product of a thought process and no doubt a medium for thinking (the bird may not have become the point until the apple tree was being rendered), also an object of thought and critical inspection revealing an internal standard ("it doesn't look right"), but it is not by any means a complete representation of the thought process. It is, however, a thing in itself, work of his hand and mind, conceived, executed, completed by him, with consciousness, reflection, inquiry (indeed she has twice felt him to be "searching," even though most of her descriptive verbs are at a much lower level of inference, e.g., "holding," "putting," "watching"), and purpose. Presumably, it becomes much harder for her to take such a product for granted now. And she knows him to be capable of all of these forms of cognition and to be capable of self-discipline, the discipline imposed by a chosen purpose. She knows him to be capable of holding her attention, even her devoted attention.

CONCLUSION

Specificity is key to the method and the ethic of the Child Study, which is very deliberately focused on individual children in their particularity and aims to interrupt any rush to generalize, categorize, presume a norm of sameness. This stress on the individual is not at odds with recognition of commonality nor with understandings of the social construction of identity. Indeed, the project is conceived and taught with an underlying assumption that what children hold in common with each other and with adults is significant; and this sustained careful attention to the particularities of an individual child's ways of being, in the company of and in exchange with colleagues similarly immersed, and perhaps in the context of simultaneous responsibility for other children, does often lead to deepened awareness of the continuities in human ways of acting in and understanding the world. But this awareness means more the more it is earned. The Child Study project likewise does not deny that knowledge of culture and cultural variety, including understanding of their own cultural locations, and of general claims of developmental and cognitive psychology, is necessary for prospective teachers and pertinent to their understanding of individual children. But all of these claims, understandings, and forms of knowledge are liable to misuse absent a steady, strong orientation and commitment to the individual child, the actual living and vulnerable, nameable being coming to school from and returning to some real specifiable family: the moral and material limit condition of the acts of teaching. Specific knowledge and attention are not only morally required, they are also indispensable for the creation of more inclusive and far-reaching conceptions, a relationship crisply expressed by William James: "No one sees farther into a generalization than his own knowledge of details extends" (in Menand, 2001, p. 131). This may serve as a foundational premise for Child Study.

From this vantage point, Child Study maps onto a larger vision of just and professional teaching, for such teaching legitimates itself—earns intellectual and moral authority—in part by practitioners' abilities to reason to and from individual children, large educational purposes, specific goals for learning, pedagogical decisions, and consequences or "outcomes." To reason like this, to connect these points, is to take responsibility for pragmatic means-ends reasoning: For example, to explain to a family why a particular course of action is chosen for their child—with what aims and merits; on the basis of what particular knowledge of the child warranting both the chosen ends and the means to their fulfillment—and to discuss what would constitute evidence of success. Being able to think and talk in these terms is a defining attribute of professionalism in teaching, that is, of just, transparent, and accountable practice. Justice, however, inheres in or is absent from the quality of purposes and aims, and in the full complement of consequences of chosen pedagogical means. Teacher educators meet only part of their responsibility to children, families, and society if we attend only to the adequacy of prospective teachers' methods. We must also attend to the ends toward which they work.

An overarching purpose of teaching and schooling toward which I endeavor to turn my students is the furthering of "children's ability and inclination to think and act with purpose, power, responsibility, and pleasure." Knowledge and appreciation of children's strengths, interests, and tendencies is a tremendous resource for a pedagogy so oriented. Child Study is a way of developing such knowledge and appreciation in a particular case and of practicing the skills necessary to create such knowledge and cultivate such appreciation in future cases. That same skill and knowledge make possible the kinds of means-ends reasoning referred to earlier; the quality of appreciation and the commitment to children's powers of thought and action give it moral weight.

A persistent challenge in teacher education is to construct a pedagogy whereby prospective teachers' attention is turned steadily—and with increasing insight, humility, and practical skill, to real students and their situated, contingent experiences of learning— to "soul-action" and "the personal play of mental powers" as Dewey poetically expressed it a century ago (1904/1964, p. 318). Understandably, prospective teachers' attention is often focused instead on management and control, methods, objectives, standards, and how their performance is being judged by others (Darling-Hammond and Bransford, 2005; Dewey, 1904/1964; Feiman-Nemser and Buchmann, 1985; Murray, 1996; Waller, 1932/1965). The challenge of keeping real children in the center of the frame is heightened today by an impoverished educational discourse in which, for example, test scores are widely accepted as proxies for children and a democratic standard of equality is displaced by an imperial stipulation of sameness. Thus the child whose personhood should be the limiting condition for educational processes is gradually reduced to object status. If teaching is at base a human relationship, the consequences of such reduction for the project of learning how to teach are potentially enormous: When the erstwhile other party in the teacher-learner relationship is repositioned as merely an object of teacher action, as a means (to the end of increasing test scores), there can be no educative relationship with learners—or between learners, subject matter, and each other—to *be* learned.

Teacher educators, working in the service of public education, also face the profound challenge of making "democracy" mean something tangible and true in the territory with which education is primarily concerned: the fostering of enduring understandings, agile habits of mind, and genuinely educative relationships.

At base, "democracy" means that each human being has the capacity as well as the right to be a *maker* of laws, to do more than merely follow—or evade—laws imposed by others. "Democracy" becomes a hollow concept if it means 'the people make the rules' without also meaning 'the people are *smart* enough, *imaginative* enough, *compassionate* enough' to be fit to make the rules. The idea of democracy rests, then, on the belief in "widely distributed human capacity to add worth to the world" (Carini, 2001, p. 52); Dewey (1939/1988, p. 226) makes the same point, asserting that democracy is "a way of life controlled by a working faith in the possibilities of human nature."

The connection between studying children and democracy is made by way of this fundamental meaning of the word *capacity*. Democracy is a proposition premised on the existence of profound and complex capacity on the part of all humans to rightly and powerfully act to shape worthwhile shared human life. The capacity is not automatically realized nor understood. All of the careful observation of and meditation on students and on the things they say, do, and make—the work of Child Study—is a discipline in perception and in valuation of capacity, in order that it become a central orientation for instruction. What is this person good at now, what kinds of materials and ideas stimulate her energy and effort and care, what questions does she favor, what struggles does she willingly return to, what is the tendency of her interests, what does she contribute to this environment? These questions, the kinds the descriptive processes engage, are asked, first, to build appreciation of the student's capacities as she is making them known to us, and, second, to help us as teachers identify the resources and opportunities that could logically extend those capacities and bring the child into a larger set of relationships and possibilities.

The performance of the Child Study work over the course of a semester, guided and critiqued by the teacher educator, entailing substantial production of observational and documentary data by prospective teachers, eventuating in the design of instruction, shapes discourse and perception. It positions the prospective teacher as a responsible and public creator of knowledge in teaching. It connects children, intending teachers, and teacher educators in a vital and generative manner. It keeps actual children at the center of the educational undertaking.

Appendix Chapter 6
Handout for Students

Keeping Real Children at the Center of Teaching: Overview of the Child Study Project

> *To describe teaches me that the subject of my attention always exceeds what I can see. I learn from describing a painting or a rock or a child or a river that the world is always larger than my conceptualization of it.*
> Patricia F. Carini

Purposes & Rationale

The Child Study is a semester-long grounded inquiry into one child's modes of thought, expression, and action, as these are manifested in classroom and school.[1] The project is premised on three related beliefs:

+ All children bring educationally (and socially) potent strengths and interests to formal learning environments;
+ Careful attention to the specifics of children's strengths and interests, as well as to needs and vulnerabilities, is a basis for powerful teaching of all children; and,
+ Observation (noticing, attending, seeing) is an ethic, a skill, and a habit, a discipline that improves with practice.

The purpose of the Child Study project is to help teacher candidates begin to acquire this discipline and begin learning how to use it as a resource for teaching; in particular, to use it as a resource for teaching intended to further children's ability and inclination to think and act with purpose, power, responsibility, and pleasure.

Thus, candidates identify one child whose particular strengths and interests, manner of connecting and communicating, modes of thinking and learning, they will take special care to learn. To accomplish this, candidates are guided in practices of observation, description, and interpretation. Gradually they build a small set of tentative understandings and working hypotheses, grounded in the data they have collected, sensitive to the observational context, and subject to reflective scrutiny and alternative interpretations—their own, and colleagues'. They use their growing understanding and awareness to develop pedagogically fruitful and socially, morally, educationally sound and justified ways of considering and speaking about the child. Eventually, they use this developing knowledge to design a "learning occasion" for the study child and several peers. The learning occasion builds upon the child's strengths and interests as a thinker, as these have become visible to the teacher candidate. The "occasion" has two aims. In the first place, it should constitute educationally worthwhile experience for the child and her/his peers. In the second case, it should further the teacher candidate's understanding of the child as a learner, thus increasing his or her ability and warrant to serve as the child's teacher.

Twice during the semester, candidates will make formal reports on their child study work, once shortly after the learning occasion, and once at the end of the semester. Throughout the semester, they keep detailed field logs; from time to time they are likely to do brief written "sketches" of the study child, memos addressed to a particular facet of their observations, and the like. Some amount of seminar time will be devoted to work on the project.

Outline

Phase I (weeks 1 – 2)

+ introduction to the project
+ getting started at the school site
+ beginning the work of observation, description, & interpretation

Phase II (weeks 2 – 7)

+ guided observation
+ reflecting on the data
+ designing & carrying out the learning occasion
+ interim report

Phase III (weeks 7 – 14)

+ continued observation & reflection
+ revised/deepened/complicated understandings
+ "final" report

Key Elements & Issues

i. Selection of study children

ii. Respect for privacy and related matters
    These will be discussed at the outset

iii. Field logs
    Specific directions for the logs, including observational foci, will be given in class. As the semester continues, candidates may also articulate their own points of observation. Logs will from time to time be turned in and/or discussed in class. It is essential that logs be kept regularly and faithfully. It will not be possible to succeed at this project if this is not done.

iv. Learning occasions

Directions will be given as the time approaches. A modest amount of in-class time will be provided for design work.

v. Interim & final reports

These will be built up out of the work you have been doing all along. Although each will contain new thought and fresh writing, neither will be created from scratch. They will not, however, be do-able without steady and detailed field logs, as already noted. Again, directions will be given as the time approaches.

1. This child study project belongs to a tradition of teacher inquiry that stretches back over a century. The project as outlined here is a continuation of work done by Dirck Roosevelt, Joseph Featherstone, Susan Donnelly, and other colleagues at Michigan State University (see Roosevelt [1998] and Levi, [1998]). The primary source for that work in turn was the work of Patricia Carini and colleagues at the Prospect School (see for example, Himley and Carini [Eds.] [2000], also Carini [2001]). Looking further back, John Dewey is an intellectual forebear, both for his conception of teachers as students of children and childhood, learning, and teaching, and for his theory of experience (as in, for example, the remark, "Every experience is a moving force. Its value can be judged only on the ground of what it moves toward and into" [Dewey, J., 1938/1963, p. 38]).

7

Discovering and Sharing Knowledge: Inventing a New Role for Cooperating Teachers

SHARON FEIMAN-NEMSER AND KATHRENE BEASLEY

This chapter describes the development of ideas and practices that were the foundation of the Team One internship. Written by a university-based teacher educator/researcher and an elementary school teacher/mentor, it tells how we invented a new role for cooperating teachers and university supervisors during our first year of collaborative research and how we then created a forum where other teachers could explore new ways of thinking about and working with student teachers. These practical experiments took place at Averill Elementary School, an urban professional development school affiliated with Michigan State University, just as the "new" teacher-education program was getting off the ground, and they influenced the way Team One conceptualized and developed the roles of university liaison and collaborating teacher and designed the internship curriculum.

We tell the story in two parts. In the first part, we recount the year we investigated Kathy's knowledge of teaching and invented new ways for her to share that knowledge with her student teacher, Debi. In the second part, we describe the early work of the Teacher Education Circle (TEC), a monthly forum at Averill where cooperating teachers learned to unpack their teaching through explanation and demonstration and help student teachers construct a reform-minded practice. We conclude with a brief discussion of how these activities influenced Team One.

In telling this story, we draw on extensive documentation, including journals we kept during the early years of our work together, minutes of TEC meetings, transcripts of presentations we made about our work at the time, and Averill's annual reports to the Michigan Partnership for a New Education. Rereading our journals and the comments we made on them fifteen years ago, we are sometimes struck by the naiveté of our former selves. Having worked with and developed these ideas for more than a decade, we are surprised to see how unsophisticated we sounded before we developed them. Still we believe that both our naiveté and our collaborative work are an important part of the Team One story.

INVENTING A NEW ROLE FOR COOPERATING TEACHERS

We began our collaboration with different ideas about what student teaching is for and what role experienced teachers should play in novice teachers' learning. We also had different hopes for our work together. Kathy wanted help with what she had come to perceive as her "problem" with student teachers. Sharon saw the collaboration as a chance to explore on a small scale a different kind of field experience for student teachers and cooperating teachers. Sharon helped transform Kathy's initial assumptions; Kathy helped refine and extend Sharon's ideas. What began as a yearlong consultation turned into a personal relationship and a collaborative inquiry about new approaches to teaching, mentoring, and learning to teach that extended over many years and had a significant impact on teacher education at Michigan State University.

The Presenting Problem

In the summer of 1990, Kathy approached Sharon at a PDS (Professional Development School) institute, having heard that Sharon was doing research on student teaching, and asked if she could help her with a problem. Every year, Kathy said, she dreaded the time her student teacher would take over the classroom. Stepping aside, Kathy would watch helplessly as everything she had worked so hard to establish during the year slowly fell apart. While Kathy tried to give her student teacher helpful advice, she always felt deep frustration for herself and a sense of loss for her students. "I came to the conclusion," Kathy told Sharon, "that I had two choices—stop taking student teachers or get some help with my 'problem.'"

At the time Kathy believed that her role in student teachers' learning was fairly minor, as she explained:

I thought my job was to provide a classroom for the student teacher to try out things she had learned at the university. I felt that I should be supportive and answer any questions she had. I also thought I should watch her teach and tell her what she was doing wrong. But I did not see that as a central role for myself.

Kathy's views had been shaped by her prior experiences as a cooperating teacher in an undergraduate teacher-education program that had been placing student teachers at her school for the previous ten years. While the program had many innovative features, including an extensive field component, it did not focus on the cooperating teacher's special knowledge or position in the classroom. With so little talk about what it meant to be a cooperating teacher, Kathy did not have a clear picture of what she could or should do. Most of her energy went into trying to find a role for her student teacher that would not disrupt classroom norms and routines and impede the pupils' learning. "If I could just figure that out, everything would be solved," she wrote in an early journal entry. She and her colleagues talked about student teaching in terms of "transferring authority to the student teacher," as though their moral and intellectual authority could be handed over like a baton. Since student teachers spent considerable time in their classrooms prior to student teaching, everyone assumed that by spring student teachers should be ready to take them over and teach on their own. There was no articulated and shared understanding of what student teachers needed to learn or how experienced teachers could guide that learning.

Listening to Kathy, Sharon thought that the so-called problem lay not in anything Kathy was doing but in a system that required the most knowledgeable and experienced person in the situation to step aside and let the novice take over. She knew from experience, from the literature on student teaching and learning to teach, and from her own research that (student) teachers viewed student teaching as the most valuable part of their teacher preparation while teacher educators worried that it "washed out" any program influence (Lortie, 1975; Zeichner, 1981). Reform-minded teacher educators were calling for extended field experiences, like yearlong internships where novices would learn to teach in the company of experienced teachers who were studying and changing their practice (Cochran-Smith, 1991; Holmes Group, 1990; Little, 1990); however, there were few models of what this could look like and what it would take to bring it about.

In an early study of eight student teachers, Sharon had been puzzled by the case of Susan, a bright student teacher placed in a fourth grade classroom where Bob, the cooperating teacher, modeled the kind of conceptually oriented subject-matter teaching advocated by the teacher-education program (Feiman-Nemser & Buchmann, 1987). Despite the close alignment between the program's orientation and the practice of the cooperating teacher, Susan did not regard Bob as a resource in her learning, mostly because she found his approach to discipline "too laissez-faire." Bob rarely spoke to Susan about teaching, his own or hers, and the university supervisors who frequently visited the classroom did not help Susan see what she could learn from Bob.

The case made Sharon wonder how teachers like Bob thought about their work with student teachers and what it would take for them to play a more educative role in novices' learning to teach. Rather than viewing student teaching as the culmination of teacher preparation, Sharon thought about student teaching as the time when novices start learning to teach in the context of teaching. Without denying the contribution of university-based study, Sharon was particularly interested in the possibilities and pitfalls of first-hand experience in learning to teach and she saw cooperating teachers as valuable sources of and guides to practical knowledge and ways of knowing (Feiman, 1983; Feiman-Nemser & Buchmann, 1987).

When Kathy approached Sharon in the summer of 1991 and asked for help, Sharon saw a wonderful opportunity to explore new ideas about the work of student teachers and cooperating teachers. She arranged to spend one day a week in Kathy's classroom, observing her teaching and her interactions with Debi, her student teacher, conferring with them, and sharing journals which all three agreed to keep.[1] During that year, Kathy discovered that she knew a lot about teaching and that some of her knowledge was implicit in her actions (Schön, 1987). She also changed the way she thought about her role and, with Sharon's help, developed new strategies for sharing her knowledge with her student teacher.

Discovering Knowledge

At the beginning of the year, Kathy underestimated how much she knew about teaching. Never having had the opportunity or encouragement to think about or articulate her knowledge and beliefs or talk much about her practice, Kathy took them for granted. At the same time, she overestimated what Debi could be expected to know from simply watching Kathy teach or spending several semesters in her classroom. Sharon tried to help Kathy see how much she knew about teaching by pointing to evidence of working knowledge in Kathy's actions. At first, this did not mean much to Kathy, as the following commentary on her first journal entry suggests:

> In my first journal entry I wrote about how Debi and I had planned the first day together, talking through all the possible things that could happen. In the margin, Sharon wrote: "This is an important clue about how much you know about teaching." At the time, I didn't really appreciate the significance of that statement. Nor did I realize how much of my knowledge of teaching was intuitive, in my actions, not explicit .

Two episodes were critical in helping us recognize and appreciate Kathy's knowledge and ways of knowing and gain insights into its nature and substance. In the first, Kathy and Debi carefully plan a lesson around a wordless picture book, only to discover, when Debi teaches the lesson, that what they did not talk about was just as important as what they did talk about. In the second, Kathy realizes that while she cannot always tell Debi ahead of time how to handle a problematic situation with a student, she is confident that she'll know what to do in the situation. Besides teaching us about the situated and tacit nature of teachers' knowledge, these episodes document Kathy's growing ability to notice and explicate her knowledge. We regularly told these two stories to illustrate Kathy's knowledge and our ways of working.

Wordless Picture Book Story

Here is how Kathy told the wordless book story to an audience of cooperating teachers, student teachers, and university teacher educators:

> Debi and I were planning a lesson for Debi to teach based on a wonderful picture book. Children had always loved this book and I was sure that Debi would have a successful experience. I thought it was important for Debi to understand the purposes behind using this book. It wasn't just a fun book to read. So, we decided that both of us would write down all the reasons for using this book as a learning opportunity for children. Then we would compare our lists and make sure we both understood the lesson. That's exactly what we did and when we finished, we felt that we had a crackerjack lesson.
>
> First Debi would read the book to the children. Then they would write words for the story which Debi would put up on chart paper. Afterwards she

would type up their story and the children would illustrate their own words. We understood that this was a language development lesson with writing skills embedded in it. It was a way to help children see how the illustrator told the story with pictures. The children would also use their reading skills and every child could participate. We knew we were ready. We couldn't wait till the next day when Debi would teach the lesson.

The next day Debi began the lesson and we both knew that something was amiss. But what was it? I knew that in previous years children were enthralled with this story and now they weren't. I was completely surprised by the way Debi had presented the book. Debi and I decided that I would do the lesson again the next day with Debi observing. As I began, it became obvious to us that there is a way to read a wordless book that engages the children. As I taught the lesson, I thought about what I was doing and thinking. Later we were able to open up the phrase "read the story from the pictures." We talked about the use of voice inflection, about the importance of exciting, descriptive language, expressive tone, pacing. I had never thought of how complex the task actually was; nor had I considered that I had some important knowledge that Debi might not have.[2]

Although Kathy had discussed the purposes and structure of the lesson with Debi, she had not thought about describing the art or technique of reading a wordless picture book. Knowing how to do this herself, she underestimated the complexity and artfulness of the task. She also assumed that Debi could interpret her directions, "Read the story from the pictures"; she did not see that these guidelines were ambiguous and incomplete, especially for a novice.

Doing the lesson helped Kathy grasp the central difference between her approach and Debi's. While Debi had described the pictures, Kathy had told a story, with all the drama and expression that good storytelling entails. Kathy's demonstration clarified the meaning of "reading the story from the pictures" by giving Debi a concrete image. With this picture in mind, they could then discuss specific elements of the reading performance like tone, pacing, inflection.

When Kathy described this incident to Sharon in their weekly meeting, Sharon was reminded of Donald Schön's (1987) *Educating the Reflective Practitioner*, in which he characterizes the tacit and spontaneous know-how that professionals reveal in skillful performances. She introduced Kathy to

Schön's concept of "knowing-in-action," and this idea entered our shared vocabulary.

The incident also gave us a powerful tool for investigating Kathy's knowledge and ways of knowing—surprise. As Jerome Bruner (1986) explains, "Surprise . . . allows us to probe what people take for granted. It provides a window on presupposition; surprise is a response to violated presupposition" (p. 46). Debi's lesson violated Kathy's image of what reading a wordless picture book should look like. Surprise spurred her to try to figure out what she knew that Debi didn't know. After this experience, we consciously used surprise to guide our inquiry. Whenever Kathy was surprised by something Debi did or failed to do in her teaching, she would think about what she would have done and how she could most effectively communicate this knowledge to Debi. Gradually, Kathy made these ideas her own, as her retelling of the "Nicole Story" reveals.

Nicole Story

In the Nicole story, which also became part of the narrative we constructed to explain what we were doing and learning together, Kathy is able to get inside her own thinking, to look at the situation from the perspective of the novice, and to figure out how to teach what she knows to Debi. She is beginning to appreciate the difference between knowing how to teach something herself, a familiar situation, and knowing how to teach someone else to teach it, a new situation:[3]

> When I became a teacher, I would hear teachers say that they had taken a student out in the hall for a talk. The implication was that this had helped resolve a serious conflict. I always wondered what teachers actually said to students in the hall. Were there certain things you were supposed to say? Were there ways of saying them that worked better than others? Over the years I've had my fair share of conversations with children and I've developed a useful repertoire of things to say and ways to say them, but somehow along the way I lost touch with that inexperienced novice in me who didn't know what to say and do.
>
> So when Debi described Nicole's sulking and asked me what to do, I responded in an offhanded way, "Why don't you take her aside and talk with her." Fortunately, Debi and I had developed the kind of relationship where she could tell me she did not know what to say. This was a familiar situation:

I knew I could talk with Nicole effectively, but I was at a loss for how to explain it to Debi. We realized that I needed to have that conversation with Debi watching.

Debi, Nicole, and I sat together at our little round table. I started by saying I had noticed that Nicole hadn't been as interested and excited about learning and working in the classroom as she usually was and I wondered if there was some problem. There was no response from Nicole. I looked as worried and concerned as I could. I reemphasized that Nicole seemed different, not the good worker and listener she usually was. Debi followed my lead and added her concerns in a warm and caring way. Then Nicole told us what the problem was—that the kids were "messing with her on the playground." When I asked Nicole how we could solve this problem, she just shrugged her shoulders. We sat silently. I made sure to look like I was thinking. Suddenly I got excited and said that I had a wonderful idea. Nicole looked interested. I suggested that we each tell our ideas and then Nicole could choose the idea she liked best. Nicole decided she liked Debi's and my solutions the best and we agreed to try them. Nicole left smiling and we had our cooperative worker back.

As Debi and I talked afterwards, I realized that I had been prepared for Nicole's sullen silences and shrugs. In fact, I had anticipated much of what actually happened, but I had never looked at this kind of interchange from the perspective of needing to teach someone else how to do it. The whole experience was familiar and new at the same time. I was framing it and analyzing it from a Sharon perspective as well as from my familiar vantage of helping a child get on with the work of learning.

Afterwards, Debi, Sharon and I articulated some important points that could be discussed with a novice embarking on a conversation with a troubled student. Let the student frame the problem. Be prepared to think and wait in silence, wait long enough and be positive enough until you feel that the student will respond to your excitement about having a possible solution. Be prepared to offer a solution that gives the student some special attention and time with you.

I won't ever again be at a loss for what to say if a novice asks me how to talk to a student about a problem. Still, I think this is one of those complex and situation-specific examples of what teaching is all about that exemplifies that saying, "You had to be there to get it."

The Nicole story reinforced our understanding of the intuitive, situated, and holistic nature of teachers' knowledge. Writing about the incident in her journal, Kathy observed: "It's almost as if I have to be in the situation and then the thinking just kicks in." While we did formulate some principles behind Kathy's approach, we realized that in teaching the whole is greater than the sum of its parts. Our discoveries about the nature and content of Kathy's knowledge and beliefs influenced our thinking about how to share that knowledge with Debi.

Sharing Knowledge

As we learned that Kathy knew more than she could say, we wondered about the best way to communicate this knowledge to Debi: When did it make sense for Kathy to explain her thinking? When was it better to show rather than tell? How much should Kathy say, and what kind of language would be helpful? How much could we expect a beginner to understand? These questions signal a second focus to our inquiry—sharing knowledge.

Strategies for sharing knowledge grew out of discoveries of and about knowledge. As the wordless book and Nicole stories reveal, Kathy and Debi discovered that demonstrations helped Debi visualize practices she could not imagine and helped Kathy to articulate some of her knowledge-in-use. As Kathy and Debi forged a new kind of relationship, they invented new forms of problem-solving and on-the-spot coaching such as "stepping in."

Stepping In

Sometimes while she observed Debi, Kathy realized that the students needed more information than Debi was giving them. Instead of waiting until the lesson was over, Kathy would find some way to intervene in the lesson and alert Debi to this need. Once we recognized the pattern and understood the purpose, we dubbed this our "step-in" strategy. We realized that being able to use this strategy depended on a different kind of relationship between cooperating teacher and student teacher than was customary. We also saw how stepping in opened new opportunities for talking about teaching and expanded the limited time available for mentoring.

Sharon first observed Kathy intervening in Debi's lesson the day Debi introduced the field guide project. As part of a unit on birds, Debi wanted students to make their own field guides to use in identifying birds in their neighborhood. She had also planned a bird-watching expedition the following week. Debi gave a rather vague introduction to the project, providing no clear reason for making the guide. On the spot, Kathy interjected a vivid story about her husband, an avid bird-watcher. She described how he gets up early, takes his binoculars and field guide, and goes out to look for birds. When he sees a bird, he uses his binoculars to observe its coloring, size, and any markings on its tail or beak. If he doesn't know what kind of bird it is, he looks at the pictures and descriptions in his field guide. Once he figures out what kind of bird it is, he writes in his log the name of the bird and the date and place of the sighting.

Talking over the incident with Sharon, Kathy explained her reasoning:

> As Debi was talking, I could tell these seven-year-olds didn't quite see why they might want to create a field guide of their own to use. So I *stepped in* and added what I felt needed to be added—a more concrete example of how a field guide is used. It would have been far more awkward to explain to Debi at that moment that she needed to be more concrete or specific. What if she didn't know how to do that?

Kathy realized that her response was rooted in her extensive knowledge about children and what they need to understand. As Kathy wrote in her journal:

> It wasn't until we talked about why the story of my husband was so powerful that I realized that it was my knowledge of children that helped me understand that they needed more information. This was another example of a specific context triggering my thinking and then through talking and questioning being able to understand a broader principle that would help guide our teaching in other settings.

As part of the bird unit, Debi bought a parakeet for the class. Sharon observed her explaining to the class how she had gone to the pet store and picked out this particular bird. Several times she said that the students would have to "take good care of the bird." Finally Kathy raised her hand and said, "Ms. C, what exactly do we have to do when we take care of the bird?" Asking Debi a question that Kathy "knew" students were thinking was another form of on-the-spot coaching that Kathy used to communicate to Debi the need to provide more information.

Building a Culture of Collaboration and Inquiry

The fact that Kathy could step into Debi's lessons meant she and Debi had formed new norms and expectations to support their new ways of working together. Typically, cooperating teachers and student teachers assume that the goal of student teaching is to move student teachers toward independent performance. The practice of university supervisors making periodic visits to conduct formal observations of the student teacher's lessons further reinforces the expectation that success in student teaching means proving that you can teach on your own.

As Debi grew more comfortable acknowledging her status as a learner, Kathy became increasingly comfortable asserting herself as Debi's teacher, even while Debi was teaching. As she explained, "We both had to understand that Debi's role was not to produce perfect lessons." Eventually we all came to see Kathy's "stepping in" and on-the-spot coaching as a way to take advantage of teachable moments and stretch the time available for mentoring.

Kathy also shared her knowledge of teaching by doing the work of teaching *with* Debi and talking about it along the way. As the year progressed, Kathy rarely stood on the sidelines watching Debi teach and giving her feedback after the lesson. More often they worked as partners, coplanning, coteaching, and then analyzing what happened. Through their "joint work" (Little, 1990, p. 494), Kathy helped Debi get inside the intellectual and practical work of teaching, and Debi learned ways of thinking and acting in context.[4] Sharon had been reading about sociocultural theories of learning (Lave & Wenger, 1990; Gallimore, Tharp, & John-Steiner, n.d.) and we came to think about this way of working as a form of "assisted performance," in which the more experienced other enables the novice to do with help what the novice is not yet ready to do on her own.

Abandoning the expectation that she should have all the answers, Kathy took the risk of sharing her own doubts and uncertainties. This marked yet another challenge to the prevailing culture of teaching, which tends to favor answers over questions, certainty over doubt. "You're not supposed to wonder about teaching," Kathy wrote in her journal. "If you're an experienced teacher, you should know how to do it. If I just had this down, Debi would have a good experience." But wonder she did, and her openness strengthened the culture of inquiry and collaboration that we were building and opened the door to the co-construction of knowledge through extended conversations about teaching.

To illustrate what our discourse was like and how it supported shared inquiry and the construction of knowledge, we highlight two segments in a pivotal conversation that occurred in November 1990. Full of surprises for everyone, this conversation led to far-reaching changes in Kathy's and

Debi's thinking and practice. It also broadened our agenda to include questions Kathy was struggling with as she moved toward a more learner-centered classroom.

The Conversation

Debi opened the conversation by sharing her new insights about what it means to create a learning community classroom. After spending two months in Kathy's classroom, she realized that you don't just set up the norms, rules, and procedures and then move on to teaching subject matter. For one thing, the rules and procedures are constantly changing. Moreover, she discovered, "learning community is connected with everything you're doing, including what you are doing with content." Actually their class had been experiencing an increase in conflicts, interruptions, and disagreements, especially when Debi was teaching. The university supervisor diagnosed "a learning community crisis," but Kathy had a different interpretation:

> I think we have taken kids who were in an authoritarian classroom last year and we've given them a lot of freedom. We've taught them to be risk-takers and now they are just heady with it. What we haven't done is give them some ways to interact with each other. They are still relying too much on us.

Debi agreed that the problems they were experiencing may have resulted from the very qualities they wanted to foster. "What we have to do," she proposed, "is teach them to deal with those conflicts."

Kathy then moved the conversation to a new level by sharing some nagging concerns. The students were "taking control of the curriculum," but she wondered if "it's in the right direction." To understand better what Kathy meant, Sharon asked for an example, and Kathy explained that three or four children were asking to start their own book-reading club. Kathy was pleased to see students excited about directing their own learning, but "silent reading was no longer silent" and she could not be sure that "all the children are really practicing their reading." Also, the school had endorsed a policy that everyone in the school would "drop everything and read" silently after lunch. Realizing that silent reading was no longer silent but rather a time when children did paired reading, asked each other for help with words, and discussed and selected books, we decided to create two different times for reading. This led us to reexamine the purposes of "silent reading" and "free reading" and develop a new plan for having students monitor their own reading activity:

> *Sharon:* You could say, "One of my concerns is that if we have more time for free reading, everyone really reads. How could we keep track of this?" It's really a chance for kids to take charge.
>
> *Kathy:* They could decide if they want to do it by time or by pages.
>
> *Sharon:* Yes.
>
> *Kathy:* I'm so used to being in control. I was thinking I would say, "We have to be sure you are practicing reading." And then I was thinking that I needed to monitor it. But you're right. They could do it.
>
> *Sharon:* As long as they show you they are doing the very things you want them to be doing, why not?
>
> *Kathy:* I love this. It's really helping me think about decisions I've made in my classroom that I'm not comfortable with, but I don't know what to do about them.

At the end of the conversation, which continued for another twenty minutes, Kathy summarized what this exchange meant for her own development as a teacher:

> I read that after a teacher has taught seven years, that was their peak. I've been sort of afraid because this is my seventh year and I was thinking, maybe I'm done teaching . . . . But today I'm really thinking differently. I was telling you some gut feelings I've been having but I don't think I would have acted on them. This really feels different, like I'm at a much deeper level in thinking about my role.

Analyzing Our Discourse

Rooted in highly contextualized examples of practice, our conversations were characterized by serious thinking, concrete language, and receptivity to questions of meaning and purpose. We worked together as colleagues, learning with and from each other. New understandings of teaching emerged from this sharing of power. Analyzing our discourse also helped us understand Sharon's role in the work.

Although we moved back and forth between the specific and the general, our conversations were always grounded in the particulars of everyday practice. The more we investigated specific incidents or framed concerns around specific examples, the more likely we were to reach powerful insights about the teacher's role or the nature of practical knowledge or learning to teach. Sharon encouraged this way of talking by asking for examples, probing the meaning of terms like "learning community," and inviting talk about purposes.

Sharon's questions stimulated Kathy to think about her decisions and actions and clarify her beliefs. In the past the question, "Why did you do that?" seemed like an implied criticism to Kathy. Once she realized that the question was genuine, Kathy welcomed the opportunity to think about what she meant or why she was doing something. She also learned to ask Debi about her purposes and to probe the meaning of abstract terms.

Conversation became a vehicle for figuring things out. Sharon rarely brought an agenda to the weekly visits. What we talked about mostly grew out of what was happening that day or what Kathy and Debi were working on. Rooted in a puzzle or problem, the conversations often embodied the kind of intellectual excitement associated with discovery. No one had all the answers. Even when Sharon threw out suggestions, they were more in the spirit of raising possibilities than of pushing a particular course of action. Kathy saw the conversations as "adventures characterized by uncertainty, excitement, and movement into the unknown." As she wrote in her journal, "We brought up doubts and problems and ideas that were not carefully thought through and often had never been said aloud to anyone before.... It was the feeling that we were exploring and discovering new ideas and the excitement of the intellectual work that kept each person deeply engaged."

Sharon regularly transformed problems into occasions for inquiry and analysis. When Kathy asked for help with her "problem" in working with student teachers, Sharon suggested that they approach their work with the following question: "How can we use conversation, observation, and writing to learn about teaching and learning to teach?" In the conversation highlighted above, Sharon interpreted what the university supervisor labeled a "classroom crisis" as evidence of Kathy's success in creating a more open classroom culture.

Sharon also helped Kathy appreciate the nature and extent of her expertise. By eliciting and labeling her practical knowledge, she enabled Kathy to see how much she knew about teaching. By conceptualizing the process, she gave value to the intellectual task of making explicit what usually remains implicit in teaching. Sharon also helped Kathy and Debi frame and investigate questions about their practice. As Sharon identified the intellectual work of teaching, Kathy came to see herself as a practical intellectual.

Both Kathy and Debi were trying to figure out the teacher's role in a learner-centered classroom. While they were at different stages in their professional development, they had similar ideas about the kind of teachers they wanted to be. Thus, Kathy's learning became a context for Debi's learning, and Debi saw that an experienced teacher can continue to study and transform her teaching.

As they worked on learning to teach in reform-minded ways, Kathy and Debi developed tools of critical colleagueship (Lord, 1994). Observation, conversation, and writing became valuable resources for learning. With Sharon's help, they learned to observe each other's teaching and document what they saw, to question their purposes and analyze their intentions, to write and talk about their practice in precise, descriptive language.

Through our collaboration, we gained new insights about what and how experienced teachers can contribute to novices' learning and how the opportunity can be a powerful professional development experience for both novice and mentor. We came to understand some of the changes in expectations and understandings that university and school people need to make before teachers will see themselves as school-based teacher educators and take on expanded roles in helping novices learn to teach. We also began to think about how we could help other teachers in our school explore this possibility.

LAUNCHING THE TEACHER EDUCATION CIRCLE

The following year (1991–92), we started the Teacher Education Circle, a monthly forum at Averill Elementary School where interested teachers could discuss questions and problems that arose in the course of their work with student teachers. We saw the project as an extension of our joint inquiry about teaching and learning to teach. Five teachers participated the first year, including Debi, who had been hired as a coteacher for the two second grades; Kathy; and three veteran teachers who each had more than twenty years' teaching experience. Since the teachers were experimenting with new ways of working with children, the TEC became a place to talk about the dual challenge of helping student teachers learn to teach while trying to learn new teaching practices yourself.

The goals of the TEC reflected the necessary connection between the professional development of cooperating teachers and the learning of student teachers as well as the importance we attached to conversation and writing as tools in that learning. In the 1991–92 Averill/PDS proposal, we listed the following goals for the project:

1. redefine the cooperating teacher's role in the student-teaching experience;
2. help cooperating teachers clarify and articulate their practical knowledge and beliefs about teaching and learning to teach;
3. develop the skills and understandings needed to help student teachers learn to teach for understanding;
4. foster thoughtful conversation and writing about teaching and learning to teach.

Bruce Rochewiak, Averill's visionary principal, arranged the schedule so that cooperating teachers had one and a half to two hours of protected time each week to meet with their student teachers. Sharon spent a day a week observing and meeting with cooperating teachers and student teachers, and she used her visits to frame questions for TEC meetings. One question that led to new ideas about mentored learning to teach concerned the difference between "scheduling" and "planning."

Sharon had noticed that teachers and student teachers often spent their planning time creating a schedule and filling in their plan books ("We'll do math from 9:00 to 9:30, then you can read a chapter from *Charlotte's Web* until 9:45 . . .") rather than talking about their instructional purposes or the pedagogy of particular learning activities. She brought this observation about difference between "scheduling" and "planning" to the TEC and it opened up an investigation across several months of how experienced teachers plan for teaching, what novices need to learn about the planning process, and how cooperating teachers could teach planning in the context of teaching. We began to use the term "coplanning" to refer to a process of thinking aloud with a novice as a way to model and teach the intellectual work of instructional planning. Sharon videotaped Kathy coplanning with her student teacher and we eventually wrote a case of coplanning (Feiman-

Nemser & Beasley, 1997) to help other teachers visualize and understand this form of mentoring.

In the spring, the members of the TEC made a presentation at the monthly PDS Forum, a time when university faculty and teachers associated with the various projects in the school shared some aspect of their ongoing work. We organized our presentation around stories illustrating how we were accomplishing the four project goals. The stories make visible the challenges of changing two practices—teaching and mentoring—at the same time. They also capture some of the early transformations of this small group of teachers who came to play a significant leadership role on Team One over the next decade. Because we tape-recorded and transcribed the presentation, it is possible to revisit this historical record.

Stories of Transformation

Kathy opened the presentation by describing how her understanding of the cooperating teacher's role had changed. Acknowledging that she used to think her job was to provide a classroom where student teachers could try out things they had learned at the university, Kathy explained that she now saw herself as a teacher of teaching:

> Now I understand that I really need to help a novice *learn to teach*; that's my job. I'm in a teaching role. I should ask questions of my student teacher, not just tell her what she did wrong but try to get at her thinking. I should help her clarify her thinking and encourage her to ask me questions about my teaching. Then I should talk about the decisions I make on my feet every day. . . . I should also help my student teacher think about the students and how they're thinking and learning. So you can see there's been a powerful change in my role.

Debi then laid out four new purposes for student teaching. Instead of thinking of student teaching as a time to "pick up some techniques" and figure out "how to teach on your own," she suggested that student teaching was a time to learn how to think and act like a teacher through coplanning and coteaching:

> The biggest idea is that student teaching is a time to continue learning. It's not that coursework isn't useful, but that's just a start. You've got to take that coursework and figure out how to put it into action in the classroom. . . .
> A second thing is that student teaching is an opportunity to learn through

joint problem solving. Kathy and I shared the same group of students so we could talk about what was going on in the classroom, what she was making decisions about, what I should be thinking about as I tried to learn how to make those decisions. . . . The third thing is that a cooperating teacher is a resource from whom I could learn teaching strategies, learn about children and how they think and learn, and learn about planning curriculum. . . . Finally, it [student teaching] is a time to study my own practice so I can continue to grow and not see student teaching as the end of my education. After this year I realize that I'm still learning and will continue to learn.

Speaking to Debi's second and third goals, Carole Shank told a story about how she learned to clarify and share her practical knowledge with her student teacher, Sarah. Carole explained that during morning meeting, Sarah would sit on the floor with the children but never intervene, even when the children next to her were messing around or not listening to the speaker. This surprised Carole, who assumed that since Sarah had been watching morning meeting for several months, she would know what to do. Talking this over with Sharon, Carole realized that she had many different ideas about morning meeting in her head that she had never discussed with Sarah—"all the decisions I make, what kids I push, why we are sitting in a circle, the specific things the kids should be doing, what kind of listening I wanted." Carole saw that "Sarah was watching but she didn't know what she was seeing." Then Carole explained that she not only met with Sarah but also talked with the students, which had a big effect on morning meeting:

> By clarifying for myself it was easier to articulate with Sarah and my kids what was going on and what we needed to have happening in that class meeting time. The kids felt safer, the class meeting was much more of a success because we were all clearer about our roles.

A final story by Jane Boyd, the most senior teacher in the group, spoke to the value of writing and conversation in teacher learning and underscored the challenge of trying to change habituated teaching practices. After many years of teaching, Jane observed, she was very good at controlling lessons and achieving closure. It was still easier to "kick back into being the teacher up in front" rather than manage the messiness of having students figure out the math problem, decide what they wanted to write about, or solve their own problems. But she was starting to question who benefits from this automatic-pilot teaching:

We've been taught that the day should end, the kids should go home happy, everything's neat, and a sub could walk in the next morning, look at your plan book and know what to do. But if you're trying to allow some student investigation, foster curiosity, let them figure things out, the day may not be tidy and there may not be closure. Sometimes that's real hard for me and as hard as I try to do it, automatic pilot kicks in. . . . So it is a dilemma of balancing thinking about kids learning in a different way and having all these years of experience telling me we could get this done a lot faster than that. I guess what this process is forcing me to do is put into words all of those things that are in my head.

Jane was not the only veteran teacher who found it difficult to experiment with new teaching practices while also trying to support and guide a student teacher. After several years of struggling to create a more learner-centered classroom while hosting student teachers, Carole decided to take a break from having student teachers. Kathy and Debi agreed to mentor Carole, and the three teachers undertook a unique peer mentoring project, using observation, conversation, and journal writing to help Carole transform her teaching practice (Beasley, Corbin, Feiman-Nemser, & Shank, 1997). When Carole resumed her work as a collaborating teacher for Team One, she was not only a confident learner-centered teacher; the experience of being mentored by Debi and Kathy had also taught her how to scaffold her interns' learning with skill and insight.

Kathy concluded the forum by reflecting on how the TEC was promoting a new way of talking about teaching, which leads to deeper understandings of the practice of teaching. Her comments resonate with a growing literature on professional discourse by researchers and teacher educators interested in clarifying the distinction between "just talk" and "consequential conversation" (Little & Horn, 2006) and studying the transformative power of professional talk among teachers. (See Ball & Cohen, 1999; Lord, 1994; Pfeifer & Featherstone, 1997):

> The way I used to talk about teaching involved story swapping, passing judgment, maybe complaining. Now for me there is a new way to talk about teaching that has a different purpose. The purpose is to deepen my own understanding of what teaching is all about. . . . This new way of talking about teaching is dependent on finding colleagues who relish trying to understand teaching, who will come to the discussion with all their wonderful ideas and

experience. This is the type of conversation we have in the TEC, and it has helped me explore more fully what teaching for understanding means.

Creating a Learning-to-Teach Curriculum

The following year, the TEC took a bold step. We decided to design and run our own student teaching program based on our new insights about the role of experienced teachers in helping novices learn to teach. We volunteered to take six student teachers each semester (the fifth-year internship had not yet started).

What followed was an intense year of experimentation. We had to figure out what to teach student teachers and how to guide, support, and assess their learning. In the past, such decisions had been made at the university, and cooperating teachers often found themselves in the position of helping student teachers do something that did not make sense to them. Now they had an opportunity to set the standards, frame the expectations, craft the assignments, and evaluate the learning.

The experience of developing a learning-to-teach curriculum deepened our understanding of teaching, mentoring, and learning to teach. It also contributed to the emergence of a schoolwide community of mentors at Averill. The monthly TEC meetings continued through the 1990s, led for a time by Dirck Roosevelt and then by a retired Averill teacher who became a liaison for Team One. As new teachers joined the faculty, they also learned to unpack their teaching practices through demonstrations and conversations and to guide novices in constructing their own innovative practices.

BRINGING THE WORK TO TEAM ONE

The formative work of Kathy, Sharon, and the Teacher Education Circle laid the conceptual and structural foundations for the yearlong internship on Team One. We redefined the roles of university supervisor and cooperating teacher, extended the TEC model to other schools, and created new forums to help those responsible for the internship get inside the practice of field-based teacher education and learn to enact their new roles. We called these new structures "study groups" because we were exploring new territory and because we wanted other teachers and liaisons to experience the kind of inquiry and conversation that had energized Sharon and Kathy.

Team One also embraced several key ideas that emerged from our original work. We framed the yearlong internship as a time for interns to learn to teach in the company of experienced teachers. We viewed those experienced teachers as "teachers of teaching" with considerable knowledge to share with their interns. Since much of this knowledge was tacit, we knew that teachers would need help uncovering and articulating it. We also recognized that learning to guide and support interns' learning could be a form of professional development for the mentors, with consequences for their own teaching.

To signal the adoption of new role definitions for cooperating teachers and university supervisors, we invented new titles, calling the former "collaborating teacher" and the latter "university liaison." We wanted teachers to see themselves as teachers of teaching collaborating with us in guiding and assessing interns' learning. Helping teachers reframe their expectations for the internship and come to see themselves as school-based teacher educators did not happen overnight. New collaborating teachers often complained that interns showed up in September not knowing how to manage the class. We would then ask whether they thought interns could learn to do that in a university course or whether it would be more effective if interns first observed how an experienced teacher established rules, expectations, and procedures at the beginning of the year; then took responsibility for managing a classroom routine; and gradually shared responsibility for directing the students and their learning while continuing to talk things through with their mentor. Usually we could count on one of the Averill teachers to make the case that teachers were in a better position than university faculty to help interns get inside the principles and practice of classroom management and guide their learning to teach across the year.

Instead of casting university teacher educators as "field supervisors," we framed their role around three responsibilities: (1) providing individualized support and guidance to four to six interns in a school; (2) leading a weekly school-based intern study group, and (3) working closely with collaborating teachers. To help liaisons who were mostly doctoral students and some retired teachers learn to do this kind of work, we created several structures. Sharon offered a practicum in field-based teacher education where doctoral students could study and develop their practice with interns and collaborating teachers. Pat Norman took the practicum and she writes about her learning in chapter 8. Team One also convened a study group for university liaisons. Meeting together every other week enabled experienced liaisons to induct newcomers into the complexities of the work and helped us to fine-tune the internship curriculum based on feedback from liaisons who were our frontline workers in the field. Over time this group accumulated considerable practical wisdom about how to guide and support interns' learning and how to work with collaborating teachers in ways that tapped their expertise and strengthened their practice as teachers and mentors.

When liaisons felt secure enough in their own mentoring practice, we encouraged them to convene a monthly study group for collaborating teachers in their school along the lines of the TEC. This, too, did not happen overnight. Many liaisons had recently left the classroom to enter the doctoral program, and they were reluctant to position themselves as guides to collaborating teachers. In chapter 9, David Carroll describes his experiences facilitating a study group for collaborating teachers in the school where he served as university liaison. He situates this work in the context of a cross-school study group that we also started in order to build more school-based leadership for collaborating teacher development.

These various structures were intended to help Team One build capacity for the internship, which required approximately one hundred mentor teachers a year in eighteen to twenty schools, each with a university liaison. We made considerable progress in developing a corps of liaisons and collaborating teachers who embraced their roles and found stimulation and satisfaction in their work with Team One, but we were never home free. First of all, there were never enough liaisons who could do the kind of labor-intensive work with collaborating teachers that Sharon had undertaken with Kathy and which she and Kathy continued through the TEC. Second, staff turnover meant that we were always inducting new liaisons and collaborating teachers into the theoretical and practical dimensions of this work. In the end, we had to face the unavoidable reality that mounting a standards-based yearlong teaching internship on a large scale requires ongoing learning opportunities for everyone involved. When we succeeded, we managed to ignite some of the intellectual excitement and sense of discovery that Sharon and Kathy felt in their early work together and forward the idea of teachers as school-based teacher educators.

8

Learning the Practice of Field-Based Teacher Education

Patricia J. Norman

Large teacher preparation programs often rely on doctoral students to supervise teacher candidates during student teaching or extended internships (Lanier & Little, 1985). Michigan State University is no exception. Doctoral students comprise most of the "university liaisons" who work in its five-year teacher-certification program. Liaisons on Team One provide three kinds of assistance during the yearlong internship. First, they support and guide interns, observing and offering them feedback on their planning and teaching. Second, they plan and convene a "guided practice seminar" for a cohort of six to eight interns placed in a single school who come together weekly to explore questions and dilemmas of practice. Finally, they support collaborating teachers in their work with interns and in their development as school-based teacher educators.

In most institutions, graduate students who work as university supervisors receive little or no training, thus they lack particular expertise in helping novices learn to teach in the context of teaching (Enz, Freeman, & Wallin, 1996; Lanier & Little, 1985). The assumption is that having been classroom teachers, doctoral students in education already know what they need to know to help novices learn to teach. What sets Michigan State apart from most other large schools of education is that doctoral students encounter both formal and informal opportunities to develop their practice as field-based teacher educators. As a novice university liaison, I received sustained support in conceptualizing my role and developing my practice, including opportunities to see models and profit from on-site coaching. For instance, I was initially paired with Dirck Roosevelt, an exceptional, experienced liaison who provided me with "images of the possible" in field-based teacher education as well as on-the-spot assistance.

In addition, I received two forms of behind-the-scenes guidance and support. Team One co-faculty leader Sharon Feiman-Nemser convened a weekly study group for liaisons in which I, along with Dirck Roosevelt, David Carroll, Susan Donnelly, Cindy Hartzler-Miller, and others, regularly participated for six years. In addition, in the spring of 1998, Sharon offered a doctoral seminar, "Becoming a Field-Based Teacher Educator," designed to help students who were currently working with interns to develop their practice as clinical teacher educators. This chapter describes how that seminar strengthened my capacity to help interns learn in and from their teaching.

Seminar on Becoming a Field-Based Teacher Educator

Sharon's seminar created a professional community where the four other doctoral students and I could clarify our role as field-based teacher educators, read about and discuss images of thoughtful mentoring, and develop our practice. Sharon helped us become a professional learning community rather than simply a support group in which we swapped stories about our work and offered each other moral support. She pushed us to engage in "critical colleagueship," an inquiry-oriented, practice-based, self-disclosing form of conversation that creates opportunities for teachers to raise questions about and carefully examine their own practice and their students' learning (Lord, 1994).

In class, we were expected to make our practice public by developing and sharing records of our field-based work with interns so that we could ground our conversations in the particulars of what was said and done. We were expected to ask hard questions of each other, support our assertions with evidence from the records of practice, consider alternative interpretations, and explore, rather than avoid, disagreement. We had to learn to separate the person from the practice and move from a defensive stance to one of openness, important elements of critical colleagueship.

Framing My Inquiry

One of the readings that we discussed early on in the seminar particularly influenced my learning. Dewey's *Experience and Education* (1938/1963) helped me think about the teacher's role in general and my role as a liaison, more specifically. Dewey explains that the teacher must pay close attention to students' internal conditions—namely their needs, desires, purposes, and capacities—in order to create the objective conditions to support further learning. As a university liaison, I was a teacher of teaching and therefore to help my interns learn in and from their own teaching needed to pay close attention to their needs and capacities. I began to wonder what it would mean to consider my interns' internal conditions so I could plan and enact educative conversations with them about their teaching.

I realized that by attending more closely to the habits and attitudes being formed by the interns, I could better shape our interactions to foster their continued learning. For example, if I could identify and take into consideration how interns were making sense of their teaching as well as our conversations, I could guide those conversations during postteaching conferences to help them to gain insights into their practice and their children's learning.

Other seminar readings about the role and practice of the university supervisor helped me articulate some of the questions I had confronted in postobservation conferences. How does this interaction fit into my evolving understanding of the intern's development? What key ideas or questions should I focus on? What if the intern's expectations and needs do not mesh with my learning agenda? What do I know or need to learn about my interns' needs and attitudes that could influence what I say and how I say it? How should I manage the tension between supporting an intern and stretching her thinking?

When Sharon invited us to conduct an inquiry around a problem encountered in our work with interns, I knew that I wanted to examine my efforts to combine support and challenge in appropriate and effective ways. I decided to focus on my work with Carole, an intern with whom I was having trouble. From the start, Carole and I had not hit it off. She seemed quite enamored of her collaborating teacher's practice, which I considered didactic and teacher-centered. When I attempted to help Carole examine her mentor's teaching and her own with a critical eye, she appeared resistant, even angry. Her stance troubled me deeply. While I knew that my efforts were not succeeding, I could not see my own role in creating our difficulties. Videotaping Carole's lessons and our postobservation conferences, then transcribing and analyzing these data in the seminar became a powerful means of helping me develop new understandings and ways of working.

Framing the Case

In this chapter, I first describe how Carole and I got stuck in an unproductive relationship or "learning bind" (Schön, 1987). Then I provide a detailed account of one observation and a series of conferences that I held with Carole. Contrary to the recommendations of Schön (1987), who argues that the coach must draw on what the student says to extend the teacher's agenda and the student's understanding, my responses to Carole's comments were completely disconnected from hers. Once I identified this problematic pattern in my practice, I worked on responding to Carole's ideas and questions in more productive ways. Planning a postobservation conference with Sharon helped solidify my ideas about what to do. In the concluding discussion, I examine how this pivotal set of experiences sensitized me to the challenges interns face as learners of teaching and to the need to attend to both what and how novices learn.

Creating a Learning Bind

When I first began working with Carole and the five other interns at Pine Ridge Elementary School, I adopted what Cochran-Smith (1991) calls a "critical dissonance" lens. I worried that the collaborating teachers' more traditional, teacher-centered practices would counteract the learner and learning-centered ideas espoused by the teacher-education program with the result that interns would perpetuate their mentors' traditional practices. Many researchers have documented the weak impact of teacher preparation compared with the strong influence of the field (Lortie, 1975; Evertson, 1990; Goodlad, 1990), and I was worried that my interns would be affected similarly.

Feeling a sense of urgency, I attempted to help the interns look critically at their collaborating teachers' teaching. I did not appreciate the tentative nature of their relationships with the collaborating teachers and with me; nor did I consider how threatening my critique of their collaborating teachers' practices felt. Instead of helping interns understand my concerns, my critiques pushed most of them closer to their collaborating teachers. Carole seemed particularly resistant to my efforts to help her bring a critical eye to teaching—her own and her collaborating teacher's.

Seminar discussions of Schön's (1987) book, *Educating the Reflective Practitioner*, helped me recognize that Carole and I were deeply caught in a "learning bind." Schön describes this as a "process of systematic miscommunication" that develops when a "student's initially resistant and defensive stance" is coupled with an equally problematic stance on the part of the instructor (pp. 126–127). Although I was aware of this learning bind, I limited my initial understanding of the causes to *Carole's* role.

I had gathered ample evidence of Carole's defensive stance. For example, when I talked to her about her first week in the classroom, she mentioned that her third-grade students were given three spelling tests in order to place them in ability groups for the year, a practice she herself supported. Alarmed by the possible messages three spelling exams might send to students (not to mention the idea of ability grouping for spelling), I tried to help Carole think about what this approach to spelling implied about her mentor's beliefs and values. Carole maintained her view that students would receive "appropriate" spelling instruction now that she and her mentor knew their "ability levels."

Our written communication mirrored our already troubled relationship. Each intern kept a teaching journal in which to write about events or questions that arose from classroom work. Instead of choosing an issue and delving into it in some detail as was expected, Carole tended to write a line or two about a specific activity without identifying an issue she was grappling with. Summarizing her first week in the classroom, Carole wrote the following entry:

> As for impressions on the day, it was great! I love Kate [Carole's collaborating teacher]. She works so well with the students and she treats me as an equal. The kids are really fun. Great to work with. . . . Friday was a sub. Good day. Overall, had a great week. Learned a lot about myself, the kids, and Kate.

Carole's ideas seemed vague, superficial, and lacking in serious thought. I remember feeling irritated by all of the smiley and sad faces that peppered her very brief entries. What did she like about Kate? What had she noticed about her students? My comments, squeezed into the margins of her first journal entries, reflected my frustration that she had written many evaluative statements without supporting details:

> *What* did you learn?

> Words like "fun," "well" and "great" are words I'd like you to stay away from unless you follow them up with an explanation of *what* actually happened that led you to those impressions.

I must have subconsciously recognized my tone of condemnation because my summative statement at the end of her first two weeks of journal writing suggests a softened stance:

Carole,

It was helpful to read your journal. . . . It gave me a sense of what you are attending to. I'd like to see you describe in greater detail what you are seeing and the questions you may have. Also, push yourself to think carefully about the messages your students are receiving through the teacher's actions. I look forward to reading your next series of entries. My comments are meant to help you push your thinking.

Pat

Unfortunately, the damage was done. Carole's searing reply illustrates that in those important opening weeks of school, we had failed utterly to understand each other. As Schön (1987) explains, once the learning bind is established, both teacher and student are locked into a no-win situation, but neither party will give up fighting. Carole's alienation was reflected in the absence of a personal salutation:

Response to Pat's comments:

I understand that my journal will be looked over by others; however, I write in my journal what I need to remember and what I thought was important. I am very open with my teacher and when I have a question I ask her. I don't write continuously in my journal because I am working with the students. I feel that I have gone beyond what time permits me to write, and what I write is for me and not what is expected of me to write. . . . These are my thoughts after getting back my journal. I think I have a different concept of journal writing.

Carole

My comments had left Carole feeling that her collaborating teacher would provide her with everything she needed, leaving little or no reason to interact with me. When, after reading her reply, I attempted to talk to her about my expectations for her journal writing, tension hung between us. She believed that she should be able to write what she deemed important. I asserted that she needed to choose one question or issue to discuss in greater depth.

I decided to focus my efforts on helping Carole prepare for teaching, rather than engaging her in examining her mentor's practice. Knowing that her mentor had asked her to design and teach a folktale unit, I invited Carole to bring *Why Mosquitoes Buzz in People's Ears* (Aardema, 1975), one of the texts to be used in the unit, to our guided practice seminar so all the interns could read the book and help Carole think about how to work with it. The seminar, which met weekly for two hours, enabled interns to talk about issues of practice that arose from their work in the classroom.

After explaining to the group that getting help with planning was a good use of seminar time, I asked Carole to share the children's book with us. Carole saw little value in reading the book to us because she had already looked through the accompanying teacher's guide and decided what to do, but she agreed to read it aloud, and an interesting conversation about the story ensued. We discussed several themes in the book that led us to generate our own list of folktale characteristics. We then considered specific activities that Carole might use to help students begin to construct their own understanding of folktales as a genre. We also discussed what Carole's third graders might find confusing about the story.

I was thrilled with this conversation. The other interns had raised many issues that I wanted Carole to consider in designing her unit. Knowing that they held more credibility for her than I did at that point, I felt confident that she would draw on our collective ideas when planning her folktale unit. In hindsight, I realize that I failed to consider what sense Carole had made of the conversation. I not only assumed that the discussion felt supportive and beneficial to Carole, I also expected that she knew how to act on the suggestions. Didn't she understand that I wanted all the interns, not just her, to do the kind of planning we had done in the seminar on a regular basis?

When I met with Carole to discuss her planned unit a week later, I was surprised to discover that she had ignored the suggestions generated the week before. Since I was still trying to win this no-win battle, my initial feelings of disappointment gave way to anger and frustration. Instead of acknowledging the reason for my frustration, I avoided being explicit about this issue, a stance guaranteed to promote further misunderstanding (Schön, 1987). She left the conversation feeling like she could do nothing right in my eyes. We had cemented our learning bind.

Could I help Carole develop a more reflective stance toward her teaching? In her own words, she liked to describe what happened while teaching and then move on. I wondered whether she avoided wading into the uncertain and muddy waters of teaching and learning because acknowledging the complexity would be too overwhelming. Still, this limited what she could learn from her teaching experiences. My assumptions led me to miss the important ways that she *was*, in fact, open to learning. Reading *Educating the Reflective Practitioner* (Schön, 1987) that spring, I finally recognized that my own defensive stance during those initial troubling months had kept me from moving forward with Carole. So I began the long and arduous process of trying to repair our damaged relationship and disentangle our learning bind.

Living with the Learning Bind

Over the weeks that followed, I managed to establish a more positive rapport with Carole by shying away from any sensitive issues about her practice. I did not trust that our relationship could sustain a challenging conversation, so I narrowed my focus, giving her positive strokes even when I was hard-pressed to find something praiseworthy about her teaching. I ignored opportunities to raise concerns.

When I observed Carole's teaching, she often wanted to know if she "was on the right track." Thinking that I should avoid talking about areas of her practice she needed to strengthen, I tried to praise Carole. Again, had I taken Schön's advice to be more explicit with Carole about my dilemma, I might have discovered a way to address the tension between Carole's wanting to know what went well and my desire to help her address the challenges that she was encountering in her work with children. I became more and more discouraged with my own practice and my inability to work toward what I considered educative ends.

Describing the situation in the doctoral seminar and voicing my frustration helped me begin to understand how my faulty thinking had led to this seeming impasse. Sharon wondered whether praising Carole was a good idea even if she seemed to want praise. "Why not be more neutral?" Sharon suggested, so that Carole could develop her own standards for assessing her teaching. This seemed like a promising idea. I also began to examine my conversations with Carole by taping and transcribing them for closer analysis.

Designing My Inquiry

Our interactions had sensitized me to the dilemma of trying to support a novice teacher while simultaneously stretching her thinking. Wanting to learn how to manage that dilemma more effectively, I framed the following set of questions to guide my inquiry:

+ What do my attempts to manage the tension between support and challenge look like in practice and with what effects?
+ When and how am I able to manage this tension productively?

In order to examine these questions, I videotaped and transcribed an hour-long lesson on adjectives Carole taught. I then audiotaped and transcribed a short postobservation conference we had immediately following the lesson. After summarizing her lesson, I describe how sharing excerpts from the video and transcript in the doctoral seminar led me to revisit the same lesson with Carole in two subsequent conversations with a resulting breakthrough.

Carole's adjectives lesson. I observed Carole teach a sixty-minute lesson on adjectives in the context of a unit on the biography, *Helen Keller* (Davidson, 1989). Carole first asked the students to define the word "adjective." After verifying their ideas with a dictionary definition, Carole elicited several examples and concluded that the students understood what an adjective is. She then held up a stuffed animal named Wrinkles and asked students, "How does it make you feel? What do you think of? You want to describe it." When students responded, "extraordinary design," "wrinkles," "snuggly," "nice," and "careful," Carole seemed flustered that they had used nouns, adverbs, and phrases instead of just adjectives.

Next Carole showed students various objects and played three different pieces of music on the computer. Each time she asked students to describe what the object or music made them think of or how it made them feel. When a student did not offer an adjective, she implored, "Give me something closer." Finally, the students worked in small groups to brainstorm "about Helen Keller, what she's like and what we think of when we hear her name." Again, the students used various parts of speech to answer. They came up with "blind," "fat," "Braille," "Scarlet Fever," "she eats like a pig," "had chickens," "horrifying," and "insane."

Initial postobservation conference. As I videotaped the lesson, I wondered why Carole had focused on adjectives and how adjectives deepened students' understanding of or connection to the biography. Carole had seemed unsure about what she was trying to teach—even though she did eight different activities in one hour.

Immediately following the lesson, we sat down to talk. Carole began by voicing her frustration that several students routinely left the classroom twice a week for language arts instruction with the reading specialist. When they rejoined the class on the remaining three days, they had missed so much that they could not meaningfully jump back into the book. How could she work with students pulled out for special services? She also expressed dissatisfaction with the lesson, suggesting a willingness to question her teaching and consider alternatives.

Instead of responding to Carole's frustration and confusion, I was intent on making her feel good about her lesson in response to what I saw as her perennial need to know that she was on the right track. I referred to several students—none of whom received resource services—who understood what adjectives were. This response reflected my continued wariness about sharing concerns that might sound critical. Even though she had raised a difficulty, I was afraid to take a risk and pick up on it.

Carole, however, was responsive to *me*. She acknowledged what I had said and shared her own sense of what students understood, working with me, not against me by abandoning her issue to explore mine. My response demonstrates that I did not clearly follow through on my earlier comment:

> I really want you to clue into the directions when you watch the videotape. When you said "I'm going to show you these six things and you're going to describe them," describing is different from saying "Give me adjectives that describe them." See the difference?

I moved from considering what the students did or did not understand to a monologue about the ambiguity in Carole's directions. Instead of helping her consider how her directions influenced students' responses, I told her what I thought was wrong. Although I was finally being explicit and direct, this move was unnecessary, since Carole could watch the videotape and draw her own insights about what she had said and how students had responded.

Second attempt to debrief Carole after her lesson. After showing video clips of Carole's lesson and analyzing the transcript of the postobservation conference with my seminar colleagues, I felt embarrassed at how poorly I had facilitated the conversation. Still determined to help Carole learn from her lesson, I suggested that she watch the video at home so that we could talk about it at a later date. When we met two weeks later, I came armed with preplanned questions that were more direct and clearly focused on her purposes for teaching adjectives. Sharon's advice to listen hard to Carole's responses echoed in my head as I opened the conversation by asking Carole to share what she thought of the video.

While the question was purposefully open-ended, I was not prepared for Carole's response. Just as she was derailed when her students offered unanticipated answers, I, too, became flustered by her unanticipated responses to my questions:

Boy, I'm boring! No, I'm kidding. That wasn't a super-exciting lesson. . . . I saw things that I miss [when teaching]. John was eating something out of his desk! I'm going to show the class the video, and then I'm gonna bust him for it.

Although I was listening closely to Carole's ideas, I did not know how to use her responses to move the conversation forward. Instead of taking advantage of the opening that Carole had created to explore why the students might have found the lesson boring, I commiserated, "It's really impossible to see all the things that go on."

Hoping to move the conversation beyond catching a boy for eating his lunch in class, I asked Carole what she had noticed about her teaching. Again, her response took me by surprise:

I noticed that I didn't reprimand anybody, but I was trying to use the positive. I walked around a lot. That's good instead of just standing. I noticed [while watching the tape] that you were just going all over. I'm like, I probably shouldn't be walking around so much because you probably got dizzy with the camera.

Personally I thought the students were incredibly complacent and good-natured, going along with the various requests and activities. So I did not understand Carole's focus on "management." Nor could I believe that this far into her yearlong internship she was still thinking about her performance without also attending to student learning. But I kept my concerns and questions to myself, saying, "You probably got dizzy watching the video. I apologize if the quality wasn't so great."

While I cared little about the video's quality, Carole again picked up on my comments. She liked how I "zoomed into one group": it gave her a chance to hear what students really talked about in their small groups. Rather than ask Carole to share what she had noticed as the small groups generated adjectives to describe Helen Keller, I sat there feeling like the conversation was going nowhere. I simply waited for Carole to state what had seemed so obvious to me while watching her teach. It had not occurred to me that Carole might not know how to learn from a classroom video.

I ignored Carole's talk when she noted her embarrassment about how she looked in the video. Sticking to my internal script, I asked about her purposes in teaching the adjectives lesson. Walking on eggshells, I asked, "I'm curious how teaching adjectives helps kids get inside the [Helen Keller] book." I had not posed such a direct question to her since a disastrous conversation several months earlier. I tensely waited for her reply. Carole responded,

> Now they seem to be excited about reading. One of the kids wanted to take the book home and reread it. It's like, "you're kidding me." Not that it was the descriptive words or adjectives that did it, but maybe he's starting to look at the words more than just reading it to get through the book. You know, instead of just saying Helen Keller was mad, you know, she was *furious*. Hopefully they are starting to find that "furious" is a much more impressive word and makes you feel something more than "mad."

I had no idea how to probe or use her ideas to get to my own agenda, which was to examine the fit between the purposes of the lesson and the learning activities. Instead, I sat there wondering how Carole could equate the adjectives lesson with students' interest in reading. I could view her answer only as a roadblock, not as an invitation or window into her thinking.

I continued to feel bewildered when Carole explained that she had watched the video with her mother, but her fiancé had quickly lost interest and left the room. Although she raised the issue of boredom again, I felt uneasy about addressing this topic. Humbled and confused, I retreated again. I had not yet realized that the concern I wanted to raise with Carole about her responses to students' ideas was the very same one I was struggling with in my work with her. Like Carole, I was anticipating certain "right" answers in response to my questions, and like Carole, I did not know how to deal with answers that did not meet my expectations.

Getting Help

After sharing a summary of this second conversation in the doctoral seminar, I expressed dismay at my inability to move Carole's thinking forward. From analyzing the transcript I realized that I lacked ideas about *how* to do this despite having clear goals for Carole's learning. I wanted to help Carole think about what makes a lesson worthwhile in the first place and see the connection between her directions and her students' responses, and consider the importance of giving clear, concise directions. With help from the seminar, I planned yet a third conference on the adjectives lesson, which we held a month later.

Even though I questioned Carole's purposes in the lesson, I knew that would feel too threatening. Instead, I decided to focus on the matter of the unclear directions. Since so much time had passed, I decided we would view the videotape together, using a research strategy I had read about in another course. We would watch a twenty-minute clip together, and Carole could stop the tape anytime something surprised her. Sharon helped me evaluate the appropriateness of this strategy by asking how it would help me to reach my stated goals. Then she suggested an alternative: she knew that a twenty-minute segment would raise too many issues, so she proposed that I use a shorter clip. We agreed that the part where Carole gave unclear directions had possibilities.

After watching the piece, Sharon suggested I ask Carole what she noticed about the directions. If she did not pick up on how confusing they were, I could bring this up directly. Imagining how this might play out, Sharon suggested some language I could use in conjunction with the lesson transcript I planned to share: "Let me tell you something that struck me. Let's go to the transcript and look at what you said." After analyzing Carole's words, we could each write a new set of directions for the task, since giving clear directions is one important teaching skill. Again, Sharon stepped into my role, talking out what I might say: "Let's both take a minute to write up directions that are clearer." Once we shared our directions, Sharon suggested that I could wrap up this segment of the conference by acknowledging the nice piece of work we had done, ask Carole what she had learned, and share my own thoughts about the importance of language in teaching.

We also discussed how to establish a positive tone for the conversation. Remembering Carole's comment about how she looked in the video of her lesson, Sharon suggested that I share my own concerns about what the video camera would do to me. Sharon also recalled that Carole had been quite frustrated during her lesson. I could show my concern for her discomfort by stating that I had been wondering about the causes of her frustration, which led me to choose this particular clip. Armed with a clear and reasonable opening, I felt confident enough to plan the remainder of the conversation, which I hoped would address the issue of Carole's purposes for teaching the lesson.

A Successful Debriefing Conference

After opening the conversation according to the new plan, Carole and I watched the video clip in which she showed students a stuffed animal, then asked them to describe how it made them feel or what it made them think of. We watched as students offered the following responses: fat, chubby, extraordinary design, cute, careful, cuddly, snugly, nice, fuzzy, Wrinkles, sleep, comfortable, and hairy. We noticed that when students did not use an adjective, Carole asked them to either "think of something closer" or "give me another one."

After watching for about five minutes, I asked Carole if she noticed anything about her directions. Immediately, she picked up on the relationship between what she had asked her students to do and how they had responded:

> I said, "Write down how you think you feel or what it makes you think of." Rachel's answer, "comfortable," totally fit into that even though you wouldn't say Wrinkles himself is comfortable. But I asked how she felt. . . . I think they were getting mixed messages.

I encouraged this analysis by suggesting that we look at her directions and the students' responses in the lesson transcript. After discussing what we noticed, I proposed that we each write a new set of directions for the "Wrinkles the Dog" activity that were clearer, explaining that giving clear directions is a skill teachers need to develop. Carole enthusiastically took up the challenge.

Next, we worked through several teacher/student exchanges, trying to generate a different teacher response. When Ryan said the stuffed animal was "careful," Carole noticed that she replied, "You think he's careful?" which led Ryan to change his answer. Carole realized that her response was not helpful. I casually asked, "So what could you have said to him?" Attempting to answer my question, she covered her mouth with her hand and spoke in much choppier, more hesitant, and softer tones. It took her three different tries to develop a response that she was comfortable with: "Ryan, I hadn't thought of that. How do you think he's careful?" When she came across other unanticipated answers, Carole tried to think of something else to say. As she worked hard to find new language to address students' responses, I saw the parallels in my own struggle to phrase questions for and responses in our previous conversations.

I also realized how challenging this was for Carole. She had quickly recognized the problematic nature of her replies to students' "wrong" answers, but this knowledge did not yield a different response. In asking, "What could you have said to him?" not only was I requiring her to think on her feet, I was also asking her to look at students' answers in a new way. Instead of treating them as either right or wrong, I wanted Carole to see each response as a window on student thinking and an opportunity to probe for understanding. Given the significance of this shift, it was not surprising that she hesitated in searching for a less evaluative response.

MENTORING THE UNIVERSITY TEACHER EDUCATOR

Finally I was able to create a space for Carole to look at teaching and learning in a new way, and she was able to risk trying on a different voice and perspective. What made this possible after so many false starts? Part of the answer lies in the jointness of our effort (Vygotsky, 1978) to make sense of and learn from Carole's teaching. I, too, took on the task of rewriting the directions. I even commented while drafting my own—"This is harder than I thought!"—which drew a laugh from us both. In this respect we were on equal footing; I was not her supervisor so much as a fellow teacher jointly engaged in an authentic teaching task. Instead of adopting an evaluative, hierarchical stance that separated us into traditional roles of supervisor and intern, we puzzled together about how to respond to students' unanticipated answers. Rather than waiting for Carole to read my mind, I suggested some different language she could use. I believe this feeling of jointness enabled us to pursue the conversation even when it moved into more threatening territory around her purposes.

What helped me to adopt a different stance in my work with Carole and actually engage her in analyzing and rethinking her practice? First, analyzing transcripts of several debriefing conferences with my colleagues helped me see that I needed to find more constructive ways to respond to Carole. Studying my practice helped me identify problematic patterns in my interactions with her, but it did not supply me with ideas about how to create new ones. Like Carole, I lacked that critical know-how. Thus another important feature of my learning occurred through what Vygotsky (1978) calls "assisted performance."

Vygotsky (1978) first wrote about assisted performance in relation to a child's zone of proximal development, those tasks a child can accomplish with assistance from a parent or teacher or more experienced other. As a learner engages in an activity to which she is committed, the teacher or mentor observes what the learner can do on her own, then provides appropriate guidance that helps the learner "to identify the nature of [her] problems and to find solutions that enable [her] to bring the activity to a satisfactory completion" (Wells, 1999, p. 159).

The seminar assisted my performance by helping me plan the final debriefing conference. While I had clear goals for the conversation, I lacked specific moves to reach those. Sharon helped me frame an analytic task to work on with Carole that redefined our roles and relationship. It would not have occurred to me to give myself the same rewriting task I gave Carole. Nor would I have thought to connect her earlier concern with how she looked in her video to my own worries about how I would appear in the video of our conference. Anticipating that Carole might not notice the problematic directions, Sharon advised me to be ready to raise the issue myself.

Sharon offered concrete language and strategies I could use to create a more productive conversation with Carole. For example, she helped me consider *how* to use the videotape of Carole's lesson as a stimulus for reflection. Mining a video and crafting a conversation around it is a practice that teacher educators must develop (Denyer, 1997; Ball & Cohen, 1999). Sharon's advice about how to use the video helped me expand my coaching repertoire. In addition, by coplanning the final debriefing conference with me, Sharon modeled a different way to approach my own supervisory practice. Sharon's questions, concrete suggestions, and joint efforts to help me anticipate potential difficulties allowed me to experience firsthand what mentoring as joint work looks and sounds like (Feiman-Nemser & Beasley, 1997). Thus Sharon's scaffolding enabled me to reframe my role as Carole's supervisor. Instead of approaching my work with her from a hierarchical, detached stance, I began to view my role as a matter of joint work between a novice and a more experienced other.

LESSONS FOR MY PRACTICE

The experience of studying my practice in the company of other teacher educators with the help of a more experienced colleague influenced my subsequent work as a field-based teacher educator in several important ways. First, I became much more sensitized to the challenges interns face as learners of teaching. When a novice begins to learn a new professional practice, she faces a seeming contradiction—she recognizes that she does not know how to do something, yet learning entails doing the very thing she does not yet know how to do. She must come to learn through action, yet at the outset she "can neither do it nor recognize it when she sees it" (Schön, 1987, p. 83). Interns are confronted by this learning paradox as they attempt to learn the practice of teaching. Prospective teachers must engage in teaching even though they are not yet able to teach.

If the internship is to be educative, novices must adopt the stance of a learner in order to recognize that important ideas about teaching and learning can be gleaned from their own initial attempts to tackle the complex art of instruction (Schön, 1987). Many times, however, interns feel an internal press to demonstrate their competence, particularly when they are exposing their practice to those in a supervisory role. This need to prove that they already know how to do the work of teaching can diminish their ability to learn from their experiences.

As a student of field-based teacher education, I, too, confronted the internal press to prove that I already knew how to do the work. Admitting to my colleagues and myself that I did not know how to break out of the dysfunctional pattern that Carole and I had established was very difficult. Experiencing firsthand the challenge of not knowing helped me better understand and respond to subsequent moments when interns seemed defensive about participating with me in the analysis of their teaching practice.

Second, my experience in the doctoral seminar helped me appreciate the importance of attending not only to *what* interns need to learn but also to *how* they can be helped to learn that. In hindsight, I realized that while some interns seem adept at figuring out how to pursue their learning to teach agenda, others require more sustained support. In other words, my practice must include not only clarifying what the intern needs to work on but also figuring out how to assist that actual learning. It is not helpful to tell an intern that she needs to improve her directions, build on students' ideas, frame worthwhile purposes if she does not know how to do these things. I also have to assist the intern's performance, often by coplanning and coteaching future lessons.

Finally, I became more aware of the power of using records of practice such as videotapes and transcripts to help interns learn from their teaching. Ball and Cohen (1999) argue that classroom teachers need opportunities to learn how to elicit students' ideas, interpret those ideas in the moment, and use what they learn about children's thinking to inform their responses to students and situations. The frenetic pace of classroom life makes it impossible for teachers to analyze and evaluate their teaching decisions in the moment and generate alternative responses. Having transcripts of lessons or videotapes can support teachers in analyzing their moves and imagining more educative possibilities.

In my current work with interns, I routinely videotape their teaching so we can ground postobservation conferences in the particulars of what the students and the intern said and did in the lesson. In addition, I help interns experience for themselves the value and even joy of self-study as they complete a semester-long action research project that grows out of an authentic problem confronting them in their practice. Thus my enthusiasm for and commitment to systematic self-study continues to shape my work as a field-based teacher educator.

Implications for Teacher Education

Beyond shaping my own practice, my experiences in the doctoral seminar have broader implications for teacher education. During my tenure as a doctoral student at Michigan State, I was fortunate to receive sustained support in becoming a serious student and practitioner of field-based teacher education. First, I had opportunities to do the work with assistance. For example,

I worked directly with more experienced university liaisons who modeled ways of relating to interns and talking with them about their work. In addition, I received behind-the-scenes support through a doctoral seminar and weekly Team One university liaison meetings where we clarified a curriculum for the interns' learning and examined difficult situations that we faced in our ongoing work. Second, I was able to learn in the context of my ongoing work as a Team One liaison. Self-study played a critical role in helping me develop my capacity to assist interns in learning to teach. Tape-recording and transcribing my interactions with interns and analyzing them with colleagues taught me the value of creating and studying records of practice as well as making public my practice for our collective scrutiny.

My experience is atypical. In most universities, graduate students who work as university supervisors may take a course on clinical supervision if they are lucky, but few have regular opportunities—both formal and informal—to discuss their work with others and receive feedback and guidance. Field-based teacher educators need and deserve professional learning opportunities. Team One understood that interns, collaborating teachers, *and* university liaisons were all constructing new practices. Interns were students of teaching. Collaborating teachers were students of mentoring. University liaisons were students of field-based teacher education. To build the capacity of all participants in the teacher preparation program, Team One provided support and guidance to everyone. This assistance extended to graduate students and included making the ongoing study of their work with interns and collaborating teachers part of their graduate program.

9

Helping Teachers Become
Teacher Educators

David Carroll

Twenty-five educators are seated around a ring of tables in a conference room at Michigan State University on a Thursday afternoon in February 2000. The cross-school liaison study group includes teacher representatives (teacher liaisons) from twelve schools, each of which is hosting five or six MSU teacher interns, plus Team One (university) liaisons and faculty leaders. Around the table are individuals with considerable teacher-education work experience—veteran and retired teachers now working as university liaisons, experienced teacher educators, plus others relatively new to mentoring and even teaching. The study group session today focuses on the challenges of leading a school-based mentor teacher study group. Team One has been encouraging the teacher and university liaisons around the table to consider initiating mentor study groups in their schools as a means of "scaling up" its efforts to support the over one hundred mentor teachers hosting interns each year. The session is intended to help everyone get inside the practice of study-group leadership.

Chapter Overview

This chapter uses the story of this cross-school liaison study group session to examine some of the challenges of engaging mentor teachers in the work of teacher education. It focuses particularly on the strategy of initiating mentor teacher study groups as a way of "scaling up" support for mentor teacher learning. To enable the reader to appreciate the background context that enabled this session and the scaling up strategy, I first introduce the ideas behind the cross-school liaison study group, and the purposes of this particular session. Next, I backtrack to review the origin of the revamped

teacher education program at Michigan State University, as it was introduced in 1993. I examine critical understandings about the program's relationship with mentor teachers, their role in the new program, and structural
changes in school placements and the deployment of resources designed to
enable those understandings. Next, I provide an extended introduction to
the mentor teacher study group I led at what I will call "Capitol Elementary School," for two-and-one-half years preceding the cross-school liaison
study-group session described in the opening paragraph. Artifacts from my
work in leading the study group at Capitol were the focus of the session. I
recount part of that history to show the origin of the artifacts and illustrate
challenges and dilemmas of leading such study groups. Finally, I return to
the group session to examine how my work at Capitol was used as a context
for exploring study group leadership and fostering our "scaling up" strategy
for mentor teacher development.

Introducing the Cross-School Liaison Study Group

Sharon Feiman-Nemser, Team One co-faculty leader, introduced the agenda
for the study group session, acknowledging that asking those assembled to
consider launching mentor study groups with their school colleagues was
a big leap in our collective work, beyond what people probably expected in
taking on this work. As she put it,

> I felt really excited last month that we stretched ourselves to imagine the
> possibility of beginning . . . some of the work that we've been doing here [in
> the cross-school liaison study group] . . . among teachers in schools who are
> working with our teacher-education students.

Typically, each session of the cross-school liaison study group, which had
been meeting monthly for three years, was organized around the examination of some artifact of practice.[1] Teaching and mentoring occur in real time,
leaving little opportunity for analysis with colleagues. Studying records of
practice allowed us to situate our learning about mentoring in actual examples, experiences, and dilemmas.

Through past investigations in the group, we had begun to develop
shared language and understandings about core aspects of mentoring, including how to help interns get inside the work of instructional planning
and how to talk with them about their teaching in analytic, nonevaluative

FIGURE 1
The Nested Contexts of Mentoring

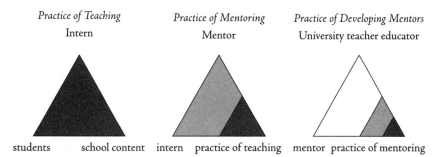

ways. We also spent time refining the internship curriculum. In the course of examining these different aspects of mentoring, we had begun to think about how the work of teaching children, teaching prospective teachers, and teaching mentor teachers to teach prospective teachers were connected. In each context, a teacher and a student come together around some engagement with content to be learned (Hawkins, 1974).

The left triangle represents the intern, taking on the role of teacher and helping her students learn the school curriculum. The middle triangle shows the intern assuming the position of learner, assisted by her mentor in the role of teacher, and learning the practice of teaching. The right triangle illustrates the cross-school liaison study group. There, university teacher educators leading the study group assist mentor teachers in learning the practice of mentoring. We found it useful to keep this visual representation in mind as we worked across these different contexts in our study group sessions. In any given episode of our work with mentor teachers, such as that unfolding in the session described here, there were considerations to be attended to at each level of the nested triangles. The artifacts we studied together—for example, a videotape of an intern's teaching—often disclosed particular ideas and issues about subject-matter teaching being enacted by interns with K–8 students. At the same time, we often used such artifacts of interns' teaching to consider mentoring issues and practices. What does a videotape of an intern's teaching suggest about mentoring moves we might use to support or stretch his/her teaching? And now, in the cross-school liaison study group session, we were about to use such artifacts to help us investigate how to lead mentor teacher study groups.

BACKTRACKING: GETTING THE NEW MICHIGAN STATE PROGRAM STARTED

Educative Mentoring

It would have been impossible to conceive of this cross-school liaison study group without the new conception of field experience envisioned by the new teacher education program—a conception that placed significant emphasis on classroom teachers as school-based teacher educators and on guided classroom experiences as central elements of learning to teach. Team One co-faculty leader Sharon Feiman-Nemser had been at work on a conception of educative mentoring that she and colleagues developed through their research in studying reform-minded teachers engaged in mentoring. This research was ongoing during the time of the development and implementation of the new teacher education program at MSU and had considerable influence on Team One.

Educative mentoring is based on the premise that mentors who take on an educative role must learn to use their practice as the context for introducing the novice to the practical and intellectual work of teaching (Feiman-Nemser & Buchmann, 1987). Since so much of the thinking that informs teaching is invisible to an observer, mentors must learn to think out loud with the novice and to share and model key tasks of teaching—such as planning for instruction, assessing student progress, and reflecting on teaching (Feiman-Nemser & Buchmann, 1987; Cochran-Smith, 1991; Zeichner, 1992; Tomlinson, 1995). Moving toward enacting a practice of educative mentoring also creates a complex and nested set of relationships among classroom students, novice teacher, classroom teacher, and university teacher educator, as illustrated previously in the "triangles" chart. Sharon Feiman-Nemser and Kathrene Beasley present the history of this work on developing the idea of educative mentoring in more detail in chapter 7.

Back in 1993, we didn't know how to harness the vision of educative mentoring on the scale that our part of the MSU program called for: one hundred interns per year. When we introduced the yearlong internship, most mentor teachers were accustomed to traditional views of student teaching, which accorded them a limited role in the novice's learning. After introducing the learner to the classroom norms and routines, the mentor teacher was supposed to step aside and let the student teacher practice teaching. Susan, one of the mentor teachers who worked closely with Team One, described her experience as a cooperating teacher for a traditional teacher preparation program at a nearby university:

> I've had two student teachers in the past. . . . It was more or less doing the modeling for the first couple of weeks, having them observe, and then literally stepping out of the classroom, which sometimes was kind of frustrating, especially the second one I had because things were not going well. But we were specifically told not to be in the classroom, that they had to do this time on their own. (Interview, December 1998)

Structural Changes to Support New Mentoring Practices

To promote ambitious mentoring for ambitious teaching, we formed sustained partnerships with a small number of districts and schools so that we could work intensively with teachers, developing their skills as mentors over time. We also deployed our resources as a team to locate and support a steady teacher education program staff person—whom we called a "university liaison"—at each school (see chapter 8 for more on the challenges of this role). These persons were charged with observing and mentoring interns in conjunction with their mentor teachers and with convening interns in weekly guided practice seminars, where they addressed emergent issues and dilemmas.

However, unless we could successfully engage reasonably large numbers of collaborating teachers in the dual process of examining and developing their own teaching and taking on the practice of educative mentoring, extending school-based field experiences would simply increase our students' exposure to traditional teaching practices and to the kind of isolated traditional student teaching experience Susan described above. Teachers' past experience with traditional teacher education, and their varying identification with reform-minded teaching, led to the need to strategize about how to help teachers become reform-minded teacher educators.

INTRODUCING CAPITOL ELEMENTARY SCHOOL AND THE MENTOR TEACHER STUDY GROUP

The work presented that day in February 2000 at the cross-school liaison study group grew out of my efforts in leading a mentor teacher study group at Capitol Elementary School. It represents a solid example of both the high hopes and recurrent dilemmas of Team One's efforts to develop teachers as school-based teacher educators. Encouraged by the outstanding reputation of principal John Mathews, I had recruited Capitol Elementary School to work with Team One three years earlier.[2] The school itself served a diverse student population challenged by poverty and its attendant discontinuities in living circumstances and resources. The turnover rate among its students was in the range of 50 percent annually. At the same time, under John Mathews's leadership, Capitol teachers were already engaged in sustained staff development activities aimed at transforming their approach to writing and mathematics in ways consistent with MSU visions of subject-matter teaching and learning.

Capitol teachers hosted five interns in their first year with Team One, and I served as university liaison for the building. That year I concentrated on getting to know the teachers and on letting them get to know me. I took part in an overnight faculty retreat at the beginning of the school year and attended many of their staff development sessions to get to know teachers and what they were working on, both individually and collectively. I also established a good working relationship with John Mathews. We met regularly, spoke candidly but confidentially about our respective perspectives on the teacher education work in the building, and coordinated our efforts in addressing ongoing issues as they arose. John made a public and consistent effort to welcome me and the interns into the building and to encourage staff members to treat us as colleagues. He also made important practical gestures, such as making sure the interns had teacher desks and that they got access cards for using the copier.

Initiating a Mentor Teacher Study Group at Capitol

Toward the end of that first year, as I clarified my own research interests in the work of mentor teacher development, I proposed that we form a mentor teacher study group at Capitol. John Mathews readily endorsed the idea, promised to attend as often as he could, and encouraged mentor teachers to take part. Perhaps in consequence, all five mentor teachers for the following year decided to participate, agreeing to meet for two-hour sessions each month to work on developing our practice as mentors.[3] I planned and led the study group sessions, where typically we shared and discussed accounts of mentoring and/or examined records of mentoring practice—written observations; transcripts; or videotapes of planning, teaching, or debriefing sessions.

TABLE 1
First-Year Mentor Teacher Study Group Participants and Their Interns

Teacher	Grade Level	Intern
Susan	Kindergarten	Ben
Pam	First Grade	Karen
Martha	First Grade	Tammy
Sandy	Second Grade	Megan
Anne	Fifth Grade	Brenda

I planned the fall study group sessions around investigating interns' perspectives on getting started in unfamiliar classrooms at the beginning of the school year and introducing some basic mentoring strategies. For example, for the first session in September, I observed and then generated a narrative account of one mentor teacher (Sandy) teaching a math lesson with assistance from her intern (Megan). I also interviewed Megan after the lesson and summarized that conversation in materials prepared for the study group session. In the study group, participants first reviewed the narrative of teaching to identify aspects of Sandy's teaching that they thought would be important for an intern to notice and begin learning about. Next they reviewed the summary of my conversation with the intern to consider what she actually seemed to have noticed. The disparity between what the mentor teachers saw and understood about a routine math lesson and what the intern noticed served to awaken participants to the perspective of their interns as learners.

I also introduced two mentoring strategies that had emerged from Sharon's previous work with the Teacher Education Circle (TEC) at Averill Elementary School: "thinking out loud" and "stepping in." In thinking out loud, the mentor shares her thinking with the novice in real time as she makes choices and decisions while teaching. This helps the novice get inside the decisions teachers make on their feet. In discussing Sandy's lesson, study-group participants recognized places in the lesson where she could have helped her intern get inside her decisions by thinking out loud. Stepping in involves a version of coteaching in which the mentor helps the novice carry out a lesson by stepping in to add explanations or additional perspectives.

In the October study group session, three mentor teachers enthusiastically shared accounts of thinking out loud and stepping in with their interns while the other two complained about their interns and the program. These early meetings illustrate two important challenges in helping these mentor teachers assume the role of school-based teacher educators: they needed both to learn a repertoire of mentoring practices and to assume an educational stance toward their interns as learners. Prior experience with traditional student teaching had predisposed these mentor teachers to view the internship as a time for their interns to apply their university course work knowledge, rather than as a time for learning to teach in the context of a real classroom through joint teaching with an experienced mentor. When some of the interns experienced difficulties, their mentor teachers responded by blaming them and the teacher education program. Only several months later, after the study group conducted an in-depth analysis of two interns' experiences with instructional planning, did they begin to see more clearly the challenges of learning to teach and how they could play an educative role in the process.

Studying Planning in the Capitol Mentor Teacher Study Group

In January, in response to interns' continuing difficulties with planning, the study group decided to study planning. One mentor teacher, Sandy, had invited me to join her with her intern, Megan, because she was stymied in figuring out how to help Megan learn to plan for teaching. In our first three-way session, Megan said very little and asked few questions. The second time we met, I got permission from Sandy and Megan to tape our interaction and I created a transcript from that session to analyze in the January study group.

From the planning session itself and from studying the transcript I had the clear impression Sandy and I had worked collaboratively and reasonably successfully in helping Megan plan a lesson. Sandy's opening remarks in the study group suggested that she saw things differently:

> Well I think it's really good to sit down and plan. . . . I'm not sure if it's necessary every single time. . . . I'm told that you guys want them planning so much but it seems to me that we took a simple thing like rules and we kind of blew it way beyond second-grade level. I think at this point in second grade things are supposed to be touched on but I don't know if they're gonna get

a real total understanding. I think some of the kids will, but then it's gonna be brought up again in third grade. . . . An hour and a half to me on one little small part is too long and I think it loses meaning that way. (Study Group Transcript, January 22, 1999)

Since our coplanning session, Sandy had decided that the session with Megan had lasted too long, probed too deeply into the content, and ended up confusing them both. I made a conscious effort to sit back and listen, rather than react defensively, as others asked Sandy further questions about the experience. I hoped to redirect the group's attention to the transcript after a few minutes of further discussion; however, instead of petering out, the discussion picked up additional fuel. Pam imagined how worrisome it might seem to Megan to spend ninety minutes planning a twenty-minute lesson when she would have to plan for six hours of daily instruction during lead teaching. Both Anne and Susan had read the transcript in advance of the meeting and felt that Megan had not understood the content very well. I shared this view. But Sandy asserted that Megan had understood the original lesson content and only became confused when I pushed the topic about "communities" too deeply. As group leader, I felt torn. By exerting her perspective as a participant in the planning conversation and as Megan's mentor, Sandy was effectively blocking any other interpretations of the event. Martha, another mentor teacher and close friend of Sandy, was reinforcing Sandy's assertions. I thought if we could look at the transcript, other possible interpretations would emerge. At the same time, I wanted Sandy and Martha to voice their concerns.

The conversation went around in circles for quite a while as Sandy and Martha advocated helping children learn about "responsibility" by taking on classroom jobs, while I argued for spending time exploring the meaning of responsibility through students' experiences. To further explain what I had in mind, I mentioned a recent exchange with Anne on teaching "patriotism," where I had distinguished between simply telling them the words and helping students get inside their meaning.

Looking back, I see that the way our planning session was being characterized challenged the viewpoint about the importance of understanding subject matter deeply that I was trying to promote in the study group. Instead of drawing out their underlying views of teaching and comparing them with my own, I responded in ways that denigrated their points of view, dismissing them as "simply telling them the words." Understandably, Sandy felt offended. We were dealing with a real difference in values and understanding. In retrospect, I realized that neither of us was able to stay open to the other's viewpoint and probe each other's meaning. Instead of investigating each other's perspectives and genuinely reconsidering our own ideas, we each steadfastly stuck to our original outlook.

Finally, I managed to move the group to examining the transcript of the planning session. Having a concrete record allowed us to analyze what actually happened at the session. We charted the sequence of topics, examined mentoring moves Sandy and I had made, and traced their apparent impact on Megan. The teachers noted how I drew out Megan's own understanding of the concepts she was teaching, explored her sense of how children understood those ideas, and periodically asked her what sense she was making of the planning session itself in order to keep the connection between the lesson's purposes and possible learning activities at the center of our joint work.

As we analyzed the transcript, the teachers began to recognize the importance of taking substantial time to help Megan get deeply involved in the subject-matter content of the lesson. They noted that we had moved back and forth between considering big ideas about responsibility and specific learning activities to address them. At the same time, responding to Sandy's concerns, they gave me workable suggestions for how to do this more efficiently in the future. The experience also reminded teachers to make explicit to interns implicit aspects of their own teaching and helped them think about how to help their interns dig more deeply into the content they were teaching. The teachers began to see that they needed to play a significant role in helping interns learn the kind of instructional planning that supports teaching for understanding. Following this session, Sandy and I continued to work with Megan on planning, and I brought more transcripts from that work to the February study group, in which Sandy attributed Megan's ultimate success in learning how to plan to our joint effort.

Applying New Understandings from the Study Group in Practice

Susan, another mentor teacher at Capitol, was also experiencing difficulties in helping her intern, Ben, learn to plan, challenges related to his understanding of content. In the same session of the Capitol study group described above, Susan had identified a new focus for her mentoring work by contrasting her observations of Ben's struggles in planning with her own practice of thoroughly researching the ideas in a new unit before planning it:

> If they fully get into it [the content of the lesson] and understand and do a little exploring, then it's going to better prepare them not only for their lesson but the reactions of their children—as Ben found out in his lesson. He was not prepared for the wide range of responses that the children gave, so he didn't know where to go because he hadn't explored it enough.
> . . . When I'm doing a new unit or a new theme, I fully research it—get into the understanding of the whole concept. If that's what we can teach them during their intern year, even if it's only in one subject area, it's going to teach them the process. (Study Group Transcript, January 22, 1999)

A few days later, Susan initiated a planning series with Ben to help him prepare for a unit on transportation for his upcoming lead teaching in their kindergarten classroom. Influenced by the study group session on teaching planning, she came to see her task as helping Ben understand the *process* of planning an integrated thematic unit.

After helping Ben map out the conceptual content of the unit and consider what kindergartners were likely to find accessible or difficult, Susan sought me out to suggest that Ben delay his lead teaching by a week or two to thoroughly plan his unit and other lessons. I was delighted by Susan's initiative and concurred with her judgment. I think that participating in the study group had helped Susan identify with her teacher educator role. Ben ended up conducting a very successful unit, several parts of which I videotaped, including a postteaching conversation between Ben and Susan, which I brought to the March study group at Capitol.

Developing the Curriculum for Learning to Teach at Capitol

Susan's work with Ben served as the focus for the March study group session. We studied clips from a videotape of their coplanning sessions, then looked at a tape of Ben's teaching and Susan's debriefing conversation with him after the lesson. Martha commented that it was awfully late in the year for Ben to be developing some of the understandings revealed in these artifacts: "There's something that needs to start way back in the fall."

The group decided to spend its last two sessions of the year outlining what mentors could do earlier in the year to introduce interns to the tasks of teaching they would be expected to perform later in the year. When the study group began to articulate those plans at its next session, Susan shared her insight about the need to combine talk and modeling:

> I'm thinking of what we do with our kids . . . model . . . model . . . model . . . and it dawned on me when I sat down with Ben. . . . He's never seen me do a lesson plan like that because we're talking it through and it's all up here . . . and even though we're talking about it that's not what we write in the plan book. I know all the pieces so I don't write them down. . . . So it's no wonder when I was asking him to do that and put it down on paper, he really didn't have a clue because that's not what we do in our plan book. (Study Group Transcript, March 25, 1999)

The study group completed its work for the year by drafting a "Curriculum for Learning to Teach at Capitol," which detailed expectations for themselves, their interns, and me and included numerous details about using their own practice as a context for interns' learning through various kinds of modeling and thinking out loud. One of the first examples of that was a reminder they made to themselves to model in-depth planning for instruction early in the coming year.

By midpoint of the following year, Capitol teachers were thinking of their teacher education work in an increasingly expansive way and were ready to have their work together stand as a solid example of the kind of impact teacher study groups could have on transforming schools into settings conducive to learning to teach. So I brought materials from our work on stretching a particular highly capable intern to the cross-school liaison study group.

Back to the Present: The Cross-School Liaison Study Group Examines My Leadership of a Capitol Study Group Session

The plan for the cross-school liaison study group session was designed to use our experience at Capitol to help mentor teachers and university liaisons from other Team One schools investigate the practice of leading mentor teacher study groups. While among our team staff we had a few individuals who were able to provide study group leadership, we could not mount study groups in all of our schools. That led us to the cross-school liaison study group strategy and the hope that we could nurture the development of teacher leaders through the activities of the study group.

Yet, was this the right time to reach for this new level of leadership on the part of mentor teachers? Was this reasonable to ask of teachers who already had full-time jobs teaching children and mentoring interns? The design of our program with its extended practicum experiences placed huge responsibilities on the shoulders of mentor teachers. We, in turn, were challenged to provide what support we could to help them become the teacher educators the program envisioned. The activities of this afternoon's study-group session would again test this strategy.

To get those assembled to understand this work, Sharon describes how the rest of the session would proceed. As she explains, we would begin by viewing a five-minute video clip from the intern's lesson, which was the focus of the study group session at Capitol. Next, she and Pat Norman, her session coleader, would interview me in front of the group to get a sense of how I thought about the purposes for the study group session at Capitol and what I did to prepare for it. After that we would watch three short clips showing conversation in the study group and discuss them in the group, with the two Capitol teachers and me remaining silent. Finally, those of us insiders who were at the Capitol session would be invited to comment. Sharon brings the interview portion of our session to a close with the following comments:

> We are calling this a study group, and David calls his activity a study group, too. In a study group, everybody's a learner. So I really want to underscore that issue—we're all trying to get smarter about how to do this together. Even if David takes responsibility to assemble the materials and think about the conversation, it's really all of us trying to figure out how to move mentor's practice and intern's teaching forward. I think that's an important stance to think about—how you even create that sort of culture or receptivity so people can come together to study something and to get smarter about how to do it.

We've reached the part of the meeting where my Capitol colleagues and I are supposed to listen silently while the teacher and university liaisons examine a videotape of one study group session, watch the moves I made and the responses they evoked, and identify dilemmas and challenges in leading such a group. The particular session we were studying involved a discussion about a math unit from the Investigations curriculum taught by a particularly capable intern, Laura, over a two-week period. This fifth-grade unit focused on gathering and interpreting data.

In preparing and organizing artifacts for the Capitol study group, I had decided to focus on the fit between the mathematical purposes of the lesson as stated in the teachers' guide and the actual purposes of the lesson as enacted by the intern and her students as a way to stretch this competent intern. We had begun the session by studying the curriculum materials and identifying what we understood as the purposes of the lesson. Then we observed and discussed three video clips of the intern teaching the lesson. I invited teachers to think about Laura's work with the following questions: "So, what are you noticing so far in relation to what Laura's doing and what we talked about before? . . . What is she able to do, what is she not being able to do?" Back at the university in the cross-school liaison study group, participants are now retracing those same steps, in somewhat briefer form, and responding to Sharon's invitation to notice how I framed the discussion and how it unfolds. The first three respondents jump in as follows:

> *Arlene [university liaison]:* I liked the way David framed it in terms of looking at it through an intern's eyes. I think we know that interns have trouble taking a prepared unit and really finding what the goal of that lesson is because that's something that we all have been working with our interns with, so that for me, hearing him say that helped me. . . .
>
> *Wendell [mentor teacher]:* I'm using Connected Math, which is sort of a sixth-grade version of Investigations but sometimes the mathematical nugget is stated quite explicitly in the teacher's manual and even so it's hard for the interns to make sense of it, in light of all of the things that they have to have the kids do. . . . And that's the thing I struggle with with my intern. She can parrot what's in the text and she can read that little nugget of information but she has a really tough time then making it explicit for the kids and, you know, opening it up for them, so that they then can own it.
>
> *Kathy [mentor teacher]:* Yeah, I thought David was trying to get the teachers to get inside the content, and I expect he did that so then they would better . . . it would be easier for them to see that the intern wasn't really inside the content, just from the questions you asked.

At that point, Pat Norman proposes an alternative way of framing my opening move in the Capitol study group as a problem of practice that I was in the middle of with Laura's collaborating teacher: "Trying to help this pretty accomplished intern make that next step." Instead of directing their attention to the specific issue I had identified ahead of time—whether or not Laura's lesson fulfilled the intentions of the Investigations unit plan— Pat proposes starting with a more general invitation to study group colleagues to consider together what approaches we might take.

Sharon chimes in with an alternative way of phrasing the idea: "We are puzzled about how to do this. Help us think about this together." As I hear these suggestions, I realize that by engaging teachers in co-constructing our approach, I may have been better able to build on their understandings of the situation and may have avoided my later efforts to redirect them toward my initial purpose. I experience that familiar feeling from past occasions of sharing my work, both as a classroom teacher and as a teacher educator, compounded of equal parts of "Why didn't I think of that?" and "That's the benefit of getting others' perspectives on my work." I jot down their ideas on my pad to remind myself to try that move in the future.

Turning to another video clip from the Capitol study group session, Pat directs us to pay attention to the "contributions of the collaborating teachers" and "what you notice David doing to facilitate or guide that conversation." In this clip, two Capitol teachers comment on the intern's introduction of the lesson in which she told students they would be gathering data and acting like researchers. The Capitol teachers wonder aloud, based on experience with their own students, how well the intern's students would understand those ideas. On the videotape, I jump in at that point, calling attention to the connection to the lesson purposes, and I ask the group how well they think the kids would "really be able to get a sense of the unit from that." I continue with my own observation about what Laura is doing in introducing her lesson:

> It was a very comfortable delivery, but to me it didn't do a very clear job of saying what was going to happen today and what pieces are going to follow from what. It felt like sort of an off-the-cuff explanation but it wasn't necessarily thought through in terms of a step-by-step layout that would be clear to understand.

As I am speaking, I apparently realize that my comments have introduced a more critical tone to the analysis of Laura's lesson. I know how protective the teachers often feel about their interns. You can hear, in the somewhat apologetic tone of my subsequent remarks, how I am trying to walk a tightrope about this issue as I hasten to explain myself:

> I should preface this by saying I'm deliberately being picky here. I mean she did this in November, and this was a magnificent performance for an intern in November. In fact it was so magnificent that we can use it as a good example of what we want interns to be working toward now. So that I think all of us were really pleased to see this then, and I'm sort of using it to get us to think about taking her to the next level. So that's why I'm sort of being more critical than I might otherwise be.

Back in the cross-school liaison study group, Pat pauses the videotape, and one of the veteran collaborating teachers comments on my move from the perspective of her own experience in a teacher study group at Averill Elementary School:

> *Kathy Beasley:* It seemed to me that it's pretty risky, I mean it would be especially in our study group, to really take someone's practice and critique it, which was what David was really asking them to do. And they were being, to me, very careful with her, very gentle. David then stepped in and said, "Let me explain the norms here. I want to make it clear, I really respect this practice." But then he said, "Come on, it's OK, we can think critically about this." I thought that was his major contribution.

Pat Norman then calls attention to a different dimension of my role, pointing to the question I had used to open the discussion, "What are you noticing about Laura, about what she's doing, and in relation to what we talked about?" Pat notes that this amounts really to two different questions, one open-ended and inviting the teachers' consideration of what they think might be worth talking about, and one more focused about what had been discussed previously in relation to the lesson purposes. Pat goes on to describe my role as enacting a sort of dance between these intentions as I try to help teachers get inside the materials but also move them toward the purposes I had identified ahead of time as worth pursuing.

Pat's thought spurs another veteran Averill teacher, Jane Boyd, now retired and working as a university liaison, to continue thinking about my efforts to get teachers to probe Laura's teaching more critically, as opposed to allowing a more open-ended entry into the materials. She recalls the opening moments of the Capitol study group discussion in which teachers wondered whether or not kids understood ideas like "data" or "researcher." Jane notes that the Capitol mentor teachers were asking genuine questions, probing what children might or might not have understood about the topic. In other words, she points out that from the start the Capitol mentor teachers are not simply making uncritical positive comments about the intern's role.

Sharon builds on Jane's idea, linking it more directly to the purposes I had set out to achieve with the study group:

> Yes, and actually, Jane, . . . what you made me think is that that is precisely what David wanted them to talk about. It is a potential bridge to "what are kids making of this?" It actually is opening the door to the very subject that he was hoping to get to. . . "What are the kids getting out of this? . . . Do they understand the language? Do they know where we're headed?" so that's helpful.

Kathy Beasley continues the idea:

> I'm really wondering, now that you brought that up, Jane: There were a lot of questions about "What does research mean," "What is evidence?" When people were asking that, I was thinking well, that really doesn't matter that they understand that. . . . I mean what's complicated about what that intern did, I keep having the sense she didn't really understand the content that she was trying to teach, and maybe that would have led to that discussion.

Jane's comment had sparked this series of interchanges, giving all of us a new vantage point for looking at the study group session and the complexities of leading it. I realized that at the time of the Capitol study group session, I had not heard the potential in teachers' initial observations about the lesson and had instead been set on moving them toward my predetermined agenda of how well Laura had enacted the stated purposes of the lesson. I was suddenly reminded of my counsel to interns about leading discussions with their students, and Susan's comments about Ben's lack of subject-matter preparation and how that limited what he was able to hear in the children's comments. Here I had tripped over the same issue in leading the Capitol mentor study group; I had not sufficiently prepared myself to anticipate different points of access the teachers might find in the materials and how those might connect to my interest in examining Laura's success in enacting the lesson purposes.

At this point, Sharon invites the group to consider what move I might have made to pick up on Jane's idea. Kathy Beasley, recalling her earlier work with Sharon at Averill (see chapter 7), suggests that I might have said, "Tell me more about what you mean by, 'they don't understand research.'" Such a comment would have enabled me to draw teachers out on their sense of the relationship between eliciting students' understandings and teaching for understanding. It might have also offered a direct bridge to questions about the stated and enacted purposes of the lesson, the topic I had wanted to discuss. Sharon summarizes these ideas, noting that Kathy's suggestion is "a chance to open the door on what is it the kids are getting, which is a question that we're trying to get at anyway. And it builds already on the fact that teachers have begun to work on that problem."

The conversation continues in the cross-school liaison study group that afternoon, as we view additional segments of the study group videotape. My Capitol colleagues and I later have a chance to comment on some of the issues raised by others. I'm still busy digesting Jane's idea and the discussion surrounding it. It has brought me face-to-face again with a familiar but often hazardous dimension of this kind of inquiry-oriented work built upon the collaborative study of artifacts and guided by visions of ambitious teaching and mentoring. How do I stay balanced in the dance to which Pat Norman had called attention, between planning and pursuing productive analytic tasks around records of practice and also staying open and responsive to the sense that participants make of those experiences? This is the same dance I try to help my interns enact in their classrooms with elementary school learners. It seemed to me that, in this case, I hadn't anticipated and didn't pick up on the connection between noticing signs of children's understanding and addressing the lesson's mathematical purposes. I didn't notice how that emergent idea about children's understanding actually was an inherent purpose of the lesson and didn't anticipate how I might also have used that as a bridge to ideas about collecting and analyzing data.

Thinking about how hard I had struggled to balance these demands in leading the study group, despite several years' experience with various kinds of study group settings, I recognized the complexity and challenge of our efforts to scale up our supports for mentor teacher development.[4] At the same time, on this particular afternoon, I was pleased that by turning this imperfect but decent experience into artifacts for our teacher liaisons to examine, and by building on each others' ideas as we studied them together, we had all pushed our understanding of the work a bit deeper and made doing it a bit more imaginable. Twenty-five people had been immersed in making collective sense of one multilayered episode of mentor teacher development in the service of helping novices learn to teach for understanding. Next month we would hear about local, school-based efforts to launch a similar study group. What else had individuals picked up on from our session? Perhaps a few were focused on the intern's teaching and may have had their thoughts jostled about teaching mathematics. Others may have gained new ideas about talking with their interns after teaching. Some were no doubt caught up by the images of participating in a mentor teacher study group. We would find out the next month how many found a way to bring these ideas to their work with students, interns, and mentor colleagues.

Conclusion: The Challenges and Dilemmas of Scaling Up

If large-scale teacher education is to meet the demands of preparing significant numbers of teacher candidates to reach ambitious standards of teaching for understanding, scaling up strategies for supporting ambitious mentoring will be necessary. This account affords a number of lessons that can contribute to that challenge.

Focusing on the Third Triangle

Given our limited resources for mentor teacher development, we chose to focus our attention on a strategy designed to engage experienced mentor teachers in leading their colleagues in mentor development activities. By pairing each of these teachers with a university colleague—usually a graduate student or a retired teacher playing the "university liaison" role—we hoped to extend our influence in mentor development to reach more teachers. While the challenges associated with this strategy are significant, as evident in the foregoing account, we believe it is still worthwhile, particularly if coupled with attention to the issues below.

Building Capacity

The insights that contributed to our enlarged understanding in the cross-school liaison study group came from many directions and represented a systematic effort to build school-based teacher education capacity going back over a decade. That effort had placed these players together in one room on this particular day. Jane Boyd and Kathy Beasley, who played important roles in this study group session, had been among the original participants in Sharon's TEC at Averill Elementary School. Jane had since retired from teaching and become a university liaison recruited by Team One. Pat Norman, a graduate student and experienced liaison, had taken a practicum course on mentoring with Sharon and conducted her own mentor teacher study group for the previous two years. Team One was also organized to support the work of graduate students who were serving as university liaisons working with interns in schools. We conducted a weekly study group to help them develop mentoring practices. Such veterans in the group were a substantial resource that prompted our collective thinking at key points. Team One played a role in both recruiting and developing these individuals over a significant time period.

Designing a Curriculum and Materials for Mentor Teacher Development

Attending to all of the tasks of designing and conducting mentor development activities is time-consuming and beyond the scope of reasonable expectations for mentor teachers who are already busy with many other responsibilities. Our strategy was based on focusing resources in particular places, such as the work that Pat Norman and I did with interns and mentors in the schools where we worked. We deliberately produced videotapes and transcripts from that work to share with other schools as they ventured into launching mentor study groups. Mentor groups could view tapes of interns teaching and of subsequent debriefing conversations to study the practice of talking with interns about their teaching. We also generated and shared video materials around coplanning with interns. Over time, we came to identify key components of a curriculum for mentor development, exemplified in the preceding account of the study group at Capitol Elementary School. We *centered our work on key practices of mentoring*—coplanning with interns; coteaching; observing and debriefing their teaching. We saw this work not as a matter of "training" mentors to use particular strategies but as *joint inquiry*—aimed at making sense of interns' experiences and our actions as mentors and *organized around records of practice*—interns' plans, videotapes, and transcripts of teaching and debriefing. Helping mentor teachers develop this kind of practice and become school-based teacher educators also requires *creating, facilitating, and sustaining opportunities for productive discourse* about the practice.

Understanding the Pedagogical Challenges
of Leading Mentor Study Groups

Study groups can provide a powerful setting for developing the kind of inquiry-oriented mentoring practices we were seeking. However, as my account of the Capitol study group's work on Laura's math lesson illustrates, leading study groups is challenging work. Here, I had to understand the pedagogical content across all levels of the triangle graphic introduced earlier. I had to recognize the implications of the Investigations math curriculum in assessing Laura's teaching and in designing a focus for the study-group session. I needed to be prepared to recognize that content in the responses of mentors reviewing Laura's teaching. I also needed to understand mentoring to facilitate our consideration of mentoring moves made by Laura's mentor teacher. Finally, I needed to balance my own judgment about the purpose of our work together with the emergent interests and understandings of study group members and to recognize and capitalize on potential connections. While this seems like a daunting agenda, we also saw that even when I did not fully overcome these challenges our efforts were productive. Like learning to teach well, the practices associated with mentor teacher development take time, ongoing study, and hard work.

10

Values and the Big University Education School

Joseph Featherstone

Team One's efforts to build a strong program rooted in the values of democratic education were supported and bounded by the realities of teacher education in a large university, key institutional contexts, and the changing national conversation on teacher education. We explained in chapter 1 how a historical moment and a reform administration at the Michigan State University College of Education launched our work and supported many of our early initiatives. Here we want to give two examples of how the context of teacher education in a large university limited us and other teams in the program in ways that are instructive for the more general reform of teacher education.

SUBJECT MATTER AND ITS ILLS

One area where Team One and the MSU teacher education program had real difficulties was in offering teacher education candidates the rich subject-matter preparation they would need for ambitious teaching. Disciplinary knowledge and subject-matter preparation are often problems for U.S. teacher education programs. The common lore of the laity has it that teacher education courses are often weak and "Mickey Mouse," while the arts and sciences courses (in subjects such as English, math, and science) give students solid academic value. There is, alas, some truth to this; many teacher education courses are flabby and content-free. Yet veterans of decent efforts at teacher education know the value of a good course that combines pedagogy and field experience with serious disciplinary content; the classroom record of teachers who come armed only with their degrees in English and biology is mixed at best. Our Team One group believed in the strong added value of teacher education courses and well-supported field experiences; we also knew that a command of subject matter is the essential foundation for learning to teach; without it, such key matters as child study, the development of curriculum, teaching for understanding, effective multicultural practice, and even one's identity as a professional, able to make vital judgments, rest on shaky ground. Teachers must know their subjects.

We started with high hopes. Judith Lanier and the Holmes Group had chided teacher education colleges for weak subject-matter preparation and advocated real subject-matter majors for elementary as well as secondary school teachers. As dean, Lanier pushed this idea vigorously. We supported this view, though we felt that the Holmes Group was naive to put such great stress on requiring subject majors in arts and science disciplines. In the rhetoric of reform, there is the assumption that while teacher education is soft, the teaching and learning of strong content are thriving in the arts and sciences. We knew that this is not so; we were critics of both teacher education and conventional university teaching in the arts and sciences. Committed to a democratic idea of teacher education, we were also worried about the way the university rations ambitious learning and the implications of this for developing teachers committed to democratic teaching.

In most universities, teacher education is hostage to other departments when it comes to majors and the like. Subject-matter courses are owned and managed by the arts and science disciplines. Complaints about the classes in these majors abound from many sources. Elementary teacher education students complain that the majors and minors are organized along specialized lines and do not address the areas of curriculum most common in schools; thus they find it hard to make connections to pedagogical content knowledge. A very common complaint about many majors at Michigan State is that the courses are boring and the pedagogy poor and unimaginative; MSU is not unique on this score. Teacher education students believe that, with some notable exceptions, university teaching offers few models of instruction that one would want to transplant to the schools, for the simple reason that the reigning methods (e.g., the long monologue on the part of the instructor) would not work with red-blooded children or live teenagers. For those advocating "teaching for understanding," too many university courses offer just the opposite—too often on our campus we pass the open doors of classrooms in which students sit passively and do not appear to be thinking or creating.

Complaints about the content of the courses took two forms: Thoughtful colleagues noted that too many courses in the disciplinary majors lacked intellectual depth and life and any thoughtful link to the big ideas in the particular discipline. Many critics also noted how rare it was for such courses to offer students a chance to actually do the discipline. Thus, science courses too often present the results of science without any real experience of actually doing a genuine (as opposed to a rigged) experiment or tackling a real problem in the field. Math is often the memorization of algorithms. English courses are rarely invitations to experience literature as one of the arts of living. History courses often give little sense of what the work of historians is like or why history matters. It is assumed that all courses—especially those that are required or attract numbers—are equally worthy in God's eyes, or at least the eyes of the provost. Yet every day students ask their teachers to demonstrate that what they teach matters. Above all, successful teachers convey values and passion. More than practitioners of any of the other educated professions, teachers need to be able to enact the living value of the subject; to do this they need to experience passionate, liberal learning themselves.

The intellectual inadequacies and weak pedagogy of university courses were especially important problems for prospective teachers; but they were not the only problems. The standard university sequences of courses and disciplines often serve prospective K–12 teachers poorly. A problem with the university hierarchy is what one of our group calls rationing and triage: introductory courses tend to have large class sizes and often require more memorization than thinking. Middle-level courses dig a bit deeper, although often in an overly specialized way, and upper-level and seminar courses sometimes actually ask students to reflect and to play intellectually with the material, but, again, frequently in a very specialized and narrowly focused way. The ladder of learning is often arranged in a hierarchy that reserves having ideas, writing and thinking about the subject, and developing broad curiosity about it for a select few who have survived the system of triage and filtration: honors seniors and grad students in seminars. The cream is saved for the top cats. But these courses are usually highly specialized and not available to elementary teacher education students.

This ladder is not suited to the educational needs of teachers, especially K–8 teachers, who need the breadth of topic as well as the depth of rich intellectual experiences. Not being liberals arts majors, these prospective elementary and middle school teachers have trouble getting to the seminar level. The university system of rationing deep thinking and real learning to seniors and a graduate elite doesn't fit the vision of teaching and learning for all that democratic classroom teachers need.

Classroom teachers need a solid and broad education that allows them, and therefore the children they teach, to make many connections to the material they are learning, to learn to be intellectually playful and at home with the large ideas and perspectives of any discipline. The constant specialist narrowing of the university knowledge pyramid does not provide good preparation for citizenship or humane teaching. A good English teacher facing seventh graders would want to know something about the relationship of the Romantic poets to industrialization and the history of democratic revolutions, but it is rare for an English major or minor to get that kind of grounding.

University specializations are not designed to prepare the generalist intellectuals we need to teach our children. This is evident both in the secondary majors Team One dealt with in the early years, and especially in the long trail of inadequate and patchy minors for prospective elementary teachers. Both groups often got a jumble of courses, more a reflection of scheduling than substance or coherence. We on Team One had hoped that the MSU reforms would make it possible to craft what we called "the liberal arts for professionals." In the early years of the team, we experimented with versions of liberal arts curricula. In TE-301, the introductory course, we tried producing, for example, units on making an opera with sets for *Where the Wild Things Are* and a curriculum unit around Verdi's *La Traviata*. We had talked of sponsoring book clubs, science clubs, arts groups, and the like, to promote a spirit of curiosity and continuous amateur learning; but we found this hard to do with MSU undergraduates, many of whom must work while attending our demanding program. Still, we had taken to heart the old progressive, democratic vision of teachers educated to make ambitious culture together with their students and sought to bring this spirit into our thinking about subject matter. We wanted our students to have ideas and to engage in serious intellectual play. We also hoped that in teacher education, at least, the spirit and content of our subject-matter courses would blend a concern with pedagogy and children's learning and a democratic commitment to knowledge and understanding for all. First graders need a discussion of *Frog and Toad* that looks and sounds more like a great discussion in a good university seminar than a lecture in a huge hall. Eighth graders need an approach to science that has them actively figuring things out. In projects such as sampling drinking water or investigating radon in their basements, they would get access to the real thing, science itself.

This grand vision remained far from reality. It was not uncommon for our students to confess that teacher education was the first MSU class in which discussion was the norm and they were actually required to write, or even to think, and in some cases attend class regularly. For a while, one member of our group made himself unpopular by proposing in many meetings that teacher education only accept course credit for our students from university departments who agreed to the following:

1. Class size is under twenty-five (our rule in our teacher education classes).
2. The teaching is such that students take part in real discussions.
3. Students write papers and get considerable feedback on them and have opportunities to rewrite.
4. The course itself grapples in some broad way with the large ideas of the discipline, connecting specialized content to some broad theme or issue or big idea.
5. Students at some point get to actually "do" the subject in some intellectually respectable form.
6. Students would end the class able to say something personal and passionate about why the subject mattered. They would have a response to the question, "So what?"

Such ideas went nowhere. Unfortunately, it was not even possible to insist on a real major for all education students. Although secondary students continued to have disciplinary majors, the majors and minors of prospective K–8 teachers remain of questionable value at MSU, as in many other universities. And there was no general reform of teaching and learning in the arts and sciences toward more ambitious learning and teaching and intellectual fare that was suitable for the combination of depth and breadth that all teachers, K–12, need. (Recently the Carnegie-sponsored Teachers for a New Era has created a dialogue between teacher education and some arts and sciences faculty on the MSU and other campuses, but the problems we point to persist.)

Still, we did see much good work in the area of subject matter over a ten-year period. Such work has many lessons for the reform of teacher education in the future. The math courses that prospective elementary teachers must take now map well onto the K–8 curriculum; many sections also integrate pedagogy and learning math with an approach that emphasizes children's thinking. We saw the development of a first-rate science course that had our students actually doing science and thinking like scientists while learning the science they will one day teach. The English department, which had a long tradition of commitment to teacher education, and a staff of people experienced in such work, continued to give many of our students a first-rate background in literature, combined with good ideas about how to create curriculum with young people.

Within our own teacher education courses, the impasse over the quality of subject-matter preparation led by default to much imaginative work. TE-301, the introductory course for juniors, was initially all about child study, with a bit of literacy thrown in; as it evolved, child study remained central, but it also turned into a course where students read first-rate children's literature (Lionni's *Frederick*, Burnett's *The Secret Garden*, Curtis's *Bud, Not Buddy*) in real depth, and used Vivian Paley's teaching in *The Girl With the Brown Crayon* as a model for creating curriculum units that would elicit children's thinking about literature and build on it in imaginative ways. Many of the TE-301 students tried out lessons they designed with the children they were studying, and they reported on the results. In effect, we were using the focus on children's thinking and the work on literature units to give our own MSU students an experience in the liberal arts for professionals, a broad and imaginative approach to literature as one of the arts of living and learning, and not just a specialized university subject. More than that, the course used these and similar books to give students an idea of how to fuse images of ambitious learning with teaching across the lines of race, class, and culture. Teacher education at Michigan State also put in place a good children's literature course that all our students took, deepening their capacity to do ambitious teaching in literacy.

In the courses for our seniors, explicitly designed to combine disciplinary content with pedagogy, there was much outstanding work. Several faculty members in science education designed courses that got our students doing science as well as investigating imaginative science curriculum. Similarly, in their math course, prospective teachers learned math through problem solving and then planned and facilitated discussions of math problems with small groups of children. Increasingly, the intern-year courses turned toward deeper subject-matter knowledge and the challenge of how to actually translate such knowledge into children's learning. Team One invested substantial time and thought in designing ways to support university teachers in combining subject matter depth with work in the field on the actual practice of teaching.

The result was that our interns did a lot of wonderful work. Evidence of this could be found in the portfolios our graduating interns presented every year. Scattered around a huge room, sitting at tables with parents and grandparents, brothers and sisters, teachers from their schools, and members of Team One, they often presented curriculum units that had real intellectual depth, as well as playfulness and imagination. Many were interdisciplinary. They reminded us of how far we had come but also, in their unevenness, of how much work remained in the area of subject-matter knowledge, pedagogy, and child study. If we had a general recommendation to make on this score, it would be in the direction of thinking of subject matter as liberal arts for professionals, a democratized version of the old liberal arts ideal. We would want more courses that rescue education students from the often deadly impact of university teaching, the scattershot of courses in majors, and from the limitations and triage of narrow university specialties. We would want students to encounter a system that sent the democratic signal that rich knowledge—culture-making—is for all, not only for the privileged. We would try to link persuasive experiences in liberal learning to teaching across lines of race, class, and culture. In our ideal university, education school faculty and committed arts and science faculty would together find ways to promote subject-matter teaching that would connect children and education students to the arts and to large questions of living and passionate learning. We would try to give our students a version of the education Lucy Sprague Mitchell imagined for her Bank Street students: an education that would help them become practical intellectuals who are at once artists, scientists, and activists.

FROM PLURAL VALUES TO MONOCULTURE

A second challenge to the democratic hopes of the team arose from teacher education's place in a research one university, and the room at MSU—in terms of ideas, imagination, and resources—for a truly ambitious version of teacher education grounded in practice in schools. We began with a future that looked bright; the Holmes Group had argued for restoring teacher preparation to a central place in the university. Strangely, in American universities teacher education tends to be a low-status cash cow, derided by professors of higher status disciplines and yet exploited by university administrators who can grant cheap degrees to students batch-processed in huge classes prior to poorly supervised student teaching placements. Paradoxically, teacher education may fare better in some lower-status universities, where at least it is seen to serve local communities with supplies of teachers. In the biggest and most prestigious research universities in the United States, as Harry Judge (1982) pointed out in a report that greatly influenced the Holmes Group, as well as Team One, the priority given to research results in a distancing of prestigious faculty and resources from schools and practice. The professional school aspect of teacher education—the clinical base in practice, the actual teaching of real children in actual schools—tends to be weakly supported in such places; few resources exist for developing schools; and faculty who take part in teacher education tend to be marginal figures. In such places, top honors and resources go to the notables of a research faculty, the production of research, and the garnering of grants. Ambitious new junior faculty and bright graduate students are advised to stay away from teacher preparation, to work on research grants instead of teaching in the certification program. Careers are shaped by these values.

Staffed with graduate students, temporary and part-time faculty, and with few resources to develop field placements, U.S. teacher certification programs are the Cinderellas of the American university. Ideas and money are rarely spent on coordinating what is learned on campus and what gets learned in schools. Even educational research done in such places is often remote from the concerns of working teachers and research about schools may be discouraged unless it is part of some large grant. The Team One group argued that a good teacher education program should be an integrated and cumulative series of experiences. Our goal was to educate "the whole student" in the same fashion that a good school aims at the whole child. Our metaphor for the team—that it should operate like a small school—guided our thinking. And the "school" would aim above all at shaping practitioners. All these concepts are harder to pull off in an institution where a monoculture of diverse research specialties calls the shots. The research monoculture of subspecialties tends to drive out the plural values that are needed for a rich and practice-oriented program. We of course knew that top-flight researchers can and do work in and support teacher education. Good research is vital to the existence of universities and plays a key role in any decent teacher education program. But any monoculture is in the long run damaging to local ecology, either in a forest or a college of education.

Our point is simply this: To sustain a rich and complex teacher education program, a college of education has to open itself deliberately to plural values, especially the necessarily uncertain and problematic values of practice. The reign of current ideals of research in big universities today, as in Harry Judge's time, makes it hard to cultivate the values a teacher education program grounded in practice needs. Without leadership that consciously aims for a (to switch metaphors) mixed economy of values, the big university will slip into the default research mode that, left to its own momentum, usually marginalizes and colonizes teacher education programs. Early in the last century, John Dewey (1904/1964) decried the dualism between theory and practice, the academic and the practical, thinking and doing. His critique rings true today.

This was not the case at Michigan State where, in the 1970s and 1980s, Lanier and strong faculty allies like Lee Shulman had reinvigorated what once was largely a plain vanilla teacher education program. When Lanier started as dean, MSU's standard certification program had huge class sizes, marginal faculty, and limited involvement with schools. By the late 1980s, Lanier and her colleagues had attracted first-rate faculty with national research reputations and set up institutes to do research on teaching and teacher education. She had also reduced class sizes and moved faculty notables into teaching roles in the certification program. The Holmes Group suggested better ways to connect with the field through heavily supported year-round internships in schools and a cluster of ambitious notions that crystallized around plans for professional development schools. (If all this keeps up, one dean from another college once complained to Lanier, educating a teacher will become as expensive as educating an engineer.) And, speaking of democracy, the new program planned to abolish the dual tracks in the existing setup, which had a cluster of specialty shops on the one hand, and a large standard program on the other. Every teacher education student at MSU was now going to get what a few used to receive. The parallel with detracking a large urban high school in the interests of giving every student an ambitious education was never far from the minds of Team One members. We wondered whether the resources, energy, and vision would last long enough to actually enact ambitious democracy. But we could be sure for a while of one thing: Any decisions about the teacher education program would be made by a group that included the notables from the teams. Lanier had found a way to prevent the colonization of teacher education by research specialties, while also furthering rich dialogue on teaching and learning among experts. (Research was flourishing in the MSU College of Education, but it nourished and was nourished by the teacher education program instead of pushing it aside.)

The first Holmes Group report, *Tomorrow's Teachers* (1986), had proposed more rigorous course work for prospective teachers, more careful cultivation of the field, and a teacher education program based on research. The report's notion of such research was vague, with a technocratic slant: Research would somehow reveal the truth, and universities would then impart the truth to teacher education and the schools. However, another more subtle, complex, and sophisticated view of research in relation to teacher education and schools was also emerging. Dean Lanier had already, in the 1980s, used the carrot of new research money to lure crack faculty toward research that spoke directly to teaching and teacher education. This was part of a significant turn toward a new mix of practice and theory and a re-emergence of the clinical throughout the MSU department of teacher education. The turn toward practice is best symbolized, perhaps, by the work in math teaching of Deborah Ball and Magdalene Lampert, two extraordinary MSU professors who arranged to divide their teaching time between university classes and elementary school classrooms. Both were gifted teachers in both settings. (See Lampert [2001] for perhaps the best book on the art of teaching for understanding ever written.) Deborah Ball and her wonderful classroom pedagogy as she taught math to third graders—available to MSU staff on videos and hypermedia—became a powerful symbol not only of teaching for understanding, but also of the new and vital connection of the college of education to schools and practice. Graduate students and faculty notables were spending more time working in schools, teaching children, and studying actual practice. MSU's current justifiable reputation as a place that attracts scholars richly engaged with schools and teaching practice emerged out of this period.

The second Holmes Group report, *Tomorrow's Schools* (1990), carried the Holmes vision even farther in the direction of a reconnection with practice, calling for long-term partnerships between universities and schools. (I was one of the authors of *Tomorrow's Schools.*) Teachers and principals were to become significant figures in teacher education. Schools were communities, the report insisted; a goal of teacher education was that they were to be democratic places in which all children learned. The kind of ambitious education historically reserved for the privileged was now to become the possession of every child. The report is notable for its appeal to democracy and its reserve in making any sweeping claims on behalf of research and the "science" of education. A careful reader would sense that research would be more of an ongoing process of reflection and scrutiny, offering fresh evidence and promoting experiment and dialogue in the new order of teacher education. Research would be vitally important, but less as the technocratic arbiter of truth, or the decider of best practice, and more as an ongoing source of good new evidence, fruitful insights, experiments, and new questions—research in the setting of the professional development school and a university in tune with practice would become a dialogue among practitioners, researchers, and teacher educators. Teaching as a craft needing the judgment of well-educated practitioners moved to the center of the report's essentially clinical vision of professional development schools. (For a very different and more critical analysis of the sharp, contrasting rhetoric of technocracy and democracy in the two Holmes reports, see Labaree, 1992.)

These two somewhat opposed visions of the relationship of research to teacher education flowed together in a climate of abundance, experiment, and easy funding. Lanier sometimes talked (particularly to funding sources) as though research could quickly discover new and better ways of teaching; she also operated in practice as though research itself was part of a complex ecology feeding a vital school of education. The analogy between professional development schools and teaching hospitals sometimes focused on the potential yields from research analogous to medical breakthroughs—like a polio vaccine—other times, the analogy sounded much more realistic and muted, more like a celebration of the capacity of well-trained veteran doctors to keep reviewing new evidence to hone their clinical skills in teaching hospitals and pass them on to novices. The unlikely promise of short-term research miracles was mixed in with the sensible vision of research for the long haul as a kind of ongoing, intimate and friendly research and development for the schools, continuous dialogue and interrogation in the interests of helping teaching practice and teacher educators grow more thoughtful and smart together.

An interesting mix emerged. On the one hand, there was a celebration of crack research, and Lanier's legendary skill at luring brilliant researchers like David Cohen to Michigan State University's rising star. On the other hand, the new prestige and interest in the teacher preparation program also brought to MSU faculty eager to mix it up with a new version of teacher education, with closer and more vital links to practice and the field. When new outside grants and some university support made the creation of professional development schools possible—at the same time that a new three-year, field-based teacher education program was adopted—a fresh vision emerged, notable for two things. The first thing was the deliberately plural set of values guiding the enterprise: Research was vital, but now alongside it stood the programmatic values of a professional school and the domain of school practice. Lanier often expressed this plural vision in the old land-grant terms of Michigan State itself: the familiar trinity of research, teaching, and service. Now, however, in both the faculty reward system and in new appointments, the vision took on a new life. Teaching (both in the certification program and in the schools) was going to be highly honored, but so was research and service, including the huge work of connecting to schools and sustaining the connection. Research never lost its sway, but the mix with other values opened resources and spaces for a new field-based teacher education program. Faculty evaluation and reward systems were jiggled a bit to send a more plural set of signals about what kind of work got honored. The institution was finding ways to reward different kinds of interests and skills and attract the mix of talent the plural vision demanded.

We on Team One were, by background and experience, unhappy with the monoculture of research in U.S. education schools. We shared Harry Judge's condemnation of the way the monoculture in prestigious universities had distanced them from certification programs and the day-to-day problems of teaching and learning. As products of progressive, democratic school reforms, we were taken with the analogies between creating good schools and establishing a first-rate teacher education program. A good teacher education program would be an entire community, like a school, and its parts—the sequence of courses and experiences—would fit together to make a whole. Its leaders would be able to make decisions shaping the program; it would not be a poor colony run from afar by research faculty or administrators. The reconnection with practice and the field was essential. We were eager to take part in a teacher education program with a renewed connection to practice and the clinical, in which teachers would play an important role. We took for granted that the plural values launching our work would remain in place. Lanier's leadership and the strong institutional ethos of the teacher education department would be the nest for a new fledgling version of teacher education.

Lanier's canny version of the plural vision touted crack research, but was also careful to tilt the institution toward research that spoke to teaching and practice. It encouraged work in school classrooms that required time to develop and might not bear immediate published fruit. Research still dominated the rewards and rating systems of the College of Education, but the new plural vision opened up many symbolic cracks in the pavement. It made it possible to hire scholars who were interested in grappling for long periods of time with the untidy realities of teaching and learning in schools, and who actually wanted to engage in the difficult long-term and continuous practice of reinventing teacher education. These plural values made it possible to staff the department with many different kinds of people: from pure and disinterested researchers, to the entrepreneurs and jungle fighters who got the big grants, to people who ate and breathed teacher education and cared passionately about working directly with teachers and schools. Graduate students and faculty began to honeycomb the schools we worked with, especially but not exclusively the schools that got professional development school status. Even the old land-grant chestnut of "service" got a fresh lift as the administration and the teams found shrewd ways to sanction the large amount of coordination and effort involved in developing teachers and meshing teacher education with schools. Faculty notables led the teams and spoke for them. The certification program and its interests as a whole were well-served and powerfully represented in the councils and committees.

Today we believe passionately that Lanier's vision of plural values makes far more sense for teacher education than the standard big university monoculture of research. Lanier saw no contradiction between promoting crack research and first-rate teacher education, but she recognized that they inhabit different worlds and march to different music. Top-flight researchers can and do become gifted practitioners, but when they do, they are shifting roles. Research as a primary value is problematic for teacher education, however. First, teacher education is a long-term enterprise, and the ideas and focus of cutting edge research in education tend to be time-bound, if not faddish. If you look at what's hot in one research decade and then skip ahead ten years, you will see how random and noncumulative education research tends to be—even though the schools' problems do not really change all that much. Even the education disciplines are different from one decade to the next; many of the hot new specializations shaping today's grant strategies and careers have a short life. Second, the real value of research in education is as a long-term process of evidence-gathering, thought, and scrutiny, rather than the search for quick fixes and ready answers. Education is a complex affair; understanding it requires insights from many disciplines. The analogy of a polio vaccine in medicine seems far-fetched in education, where the variables are often too many, and the contexts too varied, to draw simple scientific conclusions. A book like Lampert's will help teachers and scholars for generations, because it informs the reader of a whole world of thought and possibility and invites her to experiment with its insights. It opens new experience and new possibilities. The medical analogy that may come close is the development and refinement of practice: ways to improve patient care and the ability of doctors to learn and care for their patients.

The MSU experience shows how a rich climate of research invigorates a teacher-preparation program. Teacher education in the United States (often characterized by its critics as awash in faddish progressive nostrums) is, in fact, starved for ideas, thoughtful conversation, and good thinking actually related to practice. For a time, the corridors of Erickson Hall hummed with conversations that bounced back and forth from research to actual classrooms, from theory to Monday's class. The early days of professional development schools and research aimed at practice showed how research in the setting of a teacher education program partnered with schools can play an immensely fertile role in catalyzing ideas, energy, and people in classrooms. The researchers were in constant dialogue with the practitioners in schools and the teacher education program. Many played the role of both researcher and practitioner. A program with researchers in schools that are also sites for teacher education gains synergistic energy. People and resources and networks begin to overlap, creating new villagelike webs of connections. More people on both sides of the school/university divide become amphibious, at home in both worlds. Work in one area seasons work in another. Graduate students, professors, teachers, and principals begin to act together like colleagues in ways that saturate the work of the program and enrich it.

This did not happen in all of MSU's professional development schools (some were flops), but it was certainly true of the work that Team One and the staff at the Averill School in Lansing did together. (The work at Holt High School was also extraordinary and richly suggestive of what true university-school partnerships accomplish.) Averill was the jewel in Team One's crown, the complete expression of a vision of field-based teacher education that flowed from plural values.

A good teacher education program needs to maintain its identity and values as a professional school, with influential faculty able to shape a program that is a series of educative field and academic experiences that build cumulatively, not just an anthology of separate courses. First-rate teacher education requires a diverse ecology. Where specialist research reigns as a monoculture, balkanization of the teacher education program is a constant threat. In the first years of Team One, MSU maintained a balanced ecology, a broad outlook, and a successful mixed economy, but the enterprise of teacher education became more marginal over the decade or so of Team One's lifespan (it was merged with another team in 2005). Those leading the teams in the teacher education program felt marginal. Support for ongoing and sustained partnerships and connections to schools waned. There was little effort to build on the good work of the best professional development schools.

Why did the plural vision of teacher education lose ground to the monoculture of research? One answer is that in time the outside money and university funding for the professional development schools ran dry. The educational climate of the country changed from grassroots optimism to centralized gloom, and the heady democratic, progressive rhetoric of the 1990s was succeeded by a conservative emphasis on management and tighter control. Budgets were cut as times grew harder. But MSU's plural vision had actually preceded the professional development school money, so it was probably more a matter of the institutional ethos of the College of Education and the Department of Teacher Education, a matter of values and leadership. In any case, sustaining connections with schools and garnering some resources to develop teachers and coordinate field sites and campus do not require vast sums of money. They might well thrive on modest investments; indeed, it might be argued that for a time the MSU College of Education had too much professional development school money for its own good, tempting all concerned to grandiose dreams and inflated claims.

This history has had a lasting impact. To this day, the MSU Department of Teacher Education remains far more committed to practice both in university classes and in schools than most teacher education departments in most large research universities. Michigan State also remains a more collegial and cooperative place, with a research faculty committed to studying practice. Still, in the waning years of Team One, which was merged with another team in 2005, we felt that the place was reverting to the monoculture of a Research 1 university. When it came to hiring, research credentials seemed always to trump a passion for teacher education. There was little effort to recruit and develop new leadership for the teacher education program among the ranks of new faculty, and the problem of finding vital new leaders for the certification program was not even on the radar. Support within the institution for developing schools as teacher education sites evaporated. Resources for coordinating school and campus and for teacher development vanished. There was no strategy from above for cultivating the field; much of the best work with interns in schools fell to an aging and shrinking group of teachers who had developed as first-rate teacher educators in the older order of partnership. In the old land-grant language, MSU was living off its seed corn.

The lines of magnetic force operating on any big U.S. university at this time might make it hard to enact democratic, plural values. The monoculture of big research is supreme. Peer-reviewed research in scholarly journals is king; genuine intellectual values are slighted or rationed to the few. Practice does not stand high. Teachers in schools are an afterthought. This might be the American fate in higher education. Perhaps the grand plural vision was inherently unstable, but those of us who remained working in and with Team One until its end were convinced that the real issue was values, leadership, and the vision of teacher education.

CONCLUSION

In this book, we have made a case for our values: To do teacher education well, a university has to support a complex ecology, not just a research monoculture. Links to practice and schools are central. A good teacher education program has to be field-based and rooted in conversation; teachers and principals need cultivating as key figures in teacher education. Teacher education requires constant reinventing; teacher educators require the tacit knowledge and understanding of practitioners to enact a site-based program; and because so much remains unknown and forever new, all the people doing teacher education need to become a learning team, a community capable of constant self-educating and development. A teacher education program must be a coherent educational community, not a collection of specialist courses. Recall, too, that the foundation of our story is democracy. MSU's experiment in "detracking" its teacher education program was a promise to give every prospective teacher a first-rate education. A faith in human capacity and its ability to renew itself was the start of our whole enterprise. That faith has been tested and in the end strengthened by our experience. This book is its testimony.

Conclusion

DAVID CARROLL, HELEN FEATHERSTONE,
JOSEPH FEATHERSTONE, SHARON FEIMAN-NEMSER,
AND DIRCK ROOSEVELT

We came together at Michigan State University because we shared a vision of good teaching that had been shaped through the civil rights era and the democratic educational stirrings of the 1960s and 1970s. Together—and with lots of help and good work by others—we created a teacher education program that was home to about three hundred students each year. We taught students who came to us with histories in fairly conventional U.S. public schools to examine more intellectually and socially ambitious approaches to teaching subject matter to diverse learners, imagine and undertake teaching in unfamiliar ways, and develop the beginning skills and knowledge to succeed in doing this teaching.

We did not work independently: We were one of three and then four large teacher education teams of faculty, graduate students, and school partners responsible for delivering the program to our assigned students. Its structure, with its sequence of undergraduate courses and fifth year internship, was common across the four teams, as were the program's teaching standards. This meant that we had to negotiate our vision of good teaching with our colleagues and find a common language that everyone could endorse. Chapter 1 tells how the program and Team One came into being during a high tide of reform in teacher education in a university that took the lead in some of that work, (Holmes Group, 1986, 1990, 1996), and that continues to rank number one in the United States in teacher education by such popular assessments as the ratings in *U.S. News and World Report*.

In the course of creating and sustaining the program across a decade, we learned a lot about two broad topics: how to help prospective teachers learn what they need to know in order to do ambitious teaching, and how to create and sustain a correspondingly ambitious program of teacher education as an ongoing learning community. Chapters 1–10 say quite a bit about how and what we learned. In this concluding chapter we look across the previous chapters at some of the themes and larger lessons for the field that we find there. We also remind readers of the democratic progressive tradition that gave us our picture of good teaching in the first place. That tradition, and its commitment to schools as democratic communities, is a major source for this book. Our novelty has been to imagine a teacher education program as a democratic community. From it, we also borrowed the metaphor of "organizing" to convey our aspirations for a kind of professionalism that would work to share knowledge and power and help create an education that would be, in Abraham Lincoln's words, "of the people, by the people, and for the people."

LEARNING TO TEACH PROSPECTIVE TEACHERS

Those who endorse the value of teacher education agree at a general level about what teachers need to know, care about, and be able to do. That broad consensus is reflected in documents like the teaching standards developed by the National Board for Professional Teaching Standards (1989) and the Interstate New Teacher Assessment and Support Consortium (1992), which identify and elaborate on dimensions of good teaching that are hard to disagree with. It is also reflected in efforts to conceptualize central tasks of teacher preparation (Feiman-Nemser, 2001) and to codify a professional knowledge base for teaching (see, for example, Darling-Hammond & Bransford, 2005).

Chapter 3 describes how we developed our own program standards to provide "more refined ways of talking about the practices we wanted to foster." In doing so, we drew on contemporary work by national and state organizations that placed our efforts in a larger conversation about good teaching and what it entails. We discovered that the real challenge lay not so much in framing standards but in keeping them alive as an expression of our shared vision and as a useful tool in our common work—by themselves the standards are just words. We found ourselves creating a parallel set of educational processes to help faculty, students, and mentor teachers get inside the standards and learn to use them in planning, observation, and assessment.

Looking back on our collective work, we believe that our real contribution lies not so much in the formulation of teaching standards or the analysis of what beginning teachers need to know, care about, and be able to do. Rather it lies in lessons about how to help prospective teachers learn what they need to know in order to teach ambitiously and successfully and in lessons about how to create and sustain a program in which prospective teachers develop into well-started novices. In the sections that follow, we highlight some lessons for the field about doing teacher education. We also revisit the overarching theme of democracy that shaped our efforts and made the whole of the program more than the sum of its separate parts.

Lessons about Teaching Teacher Candidates

The first lesson we learned had to do with our students as learners and the stance we needed to take in teaching our teacher education courses. The doctoral students who worked in our program mostly came to MSU from classroom teaching; they regularly reminded us that teaching college classes is a lot like teaching elementary school. For one thing, it requires energy, enthusiasm, and plenty of visible evidence that the instructor is enjoying the teaching—that she delights in the subject matter and the challenges of teaching it to her students. In addition, the teacher who succeeds best, whether in second grade or in teacher education classes, is the one who figures out what her students care about and builds a curriculum that responds to those concerns. She also makes her students feel cared for, keeping one eye on the subject matter to be taught and the other on her students' needs.

These are lessons Helen Featherstone and Pat Norman initially forgot in their zeal to promote ambitious teaching. In chapter 4, Helen explains how her desire to convince students to adopt a pedagogy more focused on children's thinking hampered her ability to listen well to what her students were thinking and feeling and to dig deeper into their responses in order to understand them better. Only when she was able to lessen the distance between herself and her students and begin to "see the issues that came up through [her] students' eyes" could she form an educative alliance with them and engage them in a serious exploration of ambitious teaching. Similarly, Pat Norman, in chapter 8, found herself in a learning bind (Schön, 1987) with an intern who was unwilling to look critically at her mentor teacher's standard teaching practices. The breakthrough came when Pat learned to see the challenges of teaching through her intern's eyes and work jointly with her on the challenging tasks of instructional planning.

In applying the lessons we learned about elementary school teaching to the teaching of teacher education classes we have a chance to model the culture and practices we want our students to learn. The hidden curriculum of teacher education sends important messages about how all teachers should treat their students. Although some good university instructors see this truth and act on it, it is rare to find a teacher education program that attends to the hidden curriculum in a programmatic way. Team One was lucky to have Susan Donnelly sending out the message of attending to individual students' needs by word and deed to our entire collective. In her role as student coordinator, as David Carroll writes in chapter 2, Donnelly treated Team One students "to the kind of individualized attention they might expect from a good teacher." Paying prompt and genuine attention to their difficulties in navigating the transition from student to teacher, she let students know that they were cared for. Donnelly accomplished this in a teacher education program with approximately three hundred students a year, not in a small, boutique program where such individualized attention is the norm. The lessons from Susan Donnelly's work may be especially challenging for teacher educators working in shortened programs where there is little time to address issues of personal and professional identity formation. But such issues regularly arise when young adults learn to teach—and ignoring them does not make them go away.

Second, we learned to think in new ways about prospective teachers' resistance to our ideas. In his classic study of schoolteachers, Dan Lortie (1975) calls attention to the long years of teacher watching that candidates spend as pupils in K–12 classrooms. This "apprenticeship of observation" shapes their beliefs about teaching and contributes to the perpetuation of conventional teaching practices. Generations of teacher educators have tried to replace those images with more progressive or intellectually ambitious alternatives. But often this effort results in a kind of tug-of-war in which prospective teachers decry the uselessness of their teacher education courses—no one is telling them how to *really* teach—and the teacher educators deplore their students' resistance to enlightened ideas. Over time, we on Team One learned to ask ourselves more questions about this apparently intractable stalemate: Why were our students resistant to our ideas? Was this resistance as monolithic as it seemed? Helen Featherstone (chapter 4) got helpful insight into those questions when she took her seniors to Ms. Pricco's math class, listened to their enthusiastic responses, and read what they wrote with an analytic eye. She wondered whether she and her colleagues hadn't misread some of the resistance, whether students might not, in fact, be quite open to new images of teaching if they saw that it was feasible with the kinds of students they were likely to be teaching, liked the teacher, and saw evidence that the children in the classroom felt cared for and appreciated by their classmates and their teacher. She wondered whether she had thought enough in the past about the emotional and social climate in the classrooms of which her students were critical. Perhaps she needed a more nuanced (and respectful) word than "resistance" if she wanted to understand and connect with them.

The child study project described in chapter 6 also helped us to see the legacy of the apprenticeship of observation differently: as a team we learned that when TE-301 students designed learning occasions for children they had come to know well and appreciate deeply, they thought in imaginative, nontraditional ways about the roles they and the children would play and the lessons they designed for students. Often, they also became critical of the school curriculum and pedagogy that failed to draw on their study child's strengths.

Third, we learned to think in new ways about the role collaborating teachers could play in preparing novices. Every teacher educator knows that prospective teachers learn a great deal from their experiences in public school classrooms, and many feel discouraged by what they see happening to their students as they go through student teaching or internships. They complain that prospective teachers "lose all their progressive ideas in the schools." They also see that competent veteran teachers know many things that prospective teachers do *not* seem to learn from them during student teaching or internships—about engaging and keeping children's attention, moving through transitions, managing disruptive behavior, and dealing with reluctant students, for example. Often, student teaching seems to reinforce the notion that conventional teaching is the only kind that works in real schools, without ever teaching prospective teachers how to actually do it well.

Through the work of Sharon Feiman-Nemser, Kathy Beasley, David Carroll, and others on Team One, we learned how much of the knowledge that helps experienced public school teachers keep classrooms running smoothly is tacit, invisible to them as well as their interns. However, we also learned that when teachers and teacher educators work together, teachers can learn to unpack that knowledge, use it to help interns teach, and find a variety of other ways to support school-based intern learning. We also learned that working in a community of colleagues to craft a curriculum of school-based teacher education sometimes leads teachers to try more ambitious teaching practices themselves. In short, we learned that investing heavily in ongoing work with teachers created unimagined opportunities for interns' learning and a true dialogue among teachers and university people about teaching and learning to teach. We also learned, of course, as Joseph Featherstone shows in chapter 10, about the many ways that the monoculture of a research university can frustrate efforts to make time for this kind of collaborative work.

Fourth, we learned that forming a strong professional identity depends on gaining a sense of intellectual and moral authority as teachers. New teachers often struggle with issues of power and control; typically this is framed around whether to act as a friend or an authority figure. The familiar adage "Don't smile until Christmas" implies that teachers can get students' attention and respect by acting tough. This formulation belies the fact that forming a professional identity is a function less of how teachers act and more of how they think and feel.

Beginning teachers can never have all the confidence they need to do the complex and uncertain work of teaching. Donald Schön (1987) talks about the "paradox of the beginning professional," who cannot possibly know what she is doing but can only learn what to do by assuming the role and doing the work. Dirck Roosevelt (chapter 6) helped us appreciate that the more fundamental task in learning to teach and forming a strong teacher identity is earning intellectual and moral authority. His question—"What gives you the right to teach other people's children?"—opens new ways of thinking about what being and becoming a professional teacher entails and how teacher educators can support that process.

As Roosevelt explains, earning intellectual and moral authority as a teacher means learning to trust your professional judgment. It means seeing yourself as an agent, capable of investigating your practice, setting the standards, figuring out what and how to teach, being the author of your purposes. It means taking responsibility for these decisions. Teacher education provides an important opportunity for prospective teachers to begin developing a foundation in knowledge and skills that will enable them to make informed and principled decisions. But prospective teachers also have to understand that earning intellectual and moral authority is an ongoing process that occurs in the lived moments of teaching, not something that happens once and for all.

Fifth, we learned about the complexities and importance of making inquiry a central thread in the teacher preparation program. Inquiry is important because the challenges of teaching change from year to year, even from day to day. Teachers need to teach new and unfamiliar subject matter and work with new curricula. School populations and contexts change, and teaching is highly dependent on context. To build on their capacities and interests, a teacher must know a particular group of children well. Because teachers need the habits and skills of inquiry in order to get good at what they do, and stay good at it as they travel along a changing river, inquiry is a cross-cutting theme in the Team One program, and it threads through this book in numerous ways. In chapter 3 we see a novice teacher educator trying to engage her interns in an inquiry about their personal teaching standards. In chapter 5 we see that Julie Hanson-Eglite, a fourth-year teacher, identifies her commitment to inquiry-based practice and her ongoing and disciplined efforts to study teaching as a source of her intellectual and moral authority for teaching and as one reason that she, rather than her principal, should decide how her students should learn science.

Introducing a program-long curriculum of inquiry with child study (see chapter 6) helped prospective teachers learn the skills of careful observation and disciplined inference and become advocates for children. It also showed them how they might become makers, not just consumers, of knowledge in teaching. Child study allowed Team One students to have an early experience of truly democratic teaching by discovering the learning capacities of a child who may not look smart in school or who is a member of a traditionally marginalized group and then designing a lesson that builds on those capacities. By successfully designing and teaching a lesson that played to a child's strengths and interests, prospective teachers got a new image of what a good lesson might do and what it could mean to teach in capacity-oriented ways.

In the next two years of the program, inquiry continued to be a theme. In the senior year, for example, prospective teachers investigated some aspect of classroom culture in both their field classroom and in a hypermedia classroom; they also reported in writing on the thinking of three of their students after they facilitated discussion of a math problem with a group of five or six children. As interns they deepened their understanding of classroom management by studying the moves their collaborating teacher made to set norms and expectations in the beginning of the school year; in the spring, they designed a teacher research project around a compelling question or problem they had confronted during the year. Over time we learned to shape inquiry assignments that fed and were fed by conversation from peers and instructors in a teacher education seminar (as we see in Roosevelt's description of the child study project), that connected visibly with what prospective teachers wanted to learn, and that could be integrated into the prospective teachers' actual classroom responsibilities without becoming too burdensome. Although these guidelines sound self-evident and meshed well with the child study in the initial course, they were not always easy to follow in later semesters. The inquiry course taught in the spring of the intern year, for example, asked students to collect and analyze data that could help them investigate some question that mattered to them while assuming primary responsibility for the classroom. Their research projects were impressive, and many interns shared them proudly; others, however, felt overwhelmed by this added requirement and complained angrily about it.

Lessons about Building a Program

In addition to learning about how to help prospective teachers become well-started novice teachers, we gained much in another domain: our ten-year experiment in democratic, progressive teacher education taught us some important lessons about creating and sustaining structures that enable teacher educators at all stages of their careers and development to do good work and continue to grow collectively. In short, we learned about creating and sustaining programs. Our hunch that our efforts in teacher education would parallel the stories of the creation of small alternative schools proved true. Like a school, Team One was constantly working on becoming a better community.

The preceding chapters show why a teacher preparation program needs to create a culture of inquiry and conversation and develop structures to support the ongoing and continuous learning of all who work with prospective teachers. David Carroll, Pat Norman, and Helen Featherstone all describe situations in which they faced learning binds in their work as teacher educators. In each case, conversation with other teacher educators played a key role in turning a problem around. These are small but telling examples of how the team acted as a collective and learned as a community; they allow us to see that the solitary nature of much teacher education is as much of a problem as the isolation of classroom teachers.

The need to create structures that support serious ongoing collective growth becomes more pressing in light of the fact that the staffing of most large teacher education programs changes considerably from one year to the next, and even from semester to semester: Graduate students finish their degree programs and move to new universities, retired teachers decide they really want to retire and move to Florida, university faculty members take on responsibilities for other programs or get research grants. The staffing of many teacher education programs flows like a human river.

Team One was lucky because, for the most part, people enjoyed our egalitarian ethos and spirit of collective learning. Many graduate students and faculty members continued working with the team for longer than they might otherwise have done because they felt that the conversation about practice in our regularly scheduled meetings supported their ongoing learning and because they valued the way we arranged our field placements for the senior-year courses (with all our students in one school, so an instructor could confer with host teachers and visit students in their field placements fairly easily and thus fairly often). However, like most large teacher education programs, we still had, every fall, some new graduate students on board as course instructors and liaisons and some new public school teachers hosting seniors (in the field placement of the methods classes) and working with interns. So, we had to build support for continued learning into every component of the team.

Those teaching the senior year methods classes met regularly—once a week during some semesters—first to design the course and create a syllabus, then to discuss issues of substance, assignments, problems arising in the teaching, etc. The same was true for those who taught the introductory course, TE-301, and for the liaisons, the university instructors who worked in schools with small groups of interns and met with them weekly. We brought food to these meetings when we could, and we made sure that the agenda made room for the immediate concerns of everyone who came. Feiman-Nemser and Beasley, and also Carroll, describe some of the structures they created to support the work and learning of mentor teachers. All these meetings mixed what one of us took to calling "high and low." Because they had room for little stuff, big heavy stuff, and lofty and theoretical stuff, they managed to meet most people's needs and break down the sense that little stuff is for unimportant people and big policy or theoretical stuff is for big, important people. The mix kept things lively and at times even raucous. (The importance of pleasure in individual and collective learning is something we tried to teach our students and also enact ourselves—a truth that goes against the often grim grain of U.S. educational puritanism.)

We learned that we needed to create places for learning and, perhaps equally important, a culture of inquiry powered, shaped, and supported by conversation. At its best, a culture of inquiry encourages members of a community to try to reframe apparently intractable problems or to transform obstacles into potentially compelling questions—to turn dilemmas into sites for inquiry and group learning. In chapter 7, Feiman-Nemser and Beasley describe doing exactly that as they worked together on what had originally been formulated (by a university supervisor in the old program, and by Kathy herself) as "Kathy's problem." Likewise, Cindy Hartzler-Miller, after rejecting program standards as too rigid to be useful to her interns' growth, came to wonder, through discussion with other liaisons and faculty, whether the standards might serve as a tool to stimulate and scaffold the interns' inquiry into the dimensions of good teaching.

Of course, no sane person embraces every problem as an opportunity for learning. We did find, however, that doing the hard, sometimes impossible work of teaching in good company made an enormous difference and lifted us over the places of tribulation and despair. We got into the habit of facing trouble together and laying difficulties on the table, asking for and giving help. In the weekly meetings of faculty, doctoral students, and adjunct faculty teaching the senior year courses, we found that in the early fall those who had taught the course in the past shared concerns and raised questions more readily than those teaching for the first time. Then, as the year went by, more and more newcomers laid issues on the table; they were learning how to trust and make use of the collective. We tried to make clear that a problem was not a symptom of bad teaching (something novices almost inevitably feel) but a context for joint inquiry and learning. The more we succeeded, the more opportunities we all had to get smart.

From the outset we had much to learn about our individual jobs and roles. As time went on, we also had to create ways to develop collective intelligence. In the beginning, we placed interns in schools and classrooms assigned to us by the department. Not all of these turned out to be good places for learning to teach, but it was difficult to extricate the team from a school with which the college had a long-standing relationship. Eventually, we created a review procedure that enabled a severing of our ties with the school; this procedure became the basis for an annual review that the team did with each school, assessing what individuals (mentor teachers, university liaisons) had learned from that year's work and also what problems had arisen and how we could take further advantage of schoolwide resources to support our students' learning. When the review process revealed intractable problems—the lack of regular time for mentors to confer and plan with interns, for example, or mentors' lack of interest in thinking about more conceptually oriented approaches to subject matter teaching or more constructive management practices—we could use the evidence to support our withdrawal from the school. The steering committee, which assembled biweekly over lunch, became a place where we addressed problems large and small and gradually accumulated wisdom about the work and the care and feeding of the program. Here as elsewhere, the general lack of formal roles and hierarchy in the team, combined with emphasis on learning together, contributed to the making of a collective that could discuss any sort of problem, brainstorm solutions, and assign appropriate people to tackle it.

Each semester we also held daylong team retreats for faculty and doctoral students where we studied some aspect of our curriculum or pedagogy or some samples of our students' work. At one retreat, for instance, we analyzed student projects from the course on teaching science and tried to clarify what they revealed about our students' learning. Another time we divided into groups based on whether people were teaching sections of the introductory course, the senior year course, or internship courses. Each group studied the program's teaching standards and tried to articulate which standards they were focusing on and how this was visible in their syllabi. These programwide conversations helped shape a common conversation, strengthened the coherence of the program overall, and served as a good introduction for newcomers to the team. We always followed the meetings with potluck dinners where the food was more than lavish, illustrating Napoleon's dictum that a teacher education team marches forward on its stomach.

Teaching of any sort is an impossible task: situations are always new, students always different, the contexts change in unexpected ways. The work of teacher education often requires us to be smarter than we think we are, to have good ideas about brand new problems. Moreover, it is never exclusively intellectual work; the social, emotional, and intellectual are closely intertwined. We needed human support for our failures and difficulties as much as we needed rational analysis of our problems. Fortunately, a culture that supports inquiry, that disposes its members to see problems of practice as occasions for investigation and markers of tensions inherent in the work is in fact well situated to provide the necessary softer sorts of support. All through our enterprise, we were struck by the way the social supports the intellectual and the academic and promotes intellectual understanding and high quality. John Dewey was right—it's foolish to separate the social needs of students or faculty from their intellectual ones. Through regular meetings scheduled to investigate and solve problems, we came to know each other well. We also came to know others working in the program. Our work overlapped in ways that made it possible—even inevitable—for us to know, to have experienced, the tensions and difficulties our colleagues and students were experiencing. We became a collection of networks and villages. We knew how painful it was to have a class go poorly, to miss the boat with a depressed student, to have to choose between limiting students' learning by leaving them in bad field placements or offending the unsatisfactory teachers and principals by moving the students to new schools or classrooms.

We learned that running a teacher education program is more like running a school than we might have imagined. In work that presents problems that are emotionally and socially demanding as well as intellectually challenging, professionals need to feel cared for almost as much as college students do. Brick by brick, Susan Donnelly taught us to build a culture of caring that included teacher educators as well as prospective teachers. She did this in multiple ways. To begin with, as she explains in chapter 2, when students who were having trouble in a class came to complain about their instructor, she made sure to get the instructor's perspective on the difficulty; instructors knew that no matter what complaint students lodged, their point of view would be listened to. In addition, by treating all problems as occasions for teaching and learning, Susan took care of teacher educators as well as students. She engaged both in an educative conversation in which they felt supported—and, not incidentally, learned skills for dealing with such situations in the future. Donnelly modeled and she taught.

We learned that flattening the hierarchies that existed in the university and in the world of schools served us well in the practical and intellectual realms as well as in the moral one. Even before the creation of Team One, doctoral students and tenured faculty in the college of education at MSU often worked together as colleagues: on research projects, doctoral students' ideas were sought and respected; faculty and graduate students talked as colleagues about problems of teaching. Many of us learned as much from doctoral students as they learned from us. The culture of MSU supported our egalitarian approach to working together. (A faculty member who earned her PhD from an East Coast university noted to one of us her culture shock on coming to MSU and finding that doctoral students called her by her first name and treated her as an equal: "I'm not used to that.") Team One expanded the democratic culture of the college to include everyone who worked on the team.

Finally, we on Team One learned that putting strong effort into developing relationships with schools and working closely with teachers benefited teacher education immensely. The work that Feiman-Nemser and Beasley did together was deeply satisfying to both; it led to enormously significant changes in the way Beasley worked both with seven- and eight-year-olds and with interns, and it led to important new structures and strategies in the Team One teacher education program. The same was true of the work David Carroll and the Capitol Elementary teachers did together. We feel that despite huge obstacles, teacher education programs must renew the effort to develop relationships with teachers and schools; they must invest some resources and staff in school and teacher development, or they will never get high-quality placements and thoughtful mentoring for teacher candidates. As explored in chapter 9, for Team One, this necessitated scaling up strategies for mentor teacher development, since there were never enough excellent placements for the hundred or so interns we placed each year, plus all of the junior- and senior-year students who needed field placements. Teacher education needs to go more deeply into the field. But unless it is willing to spend time and energy and some money on creating partnerships with teachers and schools, routine school placements will continue to wash away any ambitions for a better future.

Chapter 9 illustrates two scaling up strategies: one is the mentor teacher study group based within one school, in which teachers work with a university teacher educator to investigate learning to teach and to develop mentoring practices. This work grew out of and was significantly influenced by the pioneering experiments at Averill Elementary School, described in chapter 7. Also in chapter 9, we describe the cross-school liaison study group, as a further strategy for deploying limited resources to maximum benefit. Across these different venues for mentor teacher development work are some action steps that outline an agenda of joint work for teacher educators and the mentor teachers they work with.[1] These were all part of the complex continuous work of community-building.

TRANSFORMING TEACHER EDUCATION

The core values of our group were part of the democratic and progressive tradition that has made notable contributions to schooling since the time of John Dewey. Its durable themes were the staple of our work: children and childhood, community, social justice, experience, inquiry, and the integration of theory and practice. We also embraced the metaphor of schools as communities, and teaching and activism as a kind of organizing. To us, democrats with a small "d," the organizing metaphor suggested ways to combine genuine professionalism with a commitment to grassroots democracy. Our root commitment was the assumption of capacity in all learners at all levels.

We wanted our courses to honor our students' capacity to learn. We knew there was an enormous range in quality of our students' preparation. A large public land-grant university takes in students with lots of cultural capital as well as some who are the victims of truly bad schooling; many of our students were the first in their family to walk a college campus. Our belief in capacity was not blind. Over time we saw the need for a good teacher education program to weed out students who are academically or temperamentally unsuited for teaching. But in general we assumed capacity.

The program was also ambitiously democratic in the assumption that ordinary classroom teachers can develop the capacity to play a key role in teacher education. In part this was an assumption about where knowledge of the practice of teaching is lodged and learned. Although we believed that the university had valuable knowledge to offer apprentice teachers, we were convinced that people would mainly learn to teach on site in classrooms; much of what they had to learn about putting everything together would have to take place in the field in conversations grounded in practice with a collaborating teacher. Our program did not assume the collaborating teacher was the intern's sole support: each intern was part of a school-based group that met weekly with the MSU liaison; each intern also took courses in which conversation and practice-based reflection supported the in-school learning. Yet it remained both a strength and a weakness of our effort that the collaborating teacher became a key teacher educator.

Many teachers and interns formed a team of learners, swapping strengths and covering each other's weaknesses. As time went on, some of us became convinced that an ordinary teacher willing to struggle alongside an intern (with good support for the pair from our team) was good for the intern's development, perhaps better than working with a master teacher with a dauntingly perfect repertoire. In such pairs, real learning took place; intern and teacher became colleagues, working together to develop and change their practice.

The daily practice of Team One was also rooted in the assumption of capacity. Although there were formal roles on the team, there was fluidity to particular assignments; all of us became switch hitters. If we faced a problem with a particular school, we asked: Which of us was well connected to teachers or knew the principal well enough to take on the diplomatic problem? Who would best work with a particular graduate student floundering as she taught one of our sections? Who was in the best political position to argue a point with the chair of the department?

The core group operated less as members of a hierarchy or a bureaucracy and more as organizers. The word evokes a looseness of formal definition: a constant aim of building capacity, an appeal to a vision of professionalism rooted in fellowship and solidarity and committed to sharing knowledge and power, and a constant common goal of moving forward. While not necessarily political in a partisan way, we were political in the broad sense once defined by George Orwell (1946/1953). The team worked collectively "to push the world in a certain direction, to alter other people's ideas of the kind of society they should strive after."

TIMES HAVE CHANGED

In the first chapter we explained the beginnings of Team 1, the context of the 1980s and early 1990s, and we laid out the democratic vision that provided the foundation for our work. As the story we told made clear, these were different times from the present: in education, reformers in all the major subject areas were writing standards documents that laid out visions of teaching in which students, asking important questions, and teachers, studying their own teaching, would be working together to create pedagogy and curriculum that would bring all their students, rich and poor, to durable understandings of important subject matter. There was considerable support for the idea that teachers needed to develop deep understandings of the subjects they teach and that they were professionals who should be educated to make consequential decisions about how best to teach the children in their classrooms. The establishment of the National Board for Professional Teaching Standards advanced a strong conception of accomplished teaching and what it entails.

Times have changed radically, and with them the concerns of teachers, principals, superintendents, and policymakers. The No Child Left Behind Act (NCLB) has forced all those who work in and with schools, especially city schools, to turn a major part of their attention to improving children's scores on standardized tests. We share with most of the backers of this legislation a deep concern for improving the education of poor children and children of color; like them, we would like to see the test-score gap based in race and class disappear.

In today's changed policy climate, our plea for democratic vision, ambitious curriculum for all, and teachers with the authority to make sensible judgments on behalf of the children they teach may seem fanciful and irrelevant. Teacher education itself is under attack; alternative programs proliferate, many connected with the hard-edged, managerial and top-down efforts at school reform that have been the dominant mode for some years now. Whereas we aim to strengthen the true professionalism of teachers, the current policy system seems bent on de-professionalizing it.

But is all well with the current policy regime? The reigning style of school reform through high-stakes testing, efforts to hold schools accountable through tightened controls on teaching and teacher scripts, a narrowing of the curriculum to teach to the tests, and recruitment and training programs that rob teachers of professional standing is now badly stalling, as criticism mounts from many sides. Even if test scores were the right measure (and criticism of high-stakes tests has never been louder), recent analyses of National Assessment of Education Progress data suggest that they have barely risen. There is even a spreading debate on whether it is realistic to expect schools alone to pick up the slack for the rest of society; many are beginning to ask if any amount of school reform can equalize outcomes when the lives and circumstances of U.S. children are so disparate and the gap between rich and poor so vast.

For those who accepted them in good faith, the Bush era reforms had one great merit: they were aimed at the education gap between middle-class and poor and minority children. And to their credit, these reforms have continued to keep this issue on the public agenda. Yet there is a sense in the air that one era of educational reform may be over. The outlines of any new era are far from clear.

The astute reader will have little trouble figuring out the views of the Team One group on high-stakes testing, the sort of curriculum and pedagogy we want for children, and all the rest. From our perspective, the faltering of the current regime of managerial-style school reform reinforces our basic argument about the need for more democracy in U.S. education. We of course welcome alternatives to what we view as the disasters of high-stakes testing and classrooms managed by remote control. We share the view of some critics that a single-minded focus on equalizing school outcomes between rich and poor kids without redressing other grotesque imbalances in the lives of U.S. families today is laughable. But this is not a book about the wider educational debates, still less a volume concerned with the state of American democracy today.

Implicit in what we have written in this book is the argument that today's reigning policy orthodoxies miss out on three key facts that will remain true whatever flavor of school reform prevails:

1. Reform without the active engagement of thoughtful teachers is always a fool's errand.
2. Nothing in the school lives of children matters as much to their learning as the knowledge and judgment of their teachers.
3. Teachers in classrooms will always end up subverting regimes of disrespect.

These three facts will persist whether the new policy era upon us is a renewed time of democratic hopefulness or a continuation of today's policy of centralized gloom and suspicion. In the end, teachers mediate all school reform; they are the filters, the agents, the critics, the balance wheels. They are the grownups in the classrooms with the children. We would even argue that well-educated teachers are necessary to make scripted reading series work at all, for that kind of curriculum generates problems of its own sort, whose answers are not to be found in the script. Poorly educated teachers will make a hash of lofty democratic intentions and managerial shortcuts alike. In the end, we argue, the United States will never find the cheap shortcut to educating good teachers well.

We have tried to show some of the steps a teacher education program might take to produce thoughtful teachers capable of the kind of judgment children in classrooms need, whatever the policy climate, and whatever new shifting demands the anxious public makes on schools. In the end, as Deborah Meier keeps reminding us, poor children need the kind of education that rich kids are getting. Team One has been our group's tentative shot at cultivating teachers who might begin sharing the educational wealth of our troubled republic.

We hear over and over, day in and day out, both from graduates of our program and from veteran teachers in schools, that the high stakes attached to standardized tests are actually impoverishing the education being offered to children. Greta McHaney-Trice, as she explains in Chapter 5, struggles daily with the bind that these tests put her in: she knows that it is important for her students, particularly the children of color (she worries especially about the boys) to do well on the tests. However, she also knows how important it is that they have worthwhile experiences in school that will make them think and will help them learn in deep and durable ways, experiences as rich as some she had in elementary school and in her teacher education classes. Without these experiences, she feels that the skills of reading and writing will mean little to them. Some days she follows the line of least resistance, teaching basically to the tests. She can "do the rote," she says,

> probably *better* . . . in a sense than I can the other things that I want to do. . . . It's not hard to think through, "open the page, copy the problems down, write the answers and move on." It's not hard to say that and call it teaching. . . . [But] if that's what I do and that's all that I do, I *know* that I'm taking something away from them. I know that I'm taking something away from me. Yes. Yes. Because it goes back to the beginning of the conversation . . . letting the kids choose, letting the kids explore and have experiences that are valid for them like Huck Finn is valid for me. That's learning. That's also teaching because a worthwhile product resulted. A worthwhile awareness resulted.

In her teacher education classes, McHaney-Trice says, she learned that "teaching is not an 'a, b, c, 1, 2, 3' kind of thing." Rather, it was a profession in which she would be making significant choices, changing course, making decisions that mattered. In her present context these choices are harder; the experiences that she continues to provide for her students—to get inside the thinking of a child through conversations about a good book, to discuss a child's reasoning about a math problem, for example—are not valued. More and more it's uphill work to do what a good teacher must do: pay attention.

McHaney-Trice is a professional in all the best senses of the word. She faces the hard choices every school day, taking responsibility for deciding what her students need most and for teaching what they need as well as she possibly can. Surely, she is the teacher we would all want for our own children, the one we would all, to paraphrase Dewey, want for every child in our community, our country. To get such teachers in the numbers the nation needs, we must create teacher education programs that provide time to consider the unfamiliar, to grapple with new ideas and new images of teaching, to acquire the authority of a good teacher capable of making judgments for the growth of the children she teaches.

Ultimately, we have argued, the transformation of teacher education poses the challenge of democracy in education. By democracy we mean truly visionary but also tangible, practical steps and ideas like those embedded in the work of Team One: the assumption that everyone can learn; the emphasis on learning through dialogue and conversation rooted in practice and field experience; the commitment to an ambitious curriculum for all children and an ambitious teacher education curriculum that views teachers as practical intellectuals; a vision of programs as learning communities analogous to schools; a vision of professionalism and expertise that seeks to share power and knowledge; the opening up of elite pedagogy and "higher" learning in the university to all prospective teachers, particularly elementary teachers; the flattening of university and school hierarchies to create an egalitarian team spirit; the importance of the social to the development of the academic and the intellectual; the commitment to working with schools and teachers to create excellent environments for children that will also be great places to learn to teach; the creation of partnerships with schools where teachers and principals serve as teacher educators; the notion that university experts cannot deliver knowledge of teaching except in close partnership with practitioners on site.

This agenda assumes the need for a democratization of knowledge and expertise, and a democratization of status and power that runs against the grain of some of the current assumptions and realities of the American university and the uneasy nation it mirrors. Our experience leads us to believe, however, that this is not an impossible or utopian agenda. We on Team One are proud we were able to take it far enough to hear graduates like Greta McHaney-Trice insist:

> Kids aren't cars. And that's my biggest thing: they don't go through an assembly line, you don't put on the language arts, you don't put on the writing skills, you don't put on the math, and then you get well educated Joe Blow at the end.

Notes and References

Introduction

References

Cochran-Smith, M. (2004). Taking stock in 2004: Teacher education in dangerous times. *Journal of Teacher Education, 55*(1), 3–7.

Darling-Hammond, L. (2000). Reforming teacher preparation and licensing: Debating the evidence. *Teachers College Record, 102*(1), 28–56.

Dewey, J. (1964). The relation of theory to practice in education. In R. D. Archambault (Ed.), *John Dewey on education* (pp. 313–338). Chicago: University of Chicago Press. (Original work published 1904)

Engel, B. & Martin, A. C. (Eds.), (2005). *Holding values: What we mean by progressive education: Essays by members of the North Dakota Study Group.* Portsmouth, NH: Heinemann.

Feiman-Nemser, S. (2001). From preparation to practice: Designing a continuum to strengthen and sustain teaching. *Teachers College Record, 103,* 1013–1055.

Grossman, P. L. (1990). *The making of a teacher: Teacher knowledge and teacher education.* New York: Teachers College Press.

Lortie, D. (1975). *Schoolteacher: A sociological study.* Chicago: University of Chicago Press.

Meier, D. (1995). *The power of their ideas: Lessons for America from a small school in Harlem.* Boston: Beacon Press.

Meier, D. (2002). *In schools we trust: Creating communities of learning in an era of testing and standardization.* Boston: Beacon Press.

Mitchell, L. S. (1950). *Our children and our schools: A picture and analysis of how today's public school teachers are meeting the challenge of new knowledge and new cultural needs.* New York: Simon and Schuster.

Paige, R. (2002). Meeting the highly qualified teachers challenge: The secretary's annual report on teacher quality. Washington, DC: U.S. Department of Education, Office of Postsecondary Education.

Ravitch, D. (2000). *Left back: A century of failed school reforms.* New York: Simon and Schuster.

1. FROM BOUTIQUE TO SUPERSTORE: HISTORY AND CONTEXT OF THE PROGRAM

References

Bestor, A. (1955). *The restoration of learning.* New York: Knopf.

Bruner, J. (1996). *The culture of education.* Cambridge, MA: Harvard University Press.

Conant, J. (1964). *The education of American teachers.* New York: McGraw-Hill.

Duckworth, E. (1987). The having of wonderful ideas. *"The having of wonderful ideas" and other essays on teaching and learning* (pp. 1–14). New York: Teachers College Press.

Holmes Group. (1990). *Tomorrow's schools: Principles for the design of professional development schools.* East Lansing, MI: Author.

Inzunza, V. (2002). *Years of achievement: A short history of the College of Education at Michigan State University.* East Lansing: Michigan State University, College of Education.

Jencks, C., & Riesman, D. (1968). *The academic revolution.* New York: Doubleday.

Judge, H. (1982). *American graduate schools of education: A view from abroad.* New York: Ford Foundation.

Meier, D. (1995). *The power of their ideas: Lessons for America from a small school in Harlem.* Boston: Beacon Press.

Meier, D. (2002). *In schools we trust: Creating communities of learning in an era of testing and standardization.* Boston: Beacon Press.

Silberman, C. (1970). *Crisis in the classroom: The remaking of American education.* New York: Random House.

2. CARING FOR STUDENTS WHILE GATEKEEPING FOR THE PROFESSION: THE STUDENT COORDINATOR ROLE

Notes

1. Portions of this chapter appeared previously in D. Carroll (2005).
2. The professional criteria for proceeding to the internship are available on the MSU website at http://ed-web3.educ.msu.edu/te/ele/criteria.htm.

References

Buchmann, M. (1993). Role over person: Morality and authenticity in teaching. In M. Buchmann & R. Floden (Eds.), *Detachment and concern: Conversations in the philosophy of teaching and teacher education* (pp. 145–157). New York: Teachers College Press.

Carroll, D. (2005). Developing dispositions for teaching: Teacher education programs as moral communities of practice. *New Educator 1*(2), 81–100.

Noddings, N. (2001). The caring teacher. In V. Richardson (Ed.), *Handbook of research on teaching* (pp. 99–105). Washington, DC: American Educational Research Association.

Shapiro, E. (1991). Teacher: Being and becoming. *Thought and Practice, 3*(1), 5–24.

3. PROFESSIONAL STANDARDS AS INTERPRETIVE SPACE

Notes

1. Cindy participated in a Team One study group for doctoral students and faculty working with interns in schools. Participants engaged in studies of their clinical practice. Cindy's self-study, published in the fall 1999 issue of *Action in Teacher Education*, forms the basis for this account.

2. See chapter 1 for an explanation of the label "liaison" and an elaboration of the responsibilities associated with this role.

3. Like many teacher education programs in large research universities, the Michigan State program relied heavily on doctoral students to teach courses and work with interns in the field. Team One took the support and development of doctoral students seriously. The liaison study group was one forum where doctoral students had regular opportunities to study program standards, policies, and expectations; work through problems and questions that arose in the course of their ongoing work with interns and collaborating teachers; and study and write about their practice.

4. Each team worked with approximately 350 students across the three years of the program (junior year, senior year, and internship).

5. At the time we did not address the question of how the standards would be assessed; we were still developing the curriculum. Our first cohort of interns was several years away, so we put off that task.

6. As chair of the INTASC elementary standards committee, I had the benefit of working with a group of thoughtful teachers and teacher educators from around the country on the challenges of framing standards for good beginning teaching. This work influenced my thinking about Team One's program standards. I was also studying three well-regarded induction programs around the country. In the context of this research, I learned about the California Standards for the Teaching Profession and observed skilled advisors from the Santa Cruz New Teacher Project using these standards as a critical tool in their work with beginning teachers (California Commission on Teacher Credentialing and California Department of Education, 1997). This experience gave me new ideas about how to frame and use our program's standards.

7. Each team worked with school districts close to campus and an urban school district about an hour from the university. This was a way to accommodate students

who wanted to live close to home and to offer a more diverse set of placement options. Team One placed a cohort of students in Grand Rapids schools.

8. This reconstruction of the conversation is based on two pages of notes taken by one of the liaisons who participated in the meeting.

9. Our continuum starts with an emerging stage, in which collaborating teachers plan aloud so interns can begin to get a picture of what this kind of intellectual work entails. It continues through three phases, in which the intern takes increasingly more leadership in planning by gathering appropriate materials, framing worthwhile goals, and selecting or designing learning activities and assessments. Across the stages, the collaborating teacher adjusts her role to fit the growing competence and confidence of the intern. We have used this in-house tool to help new collaborating teachers think about their interns as learners and themselves as teachers of instructional planning. In this work we were influenced by other efforts to create standards-based continua. See, for example, Danielson (1996).

References

California Commission on Teacher Credentialing and California Department of Education. (1997). *California standards for the teaching profession.* Sacramento: State of California.

Danielson, C. (1996). *Enhancing professional practice: A framework for teaching.* Alexandria, VA: Association of Supervision and Curriculum Development.

Dewey J. (1956). *The child and the curriculum.* Chicago: University of Chicago Press. (Original work published 1902)

Diez, M. (Ed.). (1998). *The role of standards and assessment: A dialogue.* Washington, DC: American Association of Colleges of Teacher Education.

Hartzler-Miller, C. (1999). Learning to teach in a standards-based program: when experience isn't enough. *Action in teacher education, 21*(3), 88–101.

Hawkins, D. (1974). I, thou, and it. In *The informed vision* (pp. 49–62). New York: Agathon Press. (Original work published 1967)

Interstate New Teacher Support and Assessment Consortium. (1992). *Model standards for beginning teacher licensing and development: A resource for state dialogue.* Washington, DC: Author.

National Board for Professional Teaching Standards. (1989). *Toward high and rigorous standards for the teaching profession.* Detroit: Author.

National Council of Teachers of Mathematics. (1989). *Curriculum and evaluation standards for school mathematics.* Reston, VA: Author.

Shulman, L. (1986). Those who understand: Knowledge growth in teaching. *Educational Researcher, 15*(2), 4–14.

4. Preparing Teachers of Elementary Mathematics: Evangelism or Education?

Notes

1. Some of the material in this chapter was included in Featherstone (2005).

2. Students in Team One took a two-course, eleven-credit sequence in the fall and spring of their senior year that served as an introductory methods course in the teaching of math, science, literacy, and social studies. Students in my TE-402 section had focused on social studies and science in the fall of 1999 and would study math and literacy with me and my partner Carolyn James in the spring of 2000.

3. Saxon math is a reductive, skills-based curriculum that rests primarily on drill in basic arithmetic facts and skills in arithmetic operations—addition, subtraction, multiplication, and division.

4. Students in our elementary teacher preparation program who are planning to teach kindergarten or preschool (and thus majoring in child development) student-teach in a nursery school or Head Start classroom during the year in which they are taking TE-401 /2 as a part of their elementary certification program. They sometimes feel pulled in opposite directions by teacher education and child development.

5. Typically, after the TE-402 students work on the horse-trading problem for a few minutes, they will offer at least two possible answers: the man made a profit of $20; the man made a profit of $10. After we discuss their solutions for a while and at least eight people have described the different ways they thought about the problem, most students agree that $20 is probably the right answer, since a number of quite different approaches, all of them apparently sensible, yield that answer. However, students are not usually able to locate and explain the logical flaw in the approach or approaches that lead to an answer of $10 profit. Since some uncertainty remains, the students almost always ask me, "What is the correct answer?" Because I have found that students continue to think about and work on the problem if I do not give them the answer immediately, I usually put off telling them my own reasoning about the problem for several days—or even several weeks.

References

Dewey, J. (1974). The relation of theory to practice in education. In R. D. Archambault (Ed.), *John Dewey on education: Selected writings* (2nd ed., pp. 313–338). Chicago: University of Chicago Press. (Original work published 1904)

Duckworth, E. (1987). *"The having of wonderful ideas" and other essays on teaching and learning.* New York: Teachers College Press.

Featherstone, H. (2000). "– Pat + Pat = 0": Intellectual play in elementary mathematics. *For the Learning of Mathematics, 20*(2), 14–23.

Featherstone, H. (2005). Learning progressive teacher education. In B. Engel and A. Martin (Eds.), *Holding values* (pp. 130–136). Portsmouth, NH: Boynton/Cook Heinemann.

Finkel, D. (2000). *Teaching with your mouth shut.* Portsmouth, NH: Boynton/Cook Heinemann.

Hawkins, D. (1974). I, thou, and it. In *The informed vision: Essays on learning and human nature* (pp. 49–62). New York: Agathon Press. (Original work published 1967)

Kant, I. (1964). *Fundamental principles of the metaphysics of morals.* New York: Harper Torchbooks. (Original work published 1785)

Kingsolver, B. (1999). *The poisonwood bible: A novel.* New York: Harperflamingo.

Lampert, M. (2001). *Teaching problems and the problems of teaching.* New Haven, CT: Yale University Press.

Lester, J. (1996). Establishing a community of mathematics learners. In D. Schifter (Ed.), *What's happening in math class? Envisioning new practices through teacher narratives* (pp. 88–101). New York: Teachers College Press.

Lortie, D. C. (1975). *Schoolteacher: A sociological study.* Chicago: University of Chicago Press.

Meier, D. (1995). *The power of their ideas: Lessons for America from a small school in Harlem.* Boston: Beacon Press.

Meier, D. (2002). *In schools we trust: Creating communities of learning in an era of testing and standardization.* Boston: Beacon Press.

National Council of Teachers of Mathematics. (1989). *Curriculum and evaluation standards for school mathematics.* Reston, VA: Author.

National Council of Teachers of Mathematics. (1991). *Professional standards for teaching mathematics.* Reston, VA: Author.

National Council of Teachers of Mathematics. (1995). *Assessment standards for school mathematics.* Reston, VA: Author.

National Council of Teachers of Mathematics. (2000). *Principles and standards for school mathematics.* Reston, VA: Author.

Paley, V. (1986). On listening to what children say. *Harvard Educational Review, 56,* 122–131.

5. "What Gives You the Right?":
Earning Moral and Intellectual Authority to Teach

Notes

1. This chapter owes its existence to Greta and Julie, two wonderful human beings whose example as teachers gives me great hope, whose conversation and friend-

ship I treasure, and whose long-ago status as my students fills me with humble surprise. Among many other friends and colleagues who have contributed to my thinking in one way or another, I must, happily, acknowledge by name Helen Featherstone and Virginia Richardson.

2. All Greta McHaney-Trice quotations are from the transcript of an interview (semi-structured, essentially a planned conversation) I conducted on May 23, 2002.

3. For thoughts about the themes of experience and *learning* from experience, important for "earned authority," I am deeply indebted to Virginia Richardson and our collaboration (see Richardson & Roosevelt, 2005).

4. Unless otherwise indicated, all Hanson-Eglite quotes are from the transcript of a semistructured interview I conducted on July 13, 2002.

5. This is an appearance I have no reason to doubt, and many reasons to accept. However, I am not neutral; I have reasons to hope that Julie is the teacher I think she is, so it may bear underscoring that I am not conducting an empirical study of Julie's practice. Primarily, I am studying a concept and the sense of professional identity. I do, however, believe that in the right conditions what people say about their practice generally reveals something about that practice. Also, the same facts that render me partial with respect to Julie's practice per se qualify me to engage her in a certain quality of conversation about it.

References

Authority. (1996). In S. Blackburn (Ed.), *The Oxford dictionary of philosophy* (Oxford Reference Online, March 15, 2003). New York: Oxford University Press.

Authority. (2002). In C. Calhoun (Ed.), *Dictionary of the social sciences* (Oxford Reference Online, March 15, 2003). Oxford University Press.

Bateson, M. C. (1989). *Composing a life.* New York: Penguin (Plume).

Curtis, C. P. (1999). *Bud, not Buddy.* New York: Scholastic.

Delpit, L. D. (1998). The silenced dialogue: Power and pedagogy in educating other people's children. *Harvard Educational Review, 58,* 280–298.

Dewey, J. (1956). *The school and society* (rev. ed. 1915). Chicago: University of Chicago Press. (Original work published 1900)

Dewey J. (1956). *The child and the curriculum.* Chicago: University of Chicago Press. (Original work published 1902)

Dewey, J. (1963). *Experience and education.* New York: Collier/Macmillan. (Original work published 1938)

Dewey. J. (1966) *Democracy and education.* New York: Macmillan. (Original work published in 1916.)

Durkheim, E. (1956). Education: Its nature and its role. In *Education and sociology* (pp. 61–90). New York: Free Press/Macmillan.

Gerth, H. H., & Mills, C. W. (Eds.). (1946). *From Max Weber: Essays in sociology.* New York: Oxford University Press.

Krieger, L. (1973). Authority. In P. Wiener (Ed.), *Dictionary of the history of ideas: Studies of selected pivotal ideas* (vol. 1, pp. 141–162). New York: Scribners.

Lowry L. (1989). *Number the Stars.* New York: Dell.

Metz, M. H. (1978). *Classrooms and corridors: The crisis of authority in desegregated secondary schools.* Berkeley: University of California Press.

Pace, J. L., & Hemmings, A. (Eds.). (2006a). *Classroom authority: Theory, research, and practice.* Mahwah, NJ: Lawrence Erlbaum Associates.

Pace, J. L., & Hemmings, A. (2006b). Understanding classroom authority as a social construction. In J. L. Pace & A. Hemmings (Eds.), *Classroom authority: Theory, research, and practice* (pp. 1–31). Mahwah, NJ: Lawrence Erlbaum Associates.

Richardson, V., & Roosevelt, D. (2005, April). *Learning well from experience.* Paper presented at the annual meeting of the American Educational Research Association, Montreal.

Twain, M. [Samuel Clemens] (1961). *Adventures of Huckleberry Finn.* (S. Bradley, R. C. Beatty, & E. H. Long, Eds.) New York: Norton. (Original work published 1885)

Twain, M. [Samuel Clemens] (1981). *The adventures of Tom Sawyer.* New York: Bantam. (Original work published 1876)

6. Keeping Real Children at the Center of Teacher Education: Child Study and the Local Construction of Knowledge in Teaching

Notes

1. This chapter and the work described in it, to the extent that they have merit, would be inconceivable without the extraordinary work of Pat Carini. For that work and for long years of friendship, I am profoundly grateful.

2. After I left Michigan State, I continued to assign child study to my students, first at the University of Michigan and now at Brandeis University. In these and other cases, it has become, for some period, a programmatic element, not just a feature of one or another professor's individual course.

3. Though this framing brings with it some threat that the arrow of influence will be reversed and Child Study reduced to evaluative judgments about the *adequacy* of the child's understanding, his or her conformity to external standards, et cetera. So bald a misconstrual is unlikely—but a slide in that direction is not so remote a possibility.

4. Although the child study may if necessary be conducted primarily through passive observation, the prospective teacher needs to have at least a couple of opportunities for direct, planned interaction with the study child.

5. This directive certainly requires explication and further prompts. One example: "If you invited your study child to explain or to demonstrate something, what would it be, and how would he/she go about it?"
6. Efrat Kussell, an elementary candidate, is a white woman in her mid-twenties; Marquis is an African American third grader. "Marquis" is a pseudonym, as are all children's names in this chapter.

References

Abu El-Haj, T. (2003). Constructing ideas about equity from the standpoint of the particular: Exploring the work of one urban teacher network. *Teachers College Record, 105,* 817–845.

Antler, J. (1982). Progressive education and the scientific study of the child: An analysis of the Bureau of Educational Experiments. *Teachers College Record, 83,* 559–591.

Antler, J. (1987). *Lucy Sprague Mitchell: The making of a modern woman.* New Haven: Yale University Press.

Bryk, A., & Hermanson, K. (1993). Educational indicator systems: Observations on their structure, interpretation, and use. *Review of research in education, 19,* 451–484.

Buber, M. (1987). *I and thou.* (2nd ed.) R. G. Smith. (Trans.) New York: Collier/Macmillan. (Original work published 1958)

Carini, P. F. (2000). A letter to parents and teachers on some ways of looking at and reflecting on children. In M. Himley (Ed.), *From another angle: Children's strengths and school standards.* New York: Teachers College Press.

Carini, P. F. (2001). *Starting strong: A different look at children, schools, and standards.* New York: Teachers College Press.

Cochran-Smith, M. & Lytle, S. (1993). *Inside/outside: Teacher research and knowledge.* New York: Teachers College Press.

Cochran-Smith, M. & Lytle, S. (1999). The teacher research movement: A decade later. *Educational Researcher, 28*(7), 15–25.

Cremin, L. A. (1961). *The transformation of the school: Progressivism in American education, 1876–1957.* New York: Alfred A. Knopf.

Darling-Hammond, L., & Bransford, J. (Eds.). (2005). *Preparing teachers for a changing world: What teachers should learn and be able to do.* San Francisco: Jossey-Bass.

Dewey, J. (1956). *The child and the curriculum.* Chicago: University of Chicago. (Original work published 1902)

Dewey, J. (1963). *Experience and education.* New York: Collier/Macmillan. (Original work published 1938)

Dewey, J. (1964). The relation of theory to practice in education. In R. D. Archambault (Ed.), *John Dewey on education: Selected writings.* (pp. 313–318). Chicago: University of Chicago Press. (Original work published 1904)

Dewey J. (1966). *Democracy and education*. New York: Macmillan. (Original work published 1916)

Dewey, J. (1988). Creative democracy—The task before us. In J. A. Boydston (Ed.), *John Dewey, the later works, 1939–1941: Vol. 14. Essays, reviews, and miscellany* (pp. 224–230). Carbondale: Southern Illinois University Press. (Original work published 1939)

Featherstone, H. (Ed.) (1998). Teachers looking closely at students and their work. *Changing Minds, 13*, 1–5.

Feiman-Nemser, S., & Buchmann, M. (1985). The pitfalls of experience in teacher education. *Teachers College Record, 87*(1), 53–65.

Gallas, K. (1994). *The languages of learning: How children talk, write, dance, draw and sing their understanding of the world*. New York: Teachers College Press.

Haberman, G. (2000). Learning to look closely at children: A necessary tool for teachers. In N. Nager & E. Shapiro (Eds.), *Revisiting a progressive pedagogy: The developmental-interaction approach* (pp. 203–219). Albany: State University of New York Press.

Hawkins, D. (1974). I, thou, and it. In *The informed vision: Essays on learning and human nature* (pp. 48–62). New York: Agathon Press. (Original work published 1967).

Himley, M. (Ed.) with Carini, P. F. (2000). *From another angle: Children's strengths and school standards*. New York: Teachers College Press.

Jennings, J. (2003). From the White House to the schoolhouse: Greater demands and new roles. In *American educational governance on trial: Change and challenges*. (102nd Yearbook of the National Society for the Study of Education, pp. 291–309). Chicago: University of Chicago Press.

Kagan, D. M. (1992). Professional growth among preservice teachers and beginning teachers. *Review of Educational Research, 62*, 129–169.

Kanevsky, R. (1993). Descriptive review of a child: A way of knowing about teaching and learning. In M. Cochran-Smith & S. Lytle (Eds.), *Inside/outside: Teacher research and knowledge* (pp. 150–162). New York: Teachers College Press.

Kant, I. (1959). *Foundation of the metaphysics of morals*. (L. W. Beck, trans.) Indianapolis: Library of Liberal Arts, Bobbs-Merrill. (Original work published 1785)

Kussell, E. (2005). *Final child study report on "Marquis."* Unpublished manuscript.

Lampert, M. (2001). *Teaching problems and the problems of teaching*. New Haven, CT: Yale University Press

Levi, J. L. (1998). "What color are birds?" Excerpts from a child study. *Changing Minds, 13*, 31–32.

Menand, L. (2001). *The metaphysical club: A story of ideas in America*. New York: Farrar, Straus, Giroux.

Mintz, S. (2004). *Huck's raft: A history of American childhood*. Cambridge, MA: Harvard University Press.

Morrison, T. (1970). *The bluest eye*. New York: Plume (Penguin).

Moss, P. A. (2004). The risks of coherence. In M. Wilson (Ed.), *Toward coherence between classroom assessment and accountability* (103rd Yearbook of the National Society for the Study of Education, part 2, pp. 217–238). Chicago: University of Chicago Press.

Murray, F. (1996). Beyond natural teaching: The case for professional education. In F. Murray (Ed.), *The teacher educator's handbook* (pp. 3–13). San Francisco: Jossey-Bass.

No Child Left Behind Act of 2001, Pub. L. No. 107-110 (H.R.1), 115 Stat. 1425 (2002).

Paley, V. (1979). *White teacher*. Cambridge, MA: Harvard University Press.

Perrone, V. (1989). *Working papers: Reflections on teachers, schools, and communities*. New York: Teachers College Press.

Reggio Children & Project Zero. (Eds.). (2001). *Making learning visible: Children as individual and group learners*. Reggio Emilia, Italy: Reggio Children.

Roosevelt, D. (1998) Teaching as an act of attention: An interview. *Changing Minds*, 13, 29–30.

Schultz, K. (2003). *Listening: A framework for teaching across differences*. New York: Teachers College Press.

Steiner, G. (2003). *Lessons of the masters*. Cambridge: Harvard University Press.

Twain, M. (Samuel Clemens). (1981). *The adventures of Tom Sawyer*. New York: Bantam. (Original work published 1876)

Vygotsky, L. (1976). Play and its role in the mental development of the child. In J. Bruner (Ed.), *Play—Its role in development and evolution* (pp. 537–554). New York: Basic Books. (Original work published 1933)

Waller, W. (1965). *The sociology of teaching*. New York: John Wiley & Sons. (Original work published 1932.)

Wenger, E. (1998). *Communities of practice: Learning, meaning, and identity*. Cambridge, England: Cambridge University Press.

Wilson, S. M. (2004). Student assessment as an opportunity to learn in and from one's teaching practice. In M. Wilson (Ed.), *Towards coherence between classroom assessment and accountability* (103rd Yearbook of the National Society for the Study of Education, part 2, pp. 264–271). Chicago: University of Chicago Press.

Zeichner, K., & Nofke, S. (2001). Practitioner research. In V. Richardson (Ed.), *Handbook of research on teaching* (4th ed., pp. 298–330). Washington, DC: American Educational Research Association.

7. DISCOVERING AND SHARING KNOWLEDGE: INVENTING A NEW ROLE FOR COOPERATING TEACHERS

Notes

1. Debi Corbin was Kathy's student teacher at the time, and she was a full participant in the study. In subsequent years she continued to be a central collaborator in this work.

2. The College of Education held a conference on alternatives in education in the spring, and Kathy, Sharon, and Debi made a presentation, which was taped, about their work during the year. The story is based on a transcript of that presentation.

3. This story is based on a transcript of a presentation that the members of the Teacher Education Circle made to the faculty at the Averill School in the spring of 1992.

4. Judith Warren Little (1990) defines "joint work" as "encounters among teachers that rest on shared responsibility for the work of teaching" (p. 494). It seems an apt way to describe the way of working that Kathy and Debi evolved.

References

Beasley, K., Corbin, D., Feiman-Nemser, S., & Shank, C. (1997). Making it happen: Creating a subculture of mentoring in a professional development school. In M. Levine & R. Trachtman (Eds.), *Professional development schools: Politics, practice, and policy* (pp. 33–51). New York: Teachers College Press.

Ball, D., & Cohen, D. K. (1999). Developing practice, developing practitioners: Toward a practice-based theory of professional education. In L. Darling-Hammond & G. Sykes (Eds.), *Teaching as the learning profession: Handbook of policy and practice* (pp. 3–32). San Francisco: Jossey-Bass.

Bruner, J. (1986). *Actual minds, possible worlds*. Cambridge, MA: Harvard University Press.

Cochran-Smith, M. (1991). Learning to teach against the grain. *Harvard Educational Review, 61*, 279–310.

Feiman, S. (1983). Learning to teach. In L. Shulman & G. Sykes (Eds.), *Handbook on teaching and policy* (pp. 150–170). New York: Longman Press.

Feiman-Nemser, S., & Beasley, K. (1997). Mentoring as assisted performance: The case of co-planning. In V. Richardson (Ed.), *Constructivist teacher education* (pp. 108–126). Basington, England: Falmer Press.

Feiman-Nemser, S., & Buchmann, M. (1985). The pitfalls of experience in teacher education. *Teachers College Record, 87*, 53–65.

Feiman-Nemser, S., & Buchmann, M. (1987). When is student teaching teacher education? *Teaching and Teacher Education, 3*, 255–273.

Gallimore, R., Tharp, R., & John-Steiner, V. (n.d.). *Developmental and socio-historical foundations of mentoring.* Unpublished manuscript.

Holmes Group. (1990). *Tomorrow's schools: Principles for the design of professional development schools.* East Lansing, MI: Author.

Lave, J. & Wenger, E. (1990). *Situated learning: Legitimate peripheral participation.* Cambridge, England: Cambridge University Press.

Little, J. W. (1990). Teachers as colleagues. In V. Richardson (Ed.), *Educator's handbook: A research perspective* (pp. 419–518). White Plains, NY: Longman.

Little, J. W., & Horn, I. (2006, April). *Resources for professional talk: From "just talk" to consequential conversation.* Paper presented at the annual meeting of the American Educational Research Association, San Francisco.

Lord, B. (1994). Teachers' professional development: Critical colleagueship and the role of professional communities. In N. Cobb (Ed.), *The future of education: Perspective on national standards in America* (pp. 175–204). New York: College Entrance Examination Board.

Lortie, D. (1975). *Schoolteacher: A sociological study.* Chicago: University of Chicago Press.

Pfeifer, L., & Featherstone, H. (1997, February). *"Toto, I don't think we're in Kansas anymore": Entering the land of public disagreement in learning to teach.* Paper presented at the Urban Ethnography Forum, Philadelphia.

Schön, D. (1987). *Educating the reflective practitioner.* San Francisco: Jossey-Bass.

Zeichner, K. (1981). Are the effects of university teacher education "washed out" by school experience? *Phi Delta Kappan, 32*(3), 11–21.

8. Learning the Practice of Field-Based Teacher Education

References

Aardema, V. (1975). *Why mosquitoes buzz in people's ears: A West African tale.* New York: Dial Press.

Ball, D., & Cohen, D. (1999). Developing practice, developing practitioners: Toward a practice-based theory of professional education. In L. Darling-Hammond & G. Sykes (Eds.), *Teaching as the learning profession: Handbook of policy and practice.* (pp. 3–32). San Francisco: Jossey-Bass.

Cochran-Smith, M. (1991). Reinventing student teaching. *Journal of Teacher Education 42*(2), 104–118.

Davidson, M. (1989). *Helen Keller.* New York: Scholastic.

Denyer, J. (1997, April). *What happens when the conversation falls apart: The potential for collaborative analysis of talk about text.* Paper presented at the annual meeting of the American Educational Research Association, Chicago.

Dewey, J. (1963). *Experience and education.* New York: Collier/Macmillan. (Original work published 1938)

Enz, B., Freeman, D., & Wallin, M. (1996). Roles and responsibilities of the student teacher supervisor: Matches and mismatches in perception. In D. McIntyre and D. Byrd (Eds.), *Preparing tomorrow's teachers: The field experience. Teacher education yearbook 4* (pp. 131–150). Reston, VA: Association of Teacher Educators.

Evertson, C. M. (1990). Bridging knowledge and action through clinical experiences. In D. D. Dill (Ed.), *What teachers need to know: The knowledge, skills, and values essential to good teaching* (pp. 94–109). San Francisco: Jossey-Bass.

Feiman-Nemser, S., & Beasley, K. (1997). Mentoring as assisted performance: The case of co-planning. In V. Richardson (Ed.), *Constructivist teacher education* (pp. 108–126). Basington, England: Falmer Press.

Goodlad, J. (1990). *Teachers for our nation's schools.* San Francisco: Jossey-Bass.

Lanier, J., & Little, J. (1985). Research on teacher education. In M. Wittrock (Ed.), *Handbook of research on teaching* (pp. 527–569). New York: Macmillan.

Lortie, D. (1975). *Schoolteacher: A sociological study.* Chicago: University of Chicago Press.

Lord, B. (1994). Teachers' professional development: Critical colleagueship and the role of professional communities. In N. Cobb (Ed.), *The future of education: Perspectives on national standards in education* (pp. 175–204). New York: College Entrance Examination Board.

Schön, D. (1987). *Educating the reflective practitioner: Toward a new design for teaching and learning in the professions.* San Francisco: Jossey-Bass.

Vygotsky, L. (1978). *Mind in society: The development of higher psychological processes.* Cambridge, MA: Harvard University Press. (Original work published 1933)

Wells, G. (1999). *Dialogic inquiry: Toward a sociocultural practice and theory of education.* Cambridge, England: Cambridge University Press.

9. Helping Teachers Become Teacher Educators

Notes

1. Sharon Feiman-Nemser introduced the strategy of analyzing artifacts of mentoring in her early work with teachers at Averill Elementary School. Several Team One staff also brought experience with artifacts of teaching and learning to the program based on their prior work at the Prospect Center in North Bennington, Vermont.

2. "John Mathews" is a pseudonym, as are the names of all teachers and interns at Capitol.

3. We began meeting after school, but by November, after interns had gained sufficient experience in leading their classrooms, study group sessions took place during the school day.

4. My first encounter with teacher study groups was as a member of the Philadelphia Teachers Learning Cooperative from 1978 to 1982. Following that, I led study groups of many kinds in conjunction with my work at Prospect Center in North Bennington, Vermont, from 1983 to 1991.

References

Cochran-Smith, M. (1991). Reinventing student teaching. *Journal of Teacher Education* 42, 104–118.

Cohen, D. K., McLaughlin, M. W., & Talbert, J. E. (Eds.). (1993). *Teaching for understanding: Challenges for policy and practice.* San Francisco: Jossey-Bass.

Feiman-Nemser, S., & Buchmann, M. (1987). When is student teaching teacher education? *Teaching and Teacher Education, 3,* 255–273.

Hawkins, D. (1974). I, thou, and it. In *The informed vision: Essays on learning and human nature* (pp. 48–62). New York: Agathon Press. (Original work published 1967)

Tomlinson, P. (1995). *Understanding mentoring: Reflective strategies for school-based teacher preparation.* Philadelphia: Open University Press.

Zeichner, K. (1992). Rethinking the practicum in the professional development school partnership. *Journal of Teacher Education, 43,* 296–307.

10. Values and the Big University Education School

References

Burnett, F. H. (2002). *The Secret Garden.* New York: Penguin Classics. (Original work published 1911)

Curtis, C. P. (1999). *Bud, not Buddy.* New York: Scholastic.

Dewey, J. (1964). *John Dewey on education: Selected writings.* (R. D. Archambault, Ed.), Chicago: University of Chicago Press. (Original work published 1904)

Holmes Group. (1986). *Tomorrow's teachers: A report of the Holmes Group.* East Lansing, MI: Author.

Holmes Group. (1990). *Tomorrow's schools: Principles for the design of professional development schools.* East Lansing, MI: Author

Holmes Group. (1996). *Tomorrow's schools of education: A report of the Holmes Group..* East Lansing, MI: Author.

Judge, H. (1982). *American graduate schools of education: A view from abroad.* New York: Ford Foundation.

Labaree, D. (1992). Doing good, doing science: The Holmes Group reports and the rhetorics of educational reform. *Teachers College Record, 93,* 628–640.

Lampert, M. (2001). *Teaching problems and the problems with teaching.* New Haven, CT: Yale University Press.

Lionni, L. (1967). *Frederick.* New York: Knopf.

Paley, V. (1999). *The girl with the brown crayon.* Cambridge, MA: Harvard University Press.

CONCLUSION

Note

1. These ideas are further developed in Carroll (2006).

References

Carroll, D. (2006). Developing joint accountability in university-school teacher education partnerships. *Action in Teacher Education, 27*(4), 3–11.

Darling-Hammond, L., & Bransford, J. (Eds.). (2005). *Preparing teachers for a changing world: What teachers should learn and be able to do.* San Francisco: Jossey-Bass.

Feiman-Nemser, S. (2001). From preparation to practice: Designing a continuum to strengthen and sustain teaching. *Teachers College Record, 103,* 1013–1055.

Holmes Group. (1986). *Tomorrow's teachers: A report of the Holmes Group.* East Lansing, MI: Author.

Holmes Group. (1990). *Tomorrow's schools: Principles for the design of professional development schools. A report of the Holmes Group.* East Lansing, MI: Author.

Holmes Group. (1996). *Tomorrow's schools of education.* East Lansing, MI: Author.

Interstate New Teacher Support and Assessment Consortium. (1992). *Model standards for beginning teacher licensing and development: A resource for state dialogue.* Washington, DC: author.

Lortie, D. (1975). *Schoolteacher: A sociological study.* Chicago: University of Chicago Press.

National Board for Professional Teaching Standards. (1989). *Toward high and rigorous standards for the teaching profession.* Detroit: Author.

Orwell, G. (1953), Why I write. In *Such, such were the joys.* New York: Harcourt Brace Jovanovich (Original work published 1946)

Schön, D. (1987). *Educating the reflective practitioner: Toward a new design for teaching and learning in the professions.* San Francisco: Jossey-Bass.

About the Contributors

Kathrene Beasley teaches at Lewton School in Lansing, Michigan. She comes from a family of teachers, and both her son and daughter are elementary school teachers. After graduating from the University of Wisconsin at Oshkosh, where she majored in French and political science and received a secondary teaching certificate, she served as a VISTA volunteer in rural north Florida, helping organize an integrated full-year Head Start program and in-school tutoring services in predominately black schools. She taught high school in Pensacola, Florida, then moved to Michigan, where she did graduate work at Michigan State and obtained an elementary teaching certificate. She has taught in the Lansing public schools for over twenty-five years.

David Carroll is an assistant professor in the elementary education department at Western Washington University. He taught previously at Michigan State University (MSU), where he served initially as manager of the professional development school network and as university coordinator for professional development school work at a large urban middle school in Lansing. With the beginning of Team One in 1993, Carroll became program coordinator, and he later also worked as a university liaison at one urban elementary school. While at MSU, Carroll also earned his PhD. Before that he served as director of the teacher education program at Prospect Center in Bennington, Vermont and conducted summer institutes and professional development consultations. He began his career in education as an elementary teacher for the School District of Philadelphia.

Susan Donnelly is head of school at Whatcom Day Academy in Bellingham, Washington. She worked previously at Michigan State University (MSU), initially as a professional development school university liaison at an urban elementary school, then as student coordinator for Team One when the new teacher education program was initiated. Before working at MSU, Donnelly served in several capacities at Prospect Center in Bennington, Vermont, including acting director, assistant director, teacher, seminar leader, and archive fellow. Donnelly worked previously in early-childhood education in Alberta, Canada, as a preschool teacher, day-care center director, and college instructor. She has a master's degree in elementary and early-childhood education.

HELEN FEATHERSTONE is associate professor of teacher education at Michigan State University, where her primary research and instructional interests are in teaching prospective elementary school teachers intellectually ambitious approaches to math instruction and in helping experienced elementary teachers to think together about math and math teaching. She began her career in the Boston Public School District and since then has taught at Harvard University and at Wellesley College, as well as at MSU. Featherstone founded the *Harvard Education Letter*, a publication that synthesizes research on education for a broad audience. She is the author of *A Difference in the Family: Life With a Disabled Child* (1980) and is currently working on a book about changes in U.S. kindergartens.

JOSEPH FEATHERSTONE is a professor of teacher education at MSU. He has taught at Harvard University and served for many years as an editor of the *New Republic*. He was the principal of the Commonwealth School in Boston. He was a faculty coleader of Team One, in which he had special responsibility for overseeing TE-301, the course that introduced students to child study. He was a coauthor of the influential Holmes Group report, *Tomorrow's Schools* (1990), and is the author of many books and articles, including most recently *Dear Josie: Witnessing the Hopes and Failures of Democratic Education* (2003). He is also a poet, author of *Brace's Cove* (2000).

SHARON FEIMAN-NEMSER is the Mandel Professor of Jewish Education at Brandeis University. She began her career as a high school English teacher in Chicago. She taught at the University of Chicago and then at Michigan State University, where she spent twenty years as a faculty member in the College of Education. At MSU, she served as faculty coleader of Team 1 and as a senior researcher at the National Center for Research on Teacher Learning. An early student of teacher learning, she has written extensively about mentoring, new teacher induction, teacher centers, and the curriculum and pedagogy of teacher education. At Brandeis, she combines her expertise in teacher education with her deep interest in Jewish education.

JULIE HANSON-EGLITE teaches high school science in the Chicago area.

GRETA McHANEY-TRICE is a fourth-grade teacher in Lansing, Michigan.

PATRICIA J. NORMAN is an associate professor in the education department at Trinity University, in San Antonio, Texas, where she came to work after earning her PhD at Michigan State University. Her research interests include field-based teacher education and mentor teacher development. As the clinical faculty at one of Trinity's four professional development schools, she works closely with elementary interns, their mentor teachers, and school faculty to create strong contexts for students, novices, and experienced teachers.

DIRCK ROOSEVELT, who earned his PhD at Michigan State University, is an associate professor and director of the master of arts in teaching program at Brandeis University. He taught at the elementary level at the Prospect School, where he also was principal, and in public schools for many years. Since 1993 he has been involved in the teaching, design, and study of teacher education at Michigan State University, the University of Michigan, and, currently, Brandeis. His present research focuses on three critical dimensions of learning to teach: valuing children, learning well from experience, and constructing intellectual and moral authority. His underlying concern is making education fit for democracy. He has published in *Theory Into Practice, Curriculum Inquiry,* and the National Society for the Study of Education yearbook.

Index